MW00526889

Narratives of Queer Desire

Also by Margaret Sönser Breen

BUTLER MATTERS: Judith Butler's Impact on Feminist and Queer Studies *(co-editor with Warren J. Blumenfeld)*

GENEALOGIES OF IDENTITY: Interdisciplinary Readings in Sex and Sexuality *(co-editor with Fiona Peters)*

MINDING EVIL: Explorations of Human Iniquity *(editor)*

TRUTH, RECONCILIATION, AND EVIL *(editor)*

UNDERSTANDING EVIL: An Interdisciplinary Approach *(editor)*

Narratives of Queer Desire

Deserts of the Heart

Margaret Sönser Breen
Associate Professor of English and Women's Studies
University of Connecticut

First published 2009 by
PALGRAVE MACMILLAN

Palgrave Macmillan in the UK is an imprint of Macmillan Publishers Limited, registered in England, company number 785998, of Houndmills, Basingstoke, Hampshire RG21 6XS.

Palgrave Macmillan in the US is a division of St Martin's Press LLC, 175 Fifth Avenue, New York, NY 10010.

Palgrave Macmillan is the global academic imprint of the above companies and has companies and representatives throughout the world.

Palgrave® and Macmillan® are registered trademarks in the United States, the United Kingdom, Europe and other countries.

ISBN-13: 978–0–230–22388–2   hardback
ISBN-10: 0–230–22388–5   hardback

This book is printed on paper suitable for recycling and made from fully managed and sustained forest sources. Logging, pulping and manufacturing processes are expected to conform to the environmental regulations of the country of origin.

A catalogue record for this book is available from the British Library.

A catalog record for this book is available from the Library of Congress.

10   9   8   7   6   5   4   3   2   1
18   17   16   15   14   13   12   11   10   09

Printed and bound in Great Britain by
CPI Antony Rowe, Chippenham and Eastbourne

For Anni and Jan
and
Hasi and Lily

Egon Schiele, *Nude on Her Stomach (Am Bauch liegender weiblicher Akt)* (1917). Gouache and black crayon, 29.8 × 46.1 cm (11.7 × 18.1 in.), Albertina, Vienna. 31452. Photograph © 2009 Albertina, Vienna.

Contents

List of Figures

Acknowledgements

Narratives of Queer Desire could never have been written without the help of so very many people. I am first and foremost indebted to my editor at Palgrave Macmillan, Paula Kennedy, and her assistant, Steven Hall, for their guidance throughout the publishing process. The anonymous reader in turn provided me with invaluable suggestions for revision. With regard to the illustrations in the book, I wish to thank Pedro Almodóvar's film company, El Deseo, and particularly Liliana Niespial; John DeFeo of the New Britain Museum of American Art; Clara Pyo of the Museum of Fine Arts, Boston; and Dr Ingrid Kastel of the Albertina Museum in Vienna. Richard Deagle, Tom Starace, and Joe Wollin also let me reprint the image of their poster, *American Flag* (1989). The Taylor and Francis Group allowed me to incorporate passages from previously published articles in *Journal of Homosexuality* 33.3–4 (1997) and the 2001 Routledge volume *The Puritan Origins of American Sex*, edited by Tracy Fessenden, Nicholas F. Radel, and Magdalena J. Zaborowska, into my analysis of Jane Rule's *Desert of the Heart* in Chapter 1. Eric van Broekhuizen of Rodopi also permitted me to draw on an earlier piece, 'The Evils of [Same] Sex: The US Gay Marriage Debate', which appeared in my 2005 edited volume *Minding Evil: Explorations of Human Iniquity*, for my discussion of marriage in Chapter 2. *Minding Evil* appeared as part of Rodopi's At the Interface series, developed and overseen by Dr Rob Fisher. Special thanks go to Rob: the idea for this project and, indeed, early versions of much of its content are the direct result of working for and with him on the series and its related conferences. Warren J. Blumenfeld, Michael T. Davies, and Isabel Hofmeyer have also offered me friendship and inspiration over the last several years.

So many of the book's chapters are rooted in my classroom experiences at the University of Connecticut. I remain indebted to my students, graduate and undergraduate, as well as to my colleagues in English and Women's Studies, especially Robert S. Tilton, Margaret Higonnet, and the late Hans Turley. University librarians Richard Bleiler and Kathy Labadorf have also helped me at every stage of research.

On a more personal note, I wish to thank Annita Sawyer and mentors George Levine, Bridget Gellert Lyons, and Barry V. Qualls. My aunt Ludmilla Rieberer and my cousins have, through their love and support, encouraged me to ground my writing in lived experience. I could also never have undertaken this project without the unwavering affection and generosity of Giuseppina Fedele and the entire Mitrano family over these past twenty years. I am grateful as well to my sister, Georgia Breen Clapham, for both her delight in words and her great kindness in a time of need.

Most immediately this project has sprung from friendship. I am grateful to Jodi O'Brien and Karen Subach; Ellen Chafee has been a continual source of encouragement and insight. My debt to Mena Mitrano and Frederick S. Roden is far greater than I can ever express: they have helped me from beginning to end; they have been my careful readers; they have encouraged me throughout. Fred is also responsible for my publishing with Palgrave Macmillan. In closing I wish to thank those who occupy my daily life. The spirit of my late father, George James Breen, hovers around this project. He, together with my mother, Anni Sönser Breen, early on taught me the importance of combining candor with stealth. My mother also instilled in me a sense of the beauty and necessity of 'squiring'; in this, as well as in her devotion to family and friends, she has had everything to do with the shaping of my understanding of desire. Keeping me company throughout the writing process have been my beautiful greyhounds, Hasi and Lily: Hasi has sat sweetly and quietly by my side and allowed me to write; Lily, the resident activist, has reminded me of the value of breaks ... and snacks. Finally, there is my partner, Jan Robes, whose kindness, patience, and wit sustain me in my work and in all aspects of my life.

Introduction

This project began in an attempt to respond to students' (and, by extension, my own) questions regarding the role that literature plays as an agent of activism and social change. 'How can reading this novel, how can analyzing this film help me fight gender inequality, sexual violence?' Over the years I have heard this question in various forms again and again, and more often than not I have felt that my answers have been lacking, bumbling, and vague. *Narratives of Queer Desire: Deserts of the Heart* seeks to explore various literary texts whose narrative patterns powerfully engage social justice issues and in so doing offer authors and readers alike strategies for thinking, reading, and articulating ways of resisting oppression, including cultural, legal, and psychological oppression, especially with regard to non-conforming expressions of gender and sexual desire.

While I have been trained as a literary critic, I regard myself primarily as a cultural critic, much of whose teaching and certainly most of whose research in feminist and queer issues have been broad-based and interdisciplinary in scope. My experience teaching interdisciplinary courses in gender and sexuality in both the Women's Studies Program and the English Department at university has afforded the particular occasions that have generated the specific inquiries of each of the chapters of this book. These chapters individually and collectively attest to literature's power to identify and come to grips with either the possibility or the impossibility of social change. Stated in a slightly different way, literature locates its readers and writers within a protean cultural space, at times political, at times not. The key role that literature plays within interdisciplinary studies is, I believe, often overlooked, and I regard my foregrounding of literary analysis within this project as an important means of furthering cultural interrogations of gender, sex, and sexuality.

1

Indeed, literature, I contend, proves a vital means for discerning and validating queer subjectivity. The acts of reading and writing literature facilitate our capacity to claim our humanity, even when that humanity is discounted or invalidated in any number of other realms, medical, political, and religious, for example. Put baldly, literature offers its readers and writers strategies for surviving even the harshest of cultural, social, and political circumstances.

That said, *Narratives of Queer Desire: Deserts of the Heart* is an inter-disciplinary project that uses literary analysis, especially close reading, along with personal testimony and the applications of gender theory, as a means for identifying, looking at, and exploring lesbian, gay, bisexual, transgender, and queer (LGBTQ) stories. Taking its subtitle from Jane Rule's 1964 novel *Desert of the Heart*, which itself encodes a tribute to W. H. Auden's 1939 elegy 'In Memory of W. B. Yeats', *Narratives of Queer Desire* considers queer yearnings for stories other than those convention-ally available, stories that, often located at the social margins ('deserts') and subject to violent regulation, engage and resist norms in literature as well as culture and politics. Within this framework, 'queer desire' oper-ates on any number of levels. For example, 'queer desire' refers to sexual fantasies, sex acts, and sexed and gendered embodiments that cross gen-der binaries and in so doing disrupt the narrative illusion of a seamless and organic or natural relation linking sex, gender, and (hetero)sexuality. More broadly, 'queer desire' speaks to a recognition and dignifying of cultural otherness, those 'deserts' of subjectivity that may be explicitly and primarily marked by gender or sex or sexuality but that may also be figured, for example, by marginal and stigmatized racial, ethnic, or class positions; that is, by some form of corporeal or social monstrosity other than or in addition to non-normative gender, sex, and/or sexual-ity. Finally, 'queer desire' refers to the yearning for stories that center on queer lives and in so doing accord them visibility and full human value and dignity; a yearning for such stories – literary and theoretical but also cultural and political – that in the process of recounting either enlarges or remakes anew traditions and conventions of narration. Recalling Shane Phelan's discussion of lesbian identity in '(Be)coming Out',[1] queer desire, then, is itself a becoming: a series of movements toward, against, and apart from the literary, cultural, and political norms; a continual questioning and re-making of the 'state' of desire.

This study necessarily engenders several questions. Some of the larger ones are as follows: How do various discourses – literary, cultural, medi-cal, political, and religious – accommodate, incorporate, and illuminate queer issues? How do queer issues change or reject those discourses? How does literature, especially its composition and its reading, offer a validating space for queer experiences and subjectivities? What can readers' engagement with literary representations of gender, sex, and sexuality learn about their own cultures' understandings of these issues? Finally, what can readers learn from the analysis and application of theories of gender and sexuality? Particular issues explored by individual chapters are as follows: literary canon formation, along with its wider social and political implications (Chapter 1); the US marriage equality movement as part of a larger social justice movement (Chapter 2); gender and sexual fantasies as a means of encountering and resisting loss (Chapter 3); lesbian authors' examination and reworking of experiences of sexual abuse (Chapter 4); translation as a figure of agency for gender and sexual minorities (Chapter 5).

Chapter 1, 'Writing Sexuality: Lesbian Novels and the Progress Narrative', begins with the question of whether it is possible to represent a lesbian story in terms of the realist conventions of the progress novel. The progress novel, which has its roots in John Bunyan's Christian allegory *The Pilgrim's Progress* (1678; 1684) and a Pauline (that is, subordinate, secondary, submissive) notion of female subjectivity, relies on a teleological narrative structure. In other words, the progress novel marks out the protagonist's life as a moral journey that, for all its struggles and setbacks, achieves an end goal; for the female protagonist especially, purpose, meaning, and development derive from her relations to others, which at times entail her subordination to others, and typically her story ends in marriage. Given these features, the answer to the question of whether one could (or would want to) represent a lesbian story in terms of a progress narrative would seem to be no. Beyond the issue of women's subservience, with which many nineteenth-century women writers working with progress narratives already grappled, there remain other problems. Why, for example, would a writer of lesbian fiction draw upon a literary tradition so invested in morality, especially if one's heroines are, as in real life, so vulnerable to being branded and dismissed as immoral? Why, too, choose a pattern of storytelling that ends in marriage, when marriage is not possible or desirable? Can one meaningfully invoke such a literary tradition in order to figure lesbian desire? Apparently, yes. Lesbian writers, beginning with Radclyffe Hall, have deliberately engaged Bunyan's text and the progress novels following it in order to carve out a dignified space for their heroines.

At first, this preoccupation with lesbian progress narratives' relation to Bunyan or a tradition of novel writing indebted to Bunyan might seem like a solely literary concern. It is not. When, for example, in 1928 well-respected British writer Radclyffe Hall published her 'Lesbian Bible', the novel *The Well of Loneliness*, which draws significantly on that tradition and on *The Pilgrim's Progress* itself, she caused a major uproar in both Great Britain and the United States. What followed was one of the most famous book trials of the twentieth century. Together, the inception and reception of the book – Hall's decision to write a story of inversion that enacting the theories of sexologists such as Havelock Ellis, would lead to an acceptance of inverts; the ensuing trials in both the UK and the US; and the novel's subsequent banning in the UK and continued publication in the US – ensured that its publication would constitute a watershed moment for the acknowledgement of lesbianism and lesbians within public and legal spheres. More generally, this chapter insists that the lesbian progress novel, beginning with Hall's *Well* and followed by Jane Rule's *Desert of the Heart* (1964) and, later, by Jeanette Winterson's *Oranges Are not the Only Fruit* (1985) and Sarah Waters' *Tipping the Velvet* (1998), needs to be read within the context of its social production and effect. Representing lesbian desire necessitates the engagement and revision and not simply or solely the dismissal of conventional narrative structures that resonate within the cultural contexts in which the writer of lesbian fiction finds herself.

Chapter 2 considers another such example of lesbian fiction's ongoing preoccupation with the representational politics of lesbian and more broadly queer desire. 'Love in the Shadows: The Same-Sex Marriage Debate and Beyond' offers a close reading of a lesbian pulp classic, Ann Bannon's *Women in the Shadows* (1959), as a means for considering the contemporary US same-sex marriage debate and the larger social justice debates that at times it blocks and obscures. Bannon's 'strange marriage' novel, in which a lesbian marries a gay man, explores characters' negotiations for sustaining queer desires within the narrow limits of heteronormative marriage. Analysis of the work offers me a literary-historical way into a larger discussion of the contemporary same-sex marriage debate and, beyond it, as the activist document 'Beyond Same-Sex Marriage' (2006) underscores, the need for legislation protecting the variety of families that, potentially occluded by the terms of this debate, are nonetheless affected by the linkage between various social and legal benefits and marriage. Stated in more specific terms, the narrative patterns structuring characters' relations to marriage in Bannon's pulp novel anticipate the very questions central to the present-day advocacy of marriage equality: most importantly, to what extent does the push for gay marriage ironically involve the disenfranchisement and elision of various groups of queers, where 'queer' may stand for non-citizens, immigrants, the aged, the working poor, various racial and ethnic minorities, as well as for non-married gay men and lesbians and transgendered people?

Chapters 3 through 5 preoccupy themselves with considering various groups of people and issues often elided by the marriage equality movement. Chapter 3, 'Reading for Fantasy in "Rip Van Winkle" and *The Farewell Symphony*', for example, takes up the issue of sexual and gender fantasies that ostensibly exist outside of marriage, that broad-based cultural fantasy of gender normativity. If marriage is core to the US cultural imagination, to what extent are foreclosed fantasies of queer yearnings central as well? With the specific concern for moving readers (especially students) beyond identity category thinking, this chapter explores how particular expressions of gender and sexuality threaten narratives of normative sexuality (and are consequently repudiated or outlawed or rendered unintelligible). In so doing, the chapter engages contemporary discussions of melancholia, especially those of Judith Butler regarding fantasy and gender, by applying them to two American literary texts: the first Washington Irving's early nineteenth-century classic 'Rip Van Winkle' (1819-20); the second Edmund White's 1997 novel, *The Farewell Symphony*. In reading these two texts in terms of recent critical, including psychoanalytical, engagements of fantasy, gender, and melancholia, I seek first, with 'Rip Van Winkle', to explore an epistemological framework that, on the one hand, identifies and legitimizes certain expressions of gender and sexuality, while, on the other hand, repudiating and relegating to the realm of forbidden yet desired fantasy others. Second, turning my attention to *The Farewell Symphony*, I wish to show how the narrative patterns at work in White's novel challenge the ways of knowing gender and sexuality that 'Rip Van Winkle' offers. Whereas Irving in his short story maintains a rigid demarcation between fantasy and reality, which in turn produces the melancholy that encircles Rip's village, White in his novel does not. He includes accounts of characters' sexual fantasies and desires. In so doing he overturns those conventional limits to telling stories about sex and sexuality: the equations of sex with sordidness and shame and narrative lapses into melancholy silence. As White's as well as Irving's text reveals, fantasy and melancholia crucially determine queer desire's narrative possibilities. Recognizing their power is especially important for the teacher of LGBT literature who would encourage students to move beyond identity category thinking in their study of the workings of gender and sexuality.

Chapter 4, 'Remaking Gendered Systems of Story: Sexual Violence in *Bastard Out of Carolina* and *The Way the Crow Flies*', concerns itself with another issue related to marriage's function as a cultural ideal and the heteronormative lynchpin within North American society: imaginative or creative resistance to the sexual violence and gender policing that take place in the name of marriage. This chapter analyzes how two lesbian writers, American Dorothy Allison and Canadian Anne-Marie MacDonald, represent lesbian desire by engaging [fictional] memories of childhood sexual abuse. In so doing both authors not only expose the widespread experience of sexual abuse especially for girls and more specifically lesbians, they also disrupt the conventional reading of lesbian desire as a result of childhood trauma and propose instead a complex interrelation between abuse and desire. Above all, the novels, written in 1992 and 2003 respectively, demonstrate the power of healing that the telling of personal stories facilitates. Stated in slightly different terms, Chapter 4 considers how lesbian writers fashion narratives in order to claim a validating and nurturing understanding of their heroines: an authorial perspective that counters broad-based social assumptions of a causal and pathologizing relation between sexual abuse and lesbianism. Personal narrative of course has a long and important place in feminist theory. Within sexuality studies, sociologist Ken Plummer has examined how the telling of sexual stories has offered visibility and healing for lesbians and gay men.[2] In this sense, this chapter defines itself within a tradition of feminist and queer writing (which is also familiar to many qualitative sociological and psychological approaches): memoir or life-writing (whether fictional or non-fictional) renders historically disenfranchised and/or effaced subjects visible; writing itself offers a powerful counter or response to the experience of trauma. It is important to note here that trauma extends to parameters laid out by second-wave feminism for the representation of lesbian desire. The section on Allison especially takes up Allison's own marginalization as a lesbian writer by lesbian feminists during the sex wars.

Finally, Chapter 5, 'Trussed/Trust/Dressed in Translation', focuses on a key, though often neglected feature of literary and cultural narratives: translation, as both a linguistic operation and a metaphor, facilitates gender and sexual others' desire for cultural belonging. Specifically, this chapter considers how translation, which is neither wholly a vehicle for social change nor a means of sustaining cultural propriety, is a monstrous feature of language; that is, while often overlooked, particularly in discussions of literature read in translation and, more broadly, within cultural narratives in which the construction of meanings goes unexamined, the figure of translation encodes the potential of queer bodies to exercise agency not only within literary but also within social and cultural contexts. Monstrous translation, I argue, proves a crucial figure of empowerment and activism for LGBTQ people, who inhabit interstices of meaning between norms for gender, sex, and sexuality. Moving from personal narrative to close reading, I analyze a range of literary texts as texts in translation: Kafka's 1912/1915 novella *The Metamorphosis* (*Die Verwandlung*), Mary Shelley's 1818/1831 *Frankenstein*, and Pedro Almodóvar's 1999 film *All About My Mother* (*Todo sobre mi madre*). Understanding how translation, whether as a metaphor or as a linguistic operation, affects narrative structure and meaning within literature and more generally within society, I contend, allows one to discern, expose, and counter not only the reduction of gender and sexual minorities to cultural monsters but also the marginalization of various ethnic, racial, and immigrant groups. Reading for translation is a powerful tool for social justice work.

Taken together, the chapters' various discussions of narratives and queer desire disclose that the overarching narrative of *Narratives of Queer Desire* is a story about the power of storytelling: within our personal, professional, and political lives and at the sites of our desire, including the classroom. Storytelling (on the part of teachers, writers, and students) ethically enacts a queer pedagogy: it reconfigures the relations among teacher, student, author, and text. Further, it grants students an accessible (if not necessarily transparent) way into the act of critical analysis. It empowers students to engage literature – to locate themselves (their I's) within the texts that they are reading and studying so that they might engage in a critique that would otherwise seem daunting, if not impossible. In so doing storytelling allows us (teachers, students, authors) to recognize and, perhaps, challenge mechanisms of oppression lodged within conventional valuations of power and authority. Ultimately, *Narratives of Queer Desire* encodes my own story about the ways in which writers and readers identify literature as a means of engaging queer individuals' and communities' experiences. This is a story about how literature encounters loss, stays off aggression, and answers erasure by offering itself as a site of care and empowerment and activism for LGBTQ people.

1
Writing Sexuality: Lesbian Novels and the Progress Narrative

1. Introduction

John Bunyan's *The Pilgrim's Progress* (1678; 1684) has long been recognized as a crucial source text for the British (and, by extension, American) novel. Through the early twentieth-century, Bunyan's work was, next to the Bible, the most widely read book in English, and its basic narrative structure, representing life as a spiritual journey, together with any number of its images (Vanity Fair and the Slough of Despond, for example), has shaped the ways in which novelists, especially during the eighteenth and nineteenth centuries, have described the lives and worlds of their heroes.[1] Even so, a connection between Bunyan's allegory and lesbian novels might well seem tenuous, forced, or even vestigial: an echo of a no longer relevant literary past. What, after all, could an allegorical account of spiritual progress have to do with a story of lesbian desire and, more broadly, a tradition of lesbian storytelling? What indeed? This is the basic question of my opening chapter, in which I examine not only how writers of lesbian fiction have directly and indirectly challenged and expanded Bunyan's two-part narrative of progress, but also how such writers have used the relation to Bunyan in order to engage their contemporary religious, social, and political understandings of same-sex desire.

While it might seem that a connection between *The Pilgrim's Progress* and twentieth-century lesbian novels is, at best, coincidental, it is, for all that, inevitable. It is also important: relevant to scholars of seventeenth-century religious allegory and modern lesbian literature alike, especially those interested in the empowerment (spiritual, social, political, or otherwise) of gender and sexual minorities through the articulation and formation of community.

That empowerment, cast as spiritual awakening, is the central pre-occupation of Part 2 of *The Pilgrim's Progress*. In contrast to Part 1, with its account of the often solitary and individuated journey of its universal and male hero, Christian, Part 2 of Bunyan's allegory focuses on Christianity's 'B' team: readers hear of the spiritual travel and travail of Christian's wife, Christiana, her sons, and her friend Mercy, as well as those of other 'weaker' pilgrims, such as Despondency, Mr. Ready-to-Halt, and Mr. Feeble-mind. Part 2 (in)famously underscores the great limitation with which the female believer must contend: her sexuality. Compensating for and distracting from that liability is the narrative attention Bunyan gives to an ever-increasing community of faithful. The sexed pilgrim's progress needs to be thought of as an inherently communal or relational effect.[2]

It is important to recognize that lesbian novels – so often themselves preoccupied with heroines' sexuality and the importance of community – have found a powerful literary touchstone not only in *The Pilgrim's Progress* but also in the wealth of progress novels that, beginning in the early eighteenth century and extending well into the twentieth century, have encoded Bunyan's text as a readers' guide to characters' strengths and failings. In the process, women writers, especially women writers of heroines, have made key revisions to the patterns of storytelling afforded female *Bildung*.

Victorian women writers were especially aware of and keen to respond to the gender markings of Bunyan's legacy. With *Jane Eyre* (1847), Charlotte Brontë provides a fascinating and problematic case in point. Brontë refuses to have her heroine, Jane, dominated by the men in her life. Because she wants an empowering story for Jane, Brontë rewrites Bunyan's narrative for female progress in three key ways: rejecting Bunyan's gender-specific linkage of sexuality with femaleness; inviting *The Pilgrim's Progress* to be deployed as a powerful textual apology for British imperialism; and, in so doing, racing the link between sexuality and community.

With regard to the first point, Brontë's heroine discovers that for her, as for Bunyan's Christiana, sexuality is a liability for a woman's spiritual progress. Passions do, at times, get the best of Jane. It must be said, however, that passions, particularly those of sexuality, also prove a liability for the two men who want to be with her: the Byronic Rochester and the sexless St John. Rochester, of course, notoriously attempts to ensnare Jane in a sham marriage: he forsakes morality in the name of desire. If by the novel's end he is chastened and reformed, he nonetheless speaks to the ever-present threat to women's sexuality that, as Bunyan underscored with Christiana, women, real and allegorical, continually encounter: the robbing of sexual consent. If from this perspective the Rochester of the first half of the novel is a character very much in line with the Evil-doers whom Christiana meets with early in her progress, St John embodies a very different kind of danger: he would marry Jane, not because he loves and desires her but because she would prove useful to him in his missionary work in India. More damagingly, I think, social propriety would require that the two working together would be married. It is her recognition that her sexuality is not so much a liability as an integral condition of her spiritual progress that allows Jane to tell him, 'If I were to marry you, you would kill me'.[3]

Importantly, though, both Jane and Brontë are content with having St John (and, by extension, English male guides in general) overseeing the moral progress of people in other parts of the world (or Empire). Brontë devotes the last paragraphs of the novel to a description of St John: 'He may be stern; he may be exacting: he may be ambitious yet; but his is the sternness of the warrior Greatheart, who guards his pilgrim convoy from the onslaught of Apollyon. His is the exaction of the apostle, who speaks but for Christ when he says – "Whosoever will come after Me, let him deny himself, and take up his cross and follow Me" '.[4] With this, Brontë's collapsing together of elements of Parts 1 and 2 of Bunyan's text,[5] readers find a key example of *The Pilgrim's Progress's* imperialist legacy. For Brontë, it's imperative that British women – by which I mean white British women – need to be in charge of not only their own sexuality but also their own spiritual progress. It's an entirely different story for those subjects of the British Empire separated from Jane by the insuperable barriers of racism.

Racial marking of spiritual capacity is arguably present in *The Pilgrim's Progress*, as in, for example, the allegory of the Flatterer, the 'man black of flesh' who momentarily leads Christian astray.[6] Bunyan's own understanding of racial constructs is not known. One can, however, assume that he had some knowledge of England's trade in slaves 'black of flesh', and it in turn seems reasonable to posit that Bunyan's figure allegorizes the black slave as a person without agency or, indeed, personhood. The Flatterer stands in contrast to Christian's friend and travel companion Faithful, who at Vanity Fair announces that they 'buy the Truth'.[7] A flatterer, would of course, be without this kind of purchasing power, a point borne home by Bunyan's description of the Flatterer, which might well suggest that the latter has himself been bought.

The racial marking that is only vaguely at work in Bunyan's text subsequently proves crucial in Brontë's novel for understanding Jane's own

spiritual location.[8] For Brontë, it is perfectly acceptable and even necessary for non-white men and women of the Empire to have an English
white male Christian guide. While in terms of Brontë's colonial vision
and her own [Irish] ancestry, race cannot be understood merely as a question of color, the power of her novel's call for Jane's spiritual autonomy
nonetheless rests partly on a construction of whiteness that reinforces
the 'naturalness' of colonial subjugation.

It is within this context, which simultaneously universalizes Jane's
story and upholds its racial privilege, that readers discern her relation
to St John. Marriage with him would become a vehicle not for Jane's
spiritual progress – as it most certainly is for Christiana – but rather for
a kind of lived Vanity Fair: a moral lapse, a fall into social convention
rather than, to paraphrase Faithful in *The Pilgrim's Progress*, a buying of
moral truth. It is this point that twentieth-century North American writer
Jane Rule makes so much of in her classic lesbian progress novel *Desert
of the Heart*, published in 1964. In that novel, heroine Evelyn Hall comes
to understand that the rites and conventions of morality, paramount
of these, marriage, can entrap one in loveless and meaningless lives.
Marriage is for Evelyn a Vanity Fair, and it is that recognition that creates
the emotional and psychological space to risk moral condemnation and
communal rejection by living the truth of her love and desire for another
woman.

When a number of years ago I examined how *Desert of the Heart* explicitly revises *The Pilgrim's Progress*, I provided little analysis of the lesbian
literary and cultural context for this engagement. With this chapter I
intend to flesh out that context and, further, to consider Bunyan's linkage to one of the earliest and most influential lesbian novels, Radclyffe
Hall's *The Well of Loneliness*, published in 1928. Novels such as Hall's
and Rule's either explicitly adopt or reject Bunyan's representations of
the dangers of sexuality experienced by female pilgrims and the consequent need for locating female progress within a context of a developing
community of faith. In writing *The Well*, Hall bequeaths *The Pilgrim's
Progress* as a master text for subsequent lesbian novelists. With *Desert
of the Heart*, Rule, in turn, critiques Hall's novel and rejects the images
of female progress codified in *The Pilgrim's Progress* and circulated and
celebrated in secular culture well past the time that Hall was writing.
Often referred to as 'the Lesbian Bible' because of both its indebtedness
to a tradition of novel writing informed by the Bible, Milton, and Bunyan, and its canonical status within a tradition of lesbian fiction, *The
Well* is a crucial 'bridge' text between Bunyan and twentieth-century
and contemporary lesbian novels; it is a text whose analysis clarifies the

inevitable relevance of *The Pilgrim's Progress* for a tradition of lesbian novels.

2.   From 'a well of English undefiled' to *The Well of Loneliness*

Between *Jane Eyre* and *Desert of the Heart* one finds key developments in the circulation and reception of *The Pilgrim's Progress*. That is to say, the recognition of Bunyan's text as a site for configuring and 'resolving' issues of race, gender, and sexuality, as seen in Brontë's *Jane Eyre*, increased as *The Pilgrim's Progress* travelled to different parts of the world, specifically Empire; at the same time the very rise of such different and distant communities of readers ensured the divergence of their textual interpretations. As Isabel Hofmeyr has demonstrated in her landmark study *The Portable Bunyan: A Transnational History of* The Pilgrim's Progress, Bunyan's text by the 1840s had already, within the context of the Baptist American South, become 'a book about black experience'. Travelling from there to Jamaica 'the text was further 'baptized' in the currents of Caribbean intellectual traditions'.[9] When, in turn, black West Indian missionaries took Bunyan with them to Africa, the book facilitated colonial critique within the context of religious conversion and belonging. Ironically, the very importance of *The Pilgrim's Progress* as a missionary text determined a growing claim within British civil service and, then, academic contexts of the book as a cultural rather than religious mainstay, whose literary power lay in its 'Englishness' and 'whiteness' rather than in the universality of its message. As Hofmeyr has pointed out, the emergence of English literary studies, which began in the 1880s and 'which acquired a strongly racial veneer under the influence of Social Darwinist thinking',[10] not only defined Bunyan as a key English literary figure, but also has largely determined the absence of race as a field of critical inquiry within Bunyan scholarship through the present day.

Within this context, sexuality fares little better. As Siobhan Somerville has pointed out, 'Although gender insubordination offers a powerful explanatory model for the 'invention' of homosexuality, ideologies of gender also ... shaped and were shaped by dominant constructions of race.'[11] Contemporaneous with the emergence of Social Darwinism and, more generally, the 'intensification and institutionalisation' of scientific racism in the latter half of the nineteenth century is the advent of sexology and, following it, the beginnings of gay and lesbian or, more broadly, queer literature in English.[12] The last part of the nineteenth century saw the appearance of discussions – many of them medical and some literary – of various sexual behaviors and, importantly, sexual and gender identities. It is at the turn of the century, for example, that the terms 'homosexual' and 'heterosexual', are coined. In the early twentieth-century American and British fiction that represents gay and lesbian characters, there is often a kind of semantic and, further, epistemological uneasiness on the part of narrators and characters. (So, Gertrude Stein in her 1903 novella *Q.E.D.* writes of 'the many *disguised* forms' of 'physical passion', and a bit later in the text she encodes lesbian desire through the repetition of the word 'nothing'.[13]) How, after all, is one to represent same-sex desire, and what should one call people who are attracted to members of the same sex? One hundred years ago the language for gay-ness and lesbianism/for queerness was very much in the making, and it was highly contested.

Writers in the early twentieth century were particularly aware of the social power and authority of medical discussions of sexuality, and even as some of those medical and psychological discussions said that gay men and lesbians needed to be treated sympathetically, the default register of these texts was typically that gay men and lesbians were monstrous and aberrant. Consider, for example, the following passage from the privately printed 1906 novel *Imre: A Memorandum* written by American expatriate Edward Prime-Stevenson:

Uranian? Similisexual? Homosexual? Dionian?
Profound and often all too oppressive, even terrible, can be the significance of those cold psychic-sexual terms to the man who – '*knows*'! *To the man who 'knows*'! Even more terrible to those who understand them not, may be the human natures of which they are but new and clumsy technical symbols, the mere labels of psychiatric study, within a few decades of medical explorers.[14]

The speaker here is the protagonist, Oscar, a well-travelled Englishman, more at home abroad than at home. Here Oscar voices his uneasiness with the scientific/medical language of same-gender desire. None of the various sexological terms he considers – Uranian, similisexual, homo-sexual – proves satisfactory. Compelling for him (if not contemporary readers) is the rather pompous euphemism '*the man who "knows"* '. Even so, the phrase anticipates the work of gender theorists in the latter part of the twentieth century, theorists such as Monique Wittig and Judith Butler, who have recognized the extent to which the relegation of homosexuality to the periphery of an epistemology of gender – to the realm of unintelligibility – has structured discourses of heterosexual or heteronormative cultural practices.[15]

In 1928, Radclyffe Hall, a well-respected, prize-winning English novelist and Catholic convert who was herself lesbian, decided to write a novel that would provide a sympathetic treatment of 'inverts', a term which today we may understand as referring not only to gay men and lesbians, but also to transgendered and transsexual people.[16] The result was *The Well of Loneliness*, a novel that, while fairly criticized for its awful writing – 'mawkish prose' is one phrase that comes to mind – and its dearth of happy lesbians, is nonetheless a key early twentieth-century British text that links Bunyanesque fiction to modernism and, at the same time, founds lesbian literature. *The Well* was also the subject of one of the most important and publicized obscenity trials in early twentieth-century Great Britain. Though banned in Great Britain, *The Well* was widely available, both on the Continent and in the US. It has never gone out of print. In writing *The Well* Hall had a strategy that was two-fold: not only would she make use of the models of gender and sexuality laid out by Havelock Ellis, who, in contrast to other sexologists, insisted that inverts should be treated with sympathy, she also would draw on a tradition of English novel writing deeply informed by Bunyan's *The Pilgrim's Progress*. While Hall was undoubtedly not the only Modernist to know her Bunyan,[17] I argue that in her case the encodings of his work have proven especially important and vexed for Bunyan and LGBT studies alike. Hall's contemporary readers would have understood that, by drawing on Bunyan's narrative, Hall was calling for the acceptance of stigmatized sexual and gender minorities as a category or community of people.

In 1928 Bunyan would have come easily to British readers' minds. 1928 was the year of the Bunyan tercentenary celebrations, with events held across Britain, the United States, and Australia.[18] British Home Secretary Sir William Joynson-Hicks, who, beginning in August, oversaw the censorship of Hall's novel, participated in a number of such events.[19] In November of that year, the same month that the ban on the book was upheld, Joynson-Hicks, appearing before the World's Evangelical Alliance, offered a tribute to Bunyan. After remarking on *The Pilgrim's Progress*'s translation into 120 languages, Joynson-Hicks spoke of both Bunyan's 'Englishness' – 'the common ordinary Puritan of his day' – and his 'marvellous' book's relevance to Britons' own everyday lives. As paraphrased in a 23 November *Times* report, he noted that in Bunyan's text, '... one met there those great difficulties that Christian met and we met them here in our own life. The pilgrimage which Christian took was here for us today and the Slough of Despond was here in our life. The Valley of Humiliation was with us, too, and not all had triumphed as had Christian.' In effect, Bunyan had demonstrated, 'the plain, simple way to salvation.' It is tempting to wonder whether *The Well of Loneliness*'s trial, which had carried into mid November, was on his mind when, a week later, he made these remarks. A month earlier, speaking to the London Diocesan Council of Youth, he indirectly referred to the necessity of banning the novel:

> It may be possible in the near future I shall have to deal with immoral and disgusting books ... I am attacked on the one hand by all those people who put freedom of speech and thought and writing before everything else in the world, as if there were freedom in God's world to pollute the young generation growing up.[20]

Even though Hall casts *The Well* as a modern-day *The Pilgrim's Progress*, Joynson-Hicks' speeches suggest a sharp contrast between the two books: Bunyan's is 'marvellous'; Hall's 'immoral and disgusting'.

The Home Secretary's assessments notwithstanding, one of the most important and problematic connections between the two texts resides in *The Well*'s sustaining of a racialized religious discourse – in the very claim of her invert-hero's 'Englishness', the very 'Englishness' that in the case of Bunyan Joynson-Hicks extols. Hall's contemporary readers would have recognized how she engages such a discourse in order to evoke their sympathy. In its reliance on what Robert Southey famously called 'a well of English undefiled',[21] *The Well of Loneliness* in effect recapitulates the kinds of questions regarding race that grew around *The Pilgrim's Progress*'s literary status during the late nineteenth century and that, within the context of literary modernism, recurred within the discourse of primitivism.[22] Regarding the former, Hofmeyr explains,

> On the one hand, a stress on white Englishness rooted the writer in England, while maintaining Bunyan as a literary icon who could confer racial distinctiveness on Britons. An ethereal universality, on the other hand, could elevate Bunyan above the black colonized societies with whom mission discourse had so long connected him. Such societies had initially provided the pre-condition for nineteenth-century ideas on Bunyan's universality. Their erasure from the critical record became one precondition for twentieth-century Bunyan scholarship to take shape and for *The Pilgrim's Progress* to become unequivocally a book of England.[23]

So, in the last paragraph of *The Well of Loneliness*, protagonist Stephen Gordon prays: 'God ... we believe; we have told You we believe ... We have not denied You, then rise up and defend us. Acknowledge us, oh God, before the whole world. Give us also the right to our existence!'[24] Casting her life as a spiritual progress, she is the sexological pilgrim seeking not only the 'Life, life, eternal life' that Bunyan's Christian sought but also the communal recognition and support experienced by Christiana.[25] Yet, Stephen's status is fraught with racial anxiety. The novel's final two pages figure her simultaneously as virgin-invert and victim of incestuous and miscegenistic rape. If, as Jean Walton has so trenchantly argued, 'to be sexually aberrant is also to be racially suspect',[26] then Stephen's call for a recognition and embrace of the community of invert believers whose existence mainstream society has either denied or demonized ultimately depends on Radclyffe Hall's claim of (the natural superiority of) whiteness, specifically English whiteness. More broadly, Stephen's call depends on Hall's disavowal of a vision of a community of readers ready to examine and critique multiple (cultural, religious, and social) sites of oppression.

A close reading reveals Bunyan's importance for the novel. From the beginning, Stephen's story resonates with allegorical significance. Hall frames Stephen's life as a Christian life *par excellence*. She is born on Christmas Eve and named after Saint Stephen, the first Christian martyr. And, too, those key questions that mark progress narratives, 'Who am I?'; 'What shall I do to be saved?', impel Stephen's maturation as she develops from a child and adolescent in need of her father's guidance into an adult committed to understanding the meaning of her life within moral and religious terms. The first question most clearly appears as 'What am I?',[27] the question of the pilgrim who, like Bunyan's Christiana, finds that her gender status and sexuality constitute the experiential stuff of her progress. The second question emerges when the adult Stephen, a novelist, acknowledges and confronts her gender and sexual unintelligibility and her consequent exclusion from mainstream society. Having learned, like Christian, that there is 'no real abiding city',[28] she leaves behind family and home. Hers is the martyr's narrative that, pointing out the moral failings of this world's social plots, offers up her own life as spiritual *pattern*.

Stephen's progress turns on her growing awareness of her embodied transgression of gender binaries: biologically a woman, but looking like, presenting as, a man, she is also a woman who desires not men but women. Born 'narrow-hipped' and 'wide-shouldered',[29] she is, in her father's words, 'all the son that I've got',[30] and he raises her to be the perfect English country gentlemen. She rides astride; she fences; she studies and writes. She is self-sacrificing, brave, athletic, and heroic. Above all, she loves the family estate, Morton, 'well-timbered, well-cottaged, well-fenced and well-watered',[31] an idyllic, paradisiacal setting. Yet, for all that, Stephen seems to her mother, 'a blemished, unworthy, maimed reproduction' of her father.[32] News of her daughter's inversion confirms this reading for her: she tells Stephen, 'this thing that you are is a sin against creation.'[33] The novel, of course, even as it continually returns to this interpretation, underscores its injustice. Stephen is no 'sin against creation'; she is rather a sign of the limited efficacy of gender norms when it comes to the interpretation of gender and sexual identity. One of 'those who stand midway between the sexes',[34] who occupies 'the no-man's-land of sex',[35] Stephen 'combine[s] the strength of a man with the gentler and more subtle strength of a woman'.[36] Even so, as a young adult she can only understand herself at best as an epistemological question mark; at worst, like her mother, she regards herself as a moral outrage: So '[s]he would think with a kind of despair: "What am I in God's name – some kind of abomination?" ... Why am I as I am – and what am I?'[37]

If as a child Stephen turns to her father to explicate the world and, significantly, herself, as an adult she confronts the question of her identity without the help of a guide. She turns instead to a set of books, the Bible and Richard von Krafft-Ebing's *Psychopathia Sexualis* (the latter first published in 1886 and perhaps the most important sexological text at the turn of the century). In this, she both recalls and extends the picture of Christian at the opening of Bunyan's text. Christian appears on the first page of *The Pilgrim's Progress*. The narrator describes him as follows:

> a man clothed with rags, standing in a certain place, with his face from his own house, a book in his hand, and a great burden upon his back. I looked, and saw him open the book, and read therein; and as he read, he wept and trembled: and not being able longer to contain, he brake out with a lamentable cry; saying, 'What shall I do?'[38]

The book that Christian is reading is, of course, the Bible. As Dayton Haskin has argued, the burden on Christian's back is the burden not only of sin but also of textual interpretation.[39] Reading the Bible, Christian learns to enact his life as spiritual text. By comparison, Stephen's invitation to a progress is founded on the exegesis of both sacred and sexological texts. In her father's library she finds 'the battered old book' written by Krafft-Ebing and 'her father's old, well-worn Bible'.[40] She reacts to *Psychopathia*'s case studies of inversion by crying out to her deceased father and, implicitly, calling out to God: 'Oh, Father – and there are so many of us – thousands of miserable, unwanted people, who have no right to compassion because they're maimed, hideously maimed and ugly – God's cruel; He let us get flawed in the making.'[41] Turning next to the Bible, she looks for 'a sign from heaven'.[42] The passage she turns to is Genesis 4:15, 'And the Lord set a mark upon Cain', and, in response, she sinks despondent, 'completely hopeless and beaten'.[43] Her reading here recalls her mother's own and seemingly affirms the inherently fallen and perverted condition of the invert, for whom salvation seems impossible and damnation inevitable.

If Stephen's burden is, like Christian's, one of textual interpretation, it is also, like Christiana's, the burden of sexuality, simultaneously the vehicle for and obstacle to her progress. For Bunyan, Christiana's sexuality is the mark of her spiritual and social inferiority. Her awakening to this knowledge enables her to undertake her spiritual journey, albeit under the protection of a male guide and within the context of an ever-growing Church community. Radclyffe Hall resolves Stephen's case differently. Early on, the adult Stephen rejects a male guide, would-be suitor Martin Hallam. Instead, sunk to the floor of her father's study, Stephen listens to the words of her friend and former governess, who implicitly answers the question 'What shall I do to be saved?' for her. The older woman calls upon Stephen to work; she urges her to write from the depth (well?) of her experiences:

> You've got work to do – come and do it! Why just because you are what you are, you may actually find that you've got an advantage. You may write with a curious double insight – write both men and women from a personal knowledge. . . . Some day the world will recognize this, but meanwhile there's plenty of work that's waiting. For the sake of all the others like you, but less strong and less gifted perhaps, many of them, it's up to you to have the courage to make good, and I'm here to help you to do it, Stephen.[44]

Much like Victorian protagonists before her, Stephen determines that through her writing she can perform the good work so necessary for a pilgrim's progress. In a self-imposed exile that takes her first to London and then to Paris, she finds that work consists of reconciling a tradition of spiritual interpretation with emerging scientific discussions so as to understand inversion as neither 'a mark of Cain' nor a sign of 'maimed' nor degenerate humanity but rather as the wound of religious and social martyrdom: the 'outward stigmata of the abnormal – verily the wounds of One nailed to a cross'.[45]

Stephen's work would seem to be the establishing of a spiritualized sexological discourse, capable of granting a community of invert-pilgrims cultural legitimacy. Arguing for Stephen's success in understanding inversion in this way or in crafting such a vindicating discourse for inversion is not easily done, particularly since that discourse depends on a racist ideology. It is not simply that Stephen, while she does become a successful writer, leads a personal life that is filled with sorrow: many of the women she befriends – Wanda, Jamie, and Barbara, for example – are damaged by the social isolation and exile that is the price of their inversion; she ultimately gives up her devoted lover, Mary Llewelyn, since she can not marry her and so legitimize their relationship; in general, she intensifies her own experience of loss by remaining invested in the very gender binaries and attendant social prescriptions that mark her as an outcast.[46] Complicating that investment is the narrator's and presumably Stephen's own understanding of self as 'some primitive thing conceived in a turbulent age of transition'.[47] In other words, Radclyffe Hall aligns Stephen's inversion with exotic primitivism and then insists on – narrates – the fallaciousness of that linkage through the construction of Stephen's whiteness as both normative and rightfully privileged.[48]

Much has been written about Modernist primitivism within both American and European contexts.[49] James F. Knapp has contended that '[b]y the early twentieth century, primitivism had become one of the languages of modernity, and we may trace in its grammar the contentiousness of change',[50] where 'contentiousness' included the contestation surrounding various kinds of identities, including class, race, gender, and sexual identities. Mary Gluck, in turn, has explained that for Europeans, avant-garde artists and consumers of mass culture alike, primitivism expressed 'the desire for escape, … attraction of the exotic, [and] … longing for the natural'. It reflected the 'empirical realities and cultural fantasies through which [they] attempted to create alternate identities that lay outside the frame of Western modernity',[51] even as it also disclosed its investment in 'the politics of imperial expansion'.[52] Hall's decision to make use of primitivism in order to convey the naturalness of Stephen's lesbian desire should be understood within these terms.

So, for example, it is on the 'holiday' island of Tenerife that Mary and Stephen consummate their relationship. As Sarah E. Chinn explains,

[t]he one place that lesbian sexuality has permission to emerge, and Stephen can let down her guard, is … on the Canary Island of Tenerife. Tenerife, the largest of a cluster of about half a dozen islands … off the border coast of Morocco and what is now Western Sahara, was – as

it still is – a Spanish colony with an already long history of tourism of the 1920s.[53]

On Tenerife, Stephen and Mary can happily explore their lesbianism because they are on vacation from the gender constraints that have determined their lives in Great Britain and France. The two women can simultaneously 'go native' and maintain their privileged status as white tourists.

This tension between identification and disavowal of the correspondence between sexual otherness and primitive exoticism resurfaces upon the lovers' return to Paris. There, Stephen meets two African-American musicians and, with them, engages primitivism via what Simon Gikandi has termed 'the curiously privileged role of the African American – in modernism'.[54] Specifically, Stephen struggles to accede to a representative voice for all [white] inverts by first co-opting and then distancing herself from a tradition of African-American discourse of spiritual and social empowerment. As Jean Walton has demonstrated, Stephen's encounter with the musician brothers Lincoln and Henry, recalling Radclyffe Hall's own 1927 engagement of American musicians Taylor Gordon and J. Rosamond Johnson, facilitates her access to a language of witnessing that acknowledges suffering and calls for righteousness: an access that, significantly, turns on her understanding of the men as 'racial primitives'.[55] Thus, Lincoln has 'the patient, questioning expression common to the eye of most animals and to those of all slowly evolving races'.[56] For Stephen as for the other inverts gathered at Valérie Seymour's salon in order to hear the brothers, Henry's singing of 'Deep River' 'channels the voices of the 'hopeless', so that these voices mysteriously interpellate the listeners in such a way that they spontaneously clasp hands with each other, acknowledging their shared status with the "hopeless" '[57] Walton effectively demonstrates that this is a moment of 'cultural ventriloquism that has by now become a familiar trope in a white modernist tradition that is characterized by its invention of, and fascination with, the "primitive" ': in other words, 'the Negroes present a model that will inform Stephen's discovery of the form for which she has been searching as invert-novelist'.[58]

That form for both Radclyffe Hall and Stephen is a novel that is scientifically updated for an early twentieth-century audience and that, crucially, replicates the dynamics of racial distinctiveness and racial erasure at work in the critical reception of *The Pilgrim's Progress* at the end of the nineteenth and well into the twentieth century.[59] Thus, *The Well* begins with a brief commentary by English sexologist Havelock Ellis, who, in contrast to Krafft-Ebing, argues against reading inversion as a sign of degeneration:

> I have read *The Well of Loneliness* with great interest because ... it possesses a notable psychological and sociological significance. So far as I know, it is the first English novel which presents, in a completely faithful and uncompromising form, one particular aspect of sexual life as it exists among us to-day. The relation of certain people – who, while different from their fellow human beings, are sometimes of the highest character and the finest aptitudes – to the often hostile society in which they move, presents difficult and still unsolved problems ...[60]

Ellis focuses on the social intolerance faced by inverts; sexual 'difference' rather than perversion marks this group of people, who at times are 'of the highest character and the finest aptitudes'. By including Ellis' perspective at the outset of the novel, Hall in effect gains the scientific authority that allows her to rebut the pathologizing portrait of inversion offered by Krafft-Ebing, particularly in the earliest editions of *Psychopathia* that Stephen encountered.[61] In setting up Stephen as 'of the highest character and the finest aptitudes', Ellis also implicitly distances Stephen from the 'racial primitivism' to which both she and Hall compare inversion in key moments in the novel. Indeed, as both Siobhan Somerville and Margot Gayle Backus have noted, Ellis's discussion of sexual inversion, particularly in the first volume of *Studies in the Psychology of Sex*, is racially coded.[62] Backus explains that in his study,

> Ellis relies on the anthropological model that emerged out of the close articulation in early twentieth-century anthropological discourse between social Darwinism, racism, and industrial capitalism. This anthropological model predicts (or requires) that 'lower' or non-white races will be less socially and psycho-sexually differentiated. Racial advancement, Ellis assumes, will invariably take for these 'lower' peoples the same forms that it took in Western Europe. Greater economic and social differentiation within an 'adaptive', 'advancing' culture will, according to Ellis, lead to the isolation and emergence of 'the invert' as a specialized class.[63]

From this perspective, Stephen's exceptionality is necessarily raced white.

More specifically, as Backus has compellingly demonstrated, it is marked as English, in contrast to a primitivism that includes Celticism.

Perhaps Hall's most powerful and intimate study in racialized contrasts is that between the English Stephen and her mother, the Irish Lady Anna. Unlike Stephen, who is 'masculine' and 'logical',[64] Lady Anna is 'emotional' and 'feminine', qualities that locate her within the 'realm that Victorian and Edwardian constructions of Irish culture . . . associated with "the Celt" '.[65] Backus continues:

> Hall's incorporation of . . . Celticism into her novel's . . . representational codes places Stephen's identity and activities, coded as 'English' as against Anna's Irishness, within a specific sphere with which most British readers would have unconsciously identified. Hall's positioning of Stephen in opposition to an Irish mother puts immense pressure on the reader to identify with Stephen and to side with her as the text's 'rightful' protagonist.[66]

Hall's representational politics push the reader to identify with Stephen, who registers as racially superior.

Even so, the text continually underscores that Stephen is herself half Irish, and both her choice of lover and her language reveal the imaginative hold that Celticism exercises over her. Stephen may be 'all things to Mary; father, mother, friend and lover, all things', in other words, the guide for Mary 'the child, the friend, the beloved, all things',[67] but, as Backus points out, Mary also 'constitutes a countervailing force . . . on the side of the colonial equation that [Victorian writer Matthew] Arnold mistakenly construes as [the Celts' and by extension] her natural place: intuitively, dreamily, and with infinite hope, the Celtic Mary is by nature inclined to restore beauty to a world that the rational, bureaucratic, and warlike Briton is by nature inclined to destroy'.[68] As such, she functions discursively much as do musician brothers Lincoln and Henry; though on a much more intimate level, she, too, serves as a projection of Stephen's own desire to arrive at a form of writing that will champion inverts' 'right to . . . existence'.[69]

The novel's inverted sentence patterns are themselves a manifestation of this desire, at work within both Stephen and Radclyffe Hall. As Backus has persuasively demonstrated, in the novel 'subject complements are frequently hooked up "backwards" to transitive clauses, as in "a happy and pleasant visit it had been" '.[70] Stephen herself takes up 'inverted constructions[, which] are crucially linked to the submerged but insistent Celticism that emerges in the text's overall construction of gender and of otherness and that is exemplified in textual representations of Stephen's mother, her Irish hunter Raftery, and her Welsh lover Mary

Llewellyn'.[71] In general, *'The Well of Loneliness*'s use of "inverted" sentence patterns suggests an early experimental attempt to develop a form of lesbian writing, to "write the lesbian body" as Hall understood that body through the available medical and psychiatric discourses of her time.'[72] Hall's – and by extension Stephen's – rhetorical strategy is necessarily an ironic one. It turns on a colonial sensibility; it upholds a politics of othering that, in the case of sexual inversion, it seeks to undo.

For Hall, writing a Bunyanesque modernist novel, in which issues of female sexuality and community prove central, entailed not only taking on the debilitating voices of sexology and religion with which Stephen contends, it also meant sustaining a vision of racial hierarchy at once scientific and aesthetic. The result is necessarily a tragedy, one that races, genders, and sexualizes the spiritual injustice of Stephen's oppression and also, importantly, forecloses the vision of a community built on an experience of linked oppressions – racism and homophobia, for example – that becomes so crucial for later twentieth-century feminist, lesbian, and queer novels.[73]

Thus, even as it tries to create a space of acceptance and respect for Stephen Gordon and the countless inverts whom she represents, *The Well* does so by participating in the very forms of marginalization that, at least in the case of inversion, it seeks to challenge. Hall's investment in discourses of spiritual and cultural righteousness participates in a racist and sexist ideology, and it accordingly exacts a heavy narrative price for the invert pilgrim. Ineluctably committed to gendered notions of progress, for which Bunyan's text offers powerful narrative models, Stephen must ultimately sacrifice her relationship with Mary, self, and community to convention. So, Stephen determines that Mary's progress, like Christiana's before her, presupposes a male guide: someone whom she can marry; someone who can sanction her sexuality, someone with whom love proves legitimate and narratable.

In other words, *The Well* is as much 'about' the anxiety of writing within a literary tradition as it is 'about' the anxiety of writing (or failing to write) a new kind of novel: one that not only can be read as thoroughly English but also scientifically up to date; one that can represent lesbian desire as emotionally normative and socially sustainable. Radclyffe Hall fails to produce such a novel, largely because of the ways in which she (together with modernists in general) conceives of narrative possibility vis-à-vis constructions of race, gender, and sexuality. So, marriage remains for her as for Bunyan and the novelists who come after him the context for narrating a woman's story. Following the distinction that Patricia E. Chu draws, the difference between Hall and, say,

nineteenth-century writers is the difference between marriage understood as contract and marriage understood as status.[74] Marriage as status,
Chu explains, means that 'individuals consent to a set of privileges and
responsibilities determined by the state and marriage changes their relationship to the state'. In other words, '[e]arly twentieth-century legal,
legislative and popular contention about the definition and purposes of
institutionalized marriage signals marriage's compatibility with admin-
istrative modernity'.[75] In terms of *The Well*, because Stephen and Mary's
relationship exists outside of marriage as the legitimizing authority of
the state, it is sustainable in terms of neither plot nor story. Stephen's
consciousness of her inability to marry her lover determines both the
rupture of the relationship and the end of Hall's novel.

Stephen's own crossings of gender, race, and sexuality also preclude
any happy resolution on either a social or a narrative level. She may
imagine herself as an invert-pilgrim, but the community she represents
'haunts' rather than houses her. Spectral inverts call upon her in the last
paragraphs of the novel. These voices of 'the quick, the dead, and the
yet unborn' recall,[76] not only, as Margot Backus has shown, the gay man
from Paris bar who calls Stephen 'ma sœur',[77] but also, as Jean Walton has
demonstrated, 'the voices conveyed by [brothers Henry and Lincoln]'.[78]
In terms of this latter reading, Stephen is 'being endowed with the same
capacity of the spirituals singers to convey the suffering of a 'multitude',
that she is on the threshold of launching a tradition of expression that
will do for inverts what spirituals have done for Negroes'.[79] Even so, the
imagery suggests incestuous and miscegenistic rape as much as it does
queer annunciation.[80] As Walton explains, 'the already racialized motif
of kinship', earlier at work in the description of the musician brothers,
'appears once more to be evoked'.[81] Stephen, in this scene, not only
recalls the brothers but is also sister and mother to the invert spirits
that 'possess' her and make 'her barren womb ... fruitful', with their
'rockets of pain, burning rockets of pain': '... In their madness to become
articulate through her, they were tearing her to pieces getting her under.
They were everywhere now, cutting off her retreat.'[82]

Ultimately, Stephen may call out to God to grant inverts 'the right to
our existence!'[83] In so doing she may invite readers to understand not
only how the earlier identity crisis has given way to a profession of faith
that underscores the moral purpose of her writing, but also the generative
structure of the novel she inhabits. Read from the perspective of these,
Stephen's final words, *The Well of Loneliness* itself performs the good work
of pilgrimage that is her writing. Still, Stephen can only imagine her
twinned sexual and interpretive burdens as 'fearful and sterile':[84] signs

of an 'authentic alterity' that remains 'linguistically dispossessed'[85] and that bears 'the misassociation with blackness'.[86] Hers is the ineluctable tragedy that Radclyffe Hall's sustained commitment to the 'Englishness' of Bunyan's text entails: a life story and a story of critical reception marked by loss and isolation; by communal fracture and liminality; by, indeed, a modernist Slough of Despond, 'a well of loneliness'.[87] Such is the inheritance that Hall bequeaths to later writers of lesbian progress novels.

3. 'There is no allegory any longer': Jane Rule's *Desert of the Heart*

In her 1975 essay collection *Lesbian Images*, Canadian novelist Jane Rule wrote,

> *The Well of Loneliness* by Radclyffe Hall ... remains *the* lesbian novel, a title familiar to most readers of fiction, either a bible or a horror story for any lesbian who reads at all. ... Along with the teachings of the church and the moral translations of those teachings by psychologists, *The Well of Loneliness* has influenced millions of readers in their attitudes toward lesbians.
>
> ...
>
> Though the novel was viciously attacked for its sympathetic idealizing of the invert, ... its survival as the single authoritative novel on lesbian love depends on it misconceptions. It supports the view that men are naturally superior. ... Stephen does not defy the social structure she was born into. Male domination is intolerable to her only when she can't assert it for herself. Women are inferior. Loving relationships must be between superior and inferior persons.
>
> ...
>
> Radclyffe Hall ... worshiped the very institutions which oppressed her, the Church and patriarchy ... Inside that framework she made and tried to redefine the only proud choice she had. The 'bible' she offered is really no better for women than the Bible she would not reject.[88]

In her own fiction, *because* she wanted to make the space for a 'happy' lesbian love story, Rule challenged the normative hierarchies upheld in Radclyffe Hall's novel. Above all, Rule interrogates conventional representations of gender, and she does so by problematizing and rejecting the Christian literary legacy that was so important for Hall.

That doubled process of literary critique is apparent from the start of Rule's 1964 novel, *Desert of the Heart*, one of whose protagonists, Evelyn, like Stephen Gordon before her, bears the 'brand of Cain on her forehead'.[89] In most of the fiction published between 1928 and 1964, lesbian characters inhabited what Catharine Stimpson has called 'the narrative of damnation':[90] they wound up either alone or dead, or they realized that, after all, they were heterosexual and they accordingly married. *Desert of the Heart* is one of the few novels from this time period that have a happy ending.[91] In an early draft of the novel, Rule gave Evelyn the surname Cross, a name that identifies her as a kind of Christian hero.[92] Significantly, by the final version, Rule had changed the name to Hall, as if to signal at least in part that her novel would revise a lesbian story's investment in Christian texts. In other words, the name that Evelyn shares with Radclyffe Hall points to the character's status as a cultural outsider; it also represents a challenge to or revision of Hall's own representation of plots available to lesbian characters.[93] The particular Christian text that Rule takes on, challenges, de-allegorizes, and, in so doing, ironically radicalizes anew is *The Pilgrim's Progress*. 'Questioning conventional morality can be the beginning of a moral education from which we can learn to make choices based on understanding rather than blind faith or great fear', observes Rule in her 1985 essay 'On a Moral Education'.[94] *Desert of the Heart*'s happy ending is absolutely predicated upon heroine Evelyn's decision to let go of a Christian moral framework for understanding her own life's progress, specifically, her love for and desire to be with a woman.

Rule describes her novel in a 1961 letter to a college friend. She remarks that, aside from Dante, Yeats, and Eliot, Bunyan 'haunt[s] the desert and the gambling casinos and the court' that constitute the novel's setting. 'I have tried to cope with what I think is a basic issue in human experience', Rule continues. For her, Bunyan and the others yield 'that rich inheritance of moral imagery which is often intellectually appreciated and philosophically rejected and emotionally experienced ...'[95]

Rule's relation to that inheritance is further indicated by the novel's title. Initially called *Permanent Resident*, the novel was published as *Desert of the Heart*, an echo of the final stanza of W. H. Auden's elegy 'In Memory of W. B. Yeats':

> In the deserts of the heart
> Let the healing fountain start,
> In the prison of his days
> Teach the free man how to praise.

In the elegy, which he composed on the eve of World War II, Auden contemplates the role of poetry, particularly at a time when, 'In the nightmare of the dark' when 'All the dogs of Europe bark'. For Auden, 'poetry makes nothing happen'. It is not an instrument of political or social change. It does, however, carry moral and social import,[96] and, accordingly, as Edward Mendelson's gloss of the final stanza indicates, poetry 'has ... powers to heal, soothe, teach, liberate, and triumph'.[97] *Desert of the Heart*, too, offers its readers possibility and promise, and it does so, importantly, even when other canonical literary works cannot.

Set in the home of casinos and 'quickie' marriages and divorces, Reno, Nevada, in 1958, *Desert of the Heart* speaks to the power of story (or stories) in the lives of so many lesbians, especially those of the 1950s and 1960s, whose desires and loves existed beyond the legitimizing and sanctioning powers of state, church, and literary canon. Jaye Zimet has termed the McCarthy/Eisenhower era paradoxical: a cultural moment in which 'straightlaced suburban sensibility' operated at the same time as 'postwar freedom, excitement, and sexual exploration'.[98] Alfred Kinsey's *Report on Sexual Behavior in the Human Male*, issued in 1948, helped facilitate a growing public awareness of sexual diversity.[99] One can, however, hardly speak of a public tolerance let alone acceptance of such diversity. For lesbians living in the United States in the 1950s, validating narratives of same-sex desire could not be found in mainstream contexts, which celebrated marriage, together with homemaking and childrearing, as the *ne plus ultra* of white, middle-class women's existence. As Betty Friedan, author of *The Feminine Mystique*, the second-wave feminist classic that was published one year before Rule's novel, remarks, 'In the fifteen years after World War II, this mystique of feminine fulfilment became the cherished and self-perpetuating core of contemporary American culture.'[100] The 'problem' as Friedan saw it was precisely a lack of fulfilment, an emptiness that permeated the lives of white, middle-class heterosexual women who conformed to normative cultural prescriptions of femininity. By contrast, the problem for lesbians, as well as gay men, was that their lives were 'ardent, dangerous, and secret',[101] and they often found themselves the study of medical and state surveillance.

Consider, for example, the following description of homosexuality put forth by the US Senate in their 1950 document 'Employment of Homosexuals and Other Sex Perverts in the US Government':

Overt acts of sex perversion, including acts of homosexuality, constitute a crime under our Federal, State, and municipal statutes and persons who commit such acts are law violators. Aside from the criminality and immorality involved in sex perversion such behavior is so contrary to the normal accepted standards of social behavior that persons who engage in such activity are looked upon as outcasts by society generally. The social stigma attached to sex perversion is so great that many perverts go to great lengths to conceal their perverted tendencies. This situation is evidenced by the fact that perverts are frequently victimized by blackmailers who threaten to expose their sexual deviations ... [102]

Within the political mainstream, lesbians and gay men were condemned as 'perverts' and 'outcasts'.

Intolerance and vilification of homosexuality even characterized progressive political circles. In her 'biomythography', *Zami: A New Spelling of My Name*, African-American lesbian poet Audre Lorde recalls the climate of left-wing activism in the United States during the early-to-mid 1950s:

I could imagine [my political] comrades, Black and white, among whom color and racial differences could be openly examined and talked about, nonetheless one day asking me accusingly, 'Are you or have you ever been a member of a homosexual relation?' For them, being gay was 'bourgeois and reactionary', a reason for suspicion and shunning. Besides, it made you 'more susceptible to the FBI'.[103]

Pre-Stonewall activists also participated in ambivalent, at times classist, attacks on aspects of lesbian and gay culture. As Suzanna Danuta Walters notes,

the Mattachine Society and the Daughters of Bilitis ... often found themselves at odds with the 'other' lesbians – the bar dykes, often working-class women whose affectional preference included the engagement in 'butch/fem' interactions. Butch/fem lesbians were seen by much of the leadership of DOB as helping to perpetuate negative stereotypes about lesbians and thus contributing to their own marginalization.[104]

In this political 'desert of the heart', it is hardly surprising that lesbians during the 1950s and 1960s turned to lesbian pulp fiction for the validation and sustenance otherwise denied them. World War II had popularized paperbacks, which were affordable readily available at newsstands and in drugstores. As Susan Stryker notes, in 1950 Fawcett published the first lesbian paperback original (pbo's), Tereska Torres'

Women's Barracks. That year it sold over a million copies.[105] (In 1951 Perma Books reprinted *The Well of Loneliness*; it sold over a one hundred thousand copies that year.[106]) By 1952, Torres' novel had come to the attention of the House of Representatives' Select Committee into Current Pornographic Materials (also known as the Gathings Committee), whose report 'singled [it] out for condemnation'.[107] Still, even as the report created an atmosphere of oppression for the industry, publishers recognized the market for lesbian paperbacks, which would be read not only by lesbians but also by [straight] men interested in salacious material. The industry responded to this double need – on the one hand, to avoid prosecution and, on the other hand, to meet reader demand – by adapting the sub-genre to the era's cultural and political intolerance of lesbianism. So, for example, in 1952 Fawcett editor Dick Carroll approached secretary Marijane Meaker about writing a lesbian-themed novel for the company's new pbo line, Gold Medal books. The 'only restriction', writes Zimet, was that the novel could not have 'a happy ending'.[108] In 1952, as Vin Packer, Meaker wrote *Spring Fire*. Zimet describes the novel as 'a relatively sincere and realistic account of a lesbian relationship',[109] at the end of which one woman goes crazy, while the other goes straight. Both outcomes prove conventional resolutions for pre-Stonewall and pre-Women's Movement lesbian pulp fiction. Carroll's formula worked: *Spring Fire* was an instant success, selling more than a million copies and even exceeding the popularity of *Women's Barracks*.

Without doubt the most acclaimed and enduring writer of the lesbian pbo, Ann Bannon offers another, doubled reason for the sub-genre's capacity to succeed. Writers of lesbian pulp, specifically women writers, whose works 'constituted a sort of industry within an industry' dominated by male writers and readers,[110] did not receive any critical attention in the 1950s or 1960s. They may have been expected to conform to the kinds of plot expectations mentioned above, in order to avoid censorship, but apart from that, Bannon observes, they were 'not even a blip on the radar screens of literary critics'. She continues:

> Not one [critic] ever reviewed a lesbian pulp paperback for the *New York Times Review of Books*, the *Saturday Review*, *The Atlantic Monthly*. We were lavishly ignored, except by the customers in the drugstores, airports, train stations, and newsstands who bought our books off the kiosks by the millions.... There was no public dialog about them in the media, either on their literary merits or their content, and that benign neglect provided a much-needed veil behind which we writers could work in peace.[111]

Importantly, that neglect also secured writers 'privacy, the chance to explore and experiment, to say the unsayable, and to fade away peacefully from the publishing scene when the paperbacks finished their popular run'.[112]

Pulp fiction might be critically dismissed as tawdry, sensational, sleazy. For a readership yearning to find its desires, particularly its sexual desires, represented, however, lesbian pulp proved a powerful and accessible medium, in part for the very reasons that critics overlooked it. As Ann Bannon observes,

> we needed stalwart social networks, we needed confirming friendships, but most of all, we needed the fire and enchantment of wonderful sex to validate our lives. Nothing else was going to help. It had to come from within us, and no aspect of human emotion is more deeply within us than that most delicate and powerful of mysteries, our sexuality. It was the glory of that sexual transport that eased the desperation of one's queerness.[113]

Thus, the sub-genre was able to offer lesbian readers a 'healing fountain': assurance that, even as they might live within 'the desert of the heart', a socio-cultural landscape in which their lesbianism had been marked out as un-American and subversive,[114] they were not alone in their desires, and their desires were liveable.[115] Lesbian readers may have had to 'read between the lines', as Zimet explains, 'and ignore the homophobic and moralistic storylines. But they were rewarded to find some sensitive portraits of lesbian characters and nuggets of gay life in the 1950s'.[116]

Jane Rule's *Desert of the Heart* owes much to the lesbian pbo's, its immediate predecessors. Even as it defies the conventional endings – such as heterosexual con- or reversion, institutionalization, marriage, and death – which constrained the kinds of stories that writers of lesbian pulps could tell, her novel also recalls those works. This is especially clear when considering Ann Bannon's fiction. One thinks, for example, of the trope of the indefinable but undeniable resemblance that exists among lesbians, a trope at work in both Bannon's second novel, *I am a Woman*, published in 1959, and Rule's own.[117] At times, the similarities only foreground the differences between the writers, and their ability to imagine lesbian possibilities. For example, one can compare the remarkably similar language of the oh-so-different endings of Bannon's first novel, *Odd*

Girl Out, published in 1957, and *Desert of the Heart. Odd Girl Out*, for instance, concludes:

> Then she turned and *walked slowly back down the steps* and over to the station. She picked up her bag where Laura had left it and walked outside into the sunshine, set it down, and looked at her watch. There was a sudden flutter of new joy in her heart.
> She had to hurry; it was almost five-thirty.[118]

Desert of the Heart ends with,

> *And they turned and walked back up the steps* toward their own image, reflected in the great, glass doors.[119]

In *Odd Girl Out*, lovers Laura and Beth part; in the last lines, Beth takes leave of Laura at the train station, and then hurries to meet her sometime boyfriend, Charlie. By contrast, in *Desert of the Heart*, lovers Evelyn and Ann turn and walk together, toward an uncertain and unscripted shared life.[120] Evelyn and Ann's happy ending is a crucial revision of Laura and Beth's. More broadly, it also reflects a crucial revision of the narrative hold that marriage exercises over (at least some of) Bannon's characters in her third and fourth novels, *Women in the Shadows* (1959) and *Journey to a Woman* (1960).

This is perhaps the crucial difference between Jane Rule and the writers of lesbian pulps: her readiness to take on both literary and social conventions. For Rule, the making – the *poesis* – of lesbian literature depends on the engagement, critique, and, in Adrienne Rich's sense of the term, revision of literary and social plots, in far bolder terms than those offered by (or permitted to) the writers of lesbian pulp. Core to that revision is her white, middle-class heroines' commitment to define themselves apart from the marriage ideal.

Desert of the Heart begins with the story of Evelyn Hall, a Berkeley English professor, who arrives in Reno in order to gain a divorce. While there she meets and falls in love with a younger woman named Ann, who works in a casino. The two women struggle with their love. They are unsure where or even how they can live together. Yet at the end of the novel, after Evelyn has obtained the divorce, the two decide to continue in their relationship, as Evelyn puts it, 'for a while ... For an indefinite period of time'. These words, in the penultimate paragraph of the novel, indicate how, for Rule, lesbian relationship is a process or progress of negotiation – negotiation that ironizes, overturns, and even abandons conventional cultural and literary expectations.

Such negotiation is apparent on the level of narrative. Rule's novel alternates between the viewpoints of its two protagonists, Evelyn and Ann. Their love story depends upon a balanced authority not only of the intertwined narratives but also of the women themselves: for each woman, desire depends upon recognizing the autonomy and power of the other. As Marilyn Schuster has noted, Rule's double narrative 'displac[es] the power of master narratives to determine fully the meanings of a woman's life'.[121] The primary master narrative that together Evelyn and Ann displace is Bunyan's or, more broadly, the popular secularized version of that narrative: Rule challenges the assumption that marriage is the primary means for understanding a woman's progress.

Explicit engagement and critique of *The Pilgrim's Progress* is present from the opening paragraphs of *Desert of the Heart*:

> Conventions, like clichés, have a way of surviving their own usefulness. They are then excused or defended as the idioms of living. For everyone, foreign by birth or by nature, convention is a mark of fluency. That is why, for any woman, marriage is the idiom of life. And she does not give it up out of scorn or indifference but only when she is forced to admit that she has never been able to pronounce it properly and has committed continually its grossest grammatical errors. For such a woman marriage remains a foreign tongue, an alien landscape, and, since she cannot become naturalized, she finally chooses voluntary exile.
>
> Evelyn Hall had been married for sixteen years before she admitted to herself that she was such a woman.[122]

This beginning identifies *Desert of the Heart* as a progress novel, even as it subverts conventional constructions of female progress. The paragraphs echo the first part of *The Pilgrim's Progress*, in which the hero, Christian, has to leave wife and children, in order to undertake his spiritual progress. At the same time, the novel's beginning radically rewrites the second part of *The Pilgrim's Progress*, in which the heroine Christiana's spiritual story depends upon her marriage: her following and eventual reunion with Christian in the Celestial City. Marriage for the female pilgrim – whether in Bunyan's text or, say, in so many nineteenth- and twentieth-century novels and, for that matter, in the socialization of generations of women – is not simply the end point but also the precondition for her travel. It is 'the idiom of life'. In Bunyan's work, Christiana's spiritual consummation and reunion with her husband merge to direct her progress. But if Bunyan insists that Christiana is at home with marriage, Rule asks whether marriage is at home with the heroine of fiction or with the woman reader. For Evelyn Hall, it is not. The words in the opening paragraph 'foreign', 'alien', and 'exile' place Evelyn in a Bunyanesque tradition that she immediately problematizes. Stephen Gordon in *The Well of Loneliness* can never relinquish her desire to participate in the 'honourable estate' of heterosexual coupling.[123] Her sense of loss at being unable to marry her lover leaves her reading her life as a 'well of loneliness'. How very different is Evelyn's trajectory. Writing some five years after *Desert of the Heart*'s publication, Adrienne Rich remarks of marriage, '[t]he "grammar" has "turned and attacked" . . .'. So in 'A Valediction Forbidding Mourning' she takes permanent leave of marriage: 'When I talk of taking a trip I mean forever.'[124] As for Rich's speaker, so for Rule's heroine: Evelyn's progress is predicated not on an inability to marry but rather on the necessity of divorce – divorce from her husband and from conventions, literary as well as social.[125]

So, for example, Evelyn's flight to Reno initially seems to reverse Bunyan's paradigm of pilgrimage, the journey from the City of Destruction to the Celestial City. Evelyn is from the Bay area, which Reno inhabitants consider 'a promised land . . . a promised sea';[126] Evelyn identifies Reno, in turn, as a modern-day Vanity Fair, a comparison suggested by her visit to a casino. There she encounters a man dressed as a minister, who quotes Bunyan. Specifically, he quotes Faithful, Christian's travelling companion in *The Pilgrim's Progress*:

> 'There can be no divine faith without the divine revelation of the will of God! Therefore, whatever is thrust into the worship of God that is not agreeable to divine revelation, cannot be done but by human faith, which faith is not profit to eternal life!'
>
> 'There can be no divine faith without the divine revelation of God!' he shouted again. 'This is Vanity Fair. Who judges me but Hate-good? Who are you, all of you, but Malice, Live-loose, Love-lust, Hate-light . . .'.

Evelyn thinks:

> Vanity Fair. Of course, she had heard it all before. He was quoting Faithful's final speech in *Pilgrim's Progress*. Faithful was tried at Vanity Fair and died there. Crackpot the old man might be, but he knew his Bunyan, and he knew Vanity Fair when he saw it? 'When they were

got out of the wilderness, they presently saw a town before them ... '.
Evelyn heard him shout just before the elevator doors closed behind
him: 'I buy the truth!'[127]

Whether the man is mad or, in fact, an overzealous cleric, whether the
city is an actual, latter-day Vanity Fair or a glitzy parody of it is not the
point; the ineluctability of such debate is. Reno and the heckler occupy
the same imaginative context, wherein the parting quote, 'I buy the
truth', is a statement not of spiritual essentialism but of the conspicuous
consumption of Christian paradigms. In his doubled role as moral critic
and allegorical figure, the would-be minister elicits Evelyn's awareness
of Reno's marketing of itself as a city of destruction.

But if Reno maps out Evelyn's spiritual desertion, it also enables her
to meet Ann Childs, with whom she falls in love. Ann is quick to point
out that the world of Christian propriety and the moral wasteland of
Reno are inextricably linked, the former indeed sanctioning the existence of the latter. Her descriptions of Reno play on the conventional
oppositions between the 'well-watered plains of the Lord'[128] and Sodom
and Gomorrah, and in so doing recall how in Genesis 13:10 – 'the plain
of Jordan ... was well watered every where, before the Lord destroyed
Sodom and Gomorrah, even as the garden of the Lord' – those places are
one and the same. For Ann, 'Every place is a Sodom and a Gomorrah ...
The faithful say the plain was well watered, even as the Garden of the
Lord, before the destroyed the cities. I don't believe it. There never was
any water here, not fresh water.'[129] Skeptical of the distinction between
desert and garden as landscapes of damnation and salvation, Ann sees
Reno as an ontological supermarket along the straight and narrow road,
where the best buys remain cultural complacency and moral smugness:
'They were perfectly ordinary people coming from all parts of the country into the evil desert ... perfectly ordinary people, free at last to be
fearful, malicious, greedy. Then home they'd go to the good, well-
watered plains of the Lord to tell what they had seen, the coarse women,
the obsessed men, the deserted children, never guessing that these picturesque inhabitants were tourists like themselves.'[130] Its clubs supplying
the church with 'both the money to be spent and the souls to be saved',
Reno is, for Ann, 'a perfect kingdom, based on nothing but the flaws
in human nature'.[131] As such it is itself a parodic allegory of spiritual
pilgrimage.

Whether a latter-day Sodom, Vanity Fair, or a city of destruction
whose alter ego is a celestial city, Reno builds its success on the com-
mercialization of the spiritual landscape. Casino life, in particular,
ironizes the female pilgrim's progress as a narrative system responding

not to individual development but to the maintenance of its own 'free' economy. At Frank's Club, where Ann works, the security system's two-way mirrors parody Bunyan's objective correlative of female progress, the mirror that in Part 2 of *The Pilgrim's Progress* Christiana brings her daughter-in-law and travelling companion Mercy.

Bunyan glosses the mirror as 'the word of God';[132] his narrator explains: 'Now the glass was one in a thousand. It would present a man one way, with his own feature exactly, and turn it but another way, and it would show one the very face and similitude of the Prince of pilgrims himself'.[133] If the two-way mirror recalls the central mystery of Christianity that Christ is both God and man, it also reflects the female believer's mediated position within the church. Unlike man, whose identification with Christ is possible on both the personal and abstract levels, woman attains only an abstract relation. So Mercy fears that without the mirror, she will 'miscarry' – both physically and spiritually. Thus the mirror images the sexual politics of Bunyan's Puritanism. Neither Christiana nor Mercy may guide herself or the other, even though the two women are travelling, 'progressing', together. The male mediation that formalizes the female pilgrim's identification with God and man obscures the immediacy of the women's bond.

In *Desert of the Heart*, in turn, the casino ceilings are lined with mirrors, which ostensibly promote employee honesty (or, at least, the image of honesty). Looking at one of these, Ann sees 'her own face separated from her ... made smaller. What a device of conscience the mirror was, for behind it, at any time, might be the unknown face of a security officer, watchful, judging; yet you could not see it. You could not get past your own minimized reflection.'[134] That reflection locates Ann within a system of surveillance, at once gendered and parodic, which reduces the importance of her actions in relation to herself. Like Christiana and travelling companion Mercy, Ann is overseen by male superiors; her behavior is subject to their approval. 'What a device of conscience that mirror was',[135] Ann muses. Yet the club has despiritualized conscience. Behind the glass is not God but rather the managers of the casino's interests.

Frank's Club offers employees and visitors alike a parodic city of God, dominated by commercial images of female sexuality that traffic in (and prostitute) Bunyan's representations of the female pilgrim. So one woman *cum* wayfarer treks ninety miles across the desert for her job as a change apron. Strapped to her belly, the fifty-pound apron itself reminds Ann of 'a fetus in its seventh month',[136] and so links Ann to Bunyan's Christiana and more nearly the pregnant Mercy, whose ineluctable burden is her sex and with it the travail of childbearing.

Ann, like Evelyn, is a critical reader of the context she inhabits. She remains removed from her co-workers, even from her lovers, Silver and Bill, whose names reflect the marketplace. Tellingly, Ann's nickname is 'Little Fish'. 'Little Fish' inscribes her within a Christian romance, where Evelyn is the fisher of [wo]men who 'hook and land' her.[137] 'Little fish' is also Virginia Woolf's term in *A Room of One's Own* for the woman's thought that, meeting prohibition rather than nurture, darts into hiding. Within the market economy, Ann is a threshold of female, more specifically, lesbian, consciousness, a thought only acknowledgeable in those cartoons that she draws in her spare time and refuses to sell. In other words, Ann's cartoons, part of her interrogation of her surrounding political and cultural landscape, gesture toward the *Bilder* of an alternative *Bildung* that is the novel itself.

Speaking of the primacy that Christian thought accords productivity, economic as well as sexual, Rule observes of her own writing, 'What interests me is watching people detached from all those requirements, figuring out ways to build a human community that is satisfying and nourishing to them.'[138] In *Desert of the Heart* the most salient metaphors are those of barrenness, which define nourishment not in terms of reproduction but in terms of self-preservation. So the desert and an alkaline lake provide the backdrop for Evelyn and Ann's romance. Where fertility demands appropriation, Evelyn and Ann's landscape remains a sterile, inviolable one, a wilderness that resists cultivation, that is itself self-sustaining. So Evelyn considers the stillness of Pyramid Lake: 'It was no wonder that a Christian God had not been at home here. It would take many animistic gods of men less confident of their own dominant spirit to describe the powers of this world.'[139] This 'dead sea' does not, however, entirely escape sexual regulation – at one point a National Guard helicopter hovers over the two women. Yet one might also say that such policing, with which Evelyn associates the endurance of Christian faith, remains a suspended possibility, in relation to which Evelyn can maintain a critical distance.

So, too, while Evelyn may initially put off Ann's lovemaking by paraphrasing the line from Auden's poem – 'I live in the desert of the heart'[140] – the younger woman draws their attention toward the figurative richness of the actual desert:

> . . . as they dropped over the crest of a hill, the rain stopped and before them was a valley of brilliant, burning sunlight, arched with rainbows, edged with lightning.
> 'This is the desert of the heart', Ann said quietly.[141]

Ann inverts Auden's metaphor for spiritual desolation: Complete with rainbows reminiscent of the one that seals the covenant between God and man in Genesis 9, the desert momentarily becomes a promised land. The desert is the landscape of self-address, the borderland that remains for the exile from convention after the possibility of defining oneself in terms of normative religious and secular plots has been swept away.

In effect, *Desert of the Heart* bewilders Bunyan's semiotic system. At the end of the novel Evelyn measures her lesbianism against Bunyan's text. Much as Bunyan's narrator walks 'through the wilderness of this world'[142] in order to dream of pilgrim's progress, Evelyn walks into the desert in order to struggle with the thought of love. But in doing so, she splits his paradigm in two – she is a pilgrim without an interpretive ground for her lesbianism:

> Evelyn had walked half a mile into her own vision of the desert before she turned and looked back at the curiously regular edge of town she had left; 'When they were got out of the wilderness, they presently saw a town ... '. And Faithful was tried there and died there, but for defending his convictions, not for giving them up. If he'd surrendered divine faith to human faith, he would not have been killed; nor would he have escaped, however. He would have stayed.
>
> Evelyn began to walk slowly back the way she had come, neither Faithful nor Christian. There is no allegory any longer, not even the allegory of love. I do not believe. Even seeing and feeling, in fact, what I do not believe, I do not believe. It's a blind faith, human faith ... That's the only faith that I have. I cannot die of that. I can only live with it, damned or not.[143]

In the desert outside Reno, Evelyn is reminded of Bunyan's Christian and Faithful entering Vanity Fair, only to find that she cannot equate her progress to theirs. Evelyn's coming out as lesbian means that she is a pilgrim without a conventionally recognizable progress. Nor does loving Ann, predicated on 'a blind faith, human faith', offer her any promise of salvation. For Evelyn, she and Ann together constitute 'a cryptic cartoon', a cartoon that Ann promises to draw 'only ... if I can live it'.[144] Where 'desert' functions as a multi-layered metaphor for an alienation from social, religious, and literary conventions and, more nearly, from 1950s American culture, Evelyn and Ann may be understood as that landscape's 'permanent residents'.

In her essay 'Morality in Literature', Jane Rule writes,

> The serious writer's job is not to segregate sexuality so that it may express only crude fantasy but to integrate sexuality with character for it to become one of the basic languages in which we can express our complex natures and communicate something far richer and more difficult than lust, not outside our morality but at its very center.[145]

Desert of the Heart upholds such a vision of sexuality: it offers a lesbian story that refuses to end in 'a well of loneliness.' In direct contrast to Stephen and Mary, Evelyn and Ann reject conventional morality and the marriage plot in order to pursue their relationship. Theirs is a progress engendered neither by the call to 'Life, life, eternal life',[146] as is Bunyan's Christian, nor by what E. M. Forster has called those 'beautiful conventions',[147] after which Stephen yearns and whose empty, parodic signs may be found everywhere in Rule's fictional Reno. Instead, written for a readership marked by the widespread vilification of homosexuality, Evelyn and Ann's story is impelled by a promise of love 'for an indefinite period of time',[148] simultaneously indeterminate, immediate, and vital.

4.   Conclusion

At the outset of this chapter I posed the question 'what could *The Pilgrim's Progress* have to do with a story of lesbian desire?' Reading *The Well of Loneliness* against Bunyan and, in turn, *Desert of the Heart* against both Bunyan and Hall, tells us something of the profound impact literature and, more specifically, a tradition of literature can have on society – even a society comprised of people who do not regard themselves as readers. While Bunyan conceived of *The Pilgrim's Progress* as a religious text addressing a Dissenting audience, by the mid-nineteenth century it had become a key source text within English literature. Through this literary absorption of Bunyan, primarily middle-class and secular, as well as through the book's cultural mission as a vehicle for both religious conversion and empire building within the British colonies, Bunyan's initially marginal, 'low' text became, by the end of the nineteenth century, a canonical literary work. Today, its widest readership is probably within literary studies. Yet, it would be a mistake to think that the book has little relevance for readers beyond the literature classroom. *The Pilgrim's Progress*'s history of reception, marked by its shifting and crossing of social and disciplinary boundaries, reflects the ways in which texts, whether initially marked as religious or literary or, for that matter, social or political, can come to occupy varying cultural placements because of their capacity to engage and address other realms of human experience.

Recognizing as much means that the outrage with which the publication of Radclyffe Hall's Bunyanesque novel met on both sides of the Atlantic proves wholly understandable. Her lesbian progress novel engendered controversy because it was not *solely* a work of literature; it was a literary work with *necessarily* important, widespread implications for the ways in which its readers thought about morality and justice and the relation between social and literary traditions.

Recognizing as much also means knowing that sometimes literature needs to divorce itself from conventional definitions of morality and justice and from social and literary tradition in order to offer readers an imaginative space apart from repressive, demeaning forces. Ironically, this statement binds Rule to Bunyan, for even as she rejects his paradigms, both writers offer their contemporary readership a new kind of story: in Bunyan's case, a spiritual allegory that, written in vernacular English and representing human behavior in realistic detail, spoke to the lives of a socially and politically marginal community of faithful; in Rule's case, a lesbian novel whose happy ending depends upon the dismissal of both the genre's conventional happy ending of marriage and the emerging sub-genre's conventional unhappy ending of isolation. In this manner, *Desert of the Heart* offered lesbian readers in the mid 1960s a literary model for respecting and nurturing their own lives. Writing this chapter in the early twenty-first century, at a time when neither the US federal government nor a majority of the states offer adequate protection and support for either women or gender and sexual minorities, and at a time when the most readily identifiable gay and lesbian issue within mainstream culture is that of same-sex marriage, or, again, in evangelical political terms, 'the sanctity of marriage', I find that Rule's novel, with its refusal to inscribe its heroines within expected narratives of white, middle-class female progress, still proves relevant to and powerful for readers.

For subsequent lesbian novelists, relevant and powerful, too, are the alternative visions of Bunyan set forth by Hall and Rule in their canonical works of lesbian fiction. Writers such as Jeanette Winterson and Sarah Waters have inherited Bunyan as a literary problem to be solved, for example, either by placing a Christian heritage in conversation with other literary sources, as does Winterson in her semi-autobiographical novel *Oranges Are Not the Only Fruit* (1985), or by allying the struggles of sexual minorities with those of other disenfranchised groups, as does

Waters in *Tipping the Velvet* (1998). While it is not within the scope of this chapter to offer an extended analysis of these more recent examples of lesbian fiction, a brief reading of each suggests how Bunyan, particularly as filtered by Hall and Rule, remains a literary touchstone for lesbian progress novels.

So, *Oranges Are Not the Only Fruit*, acclaimed by literary critics and lesbian readers alike,[149] is clearly informed by the progress novel tradition. Structuring her own story in terms of Old Testament books, narrator-protagonist Jeanette, sharing her first name with the author, identifies herself initially as a Christ-like figure, a latter-day prophet and interpreter of texts, understandings of self that her strong-minded, idiosyncratic adoptive mother actively encourages. Raised within her mother's Evangelical Christian community, Jeanette as an adolescent realizes her lesbianism, which, in contrast to Stephen Gordon, she refuses to align with sin. Consequently cast out of church and home, she nonetheless maintains an understanding of her sexuality free from guilt. And she does not remain in exile. By novel's end, Jeanette is able to return home to visit her mother. In many ways reminiscent of the 'indefinite' vision of Ann and Evelyn's reality that Jane Rule offers readers at the close of *Desert of the Heart*, the final scene of *Oranges* is of a contradictory but persisting mother–daughter relationship, sustained both despite and because of Jeanette's challenge to social and religious conventions. Importantly, that challenge also occurs on a meta-fictional level, which might be said to extend the implications of Rule's critique of realist conventions. *Oranges* is a postmodernist text that ruptures the texture of realism itself and in the process reworks the relation between spiritual narrative and hero's development. That is, unlike Rule, Winterson retains the stories of spiritual progress as markers of the hero's progress. Her innovation is in qualifying these stories' narrative authority. As Anita Gnagnatti observes, Winterson 'undermines' or delimits the power of the novel's biblical underpinnings through the 'juxtaposition of reworked biblical tales with fairy tales and Arthurian myth'.[150] Much as the title's 'oranges' signify the fruit of knowledge, particularly sexual knowledge, they also refer to the multiple narratives that inform Jeanette's understanding of reality. In other words, the Bible – or Bunyan, for that matter – is not the *only* narrative model for understanding individual progress: it is one of many.

Like *Oranges,* Sarah Waters' *Tipping the Velvet* is a progress novel written in the first person. It is also an historical novel. Set in Victorian England, *Tipping* recounts the sexual adventures of Nan King, adventures that, within a matter of a few years, propel Nan from shucking oysters in her father's seaside business, to performing in London music halls, to cross-dressing and servicing male clientele on the streets, to sojourning in the stylized world of patrician sapphism, and finally to working for the rights of women, workers, and immigrants. Taken together, Nan's experiences read like a primer for late twentieth-century lesbians, feminists, and queers. Her journey, part picaresque, part *Bildung*, raises such contemporary issues and concerns as the lesbian sex wars, gender performativity, and coalition activism. This in effect is Waters' narrative innovation for the lesbian progress novel. While in general the historical novel provides author and readers alike a means of contemplating the present from a safe remove, the 'Victorian' *Tipping* specifically offers a witty allegorical reprise of contemporary gender and sexual politics that also, as Mark Wormald has observed, 'bring[s] to vivid life episodes in the history of sexuality' that 'may or may not be 'real', but in Waters' hands ... manage to escape the limitations of the genres which inspired them'.[151] Waters' strategy of encouraging readers to understand *Tipping* as a deeply literary and political text offsets and so answers the eradicating force of realism's regulation of female sexuality within traditional progress narratives.[152] Nan's sexual relationships are the basis for a moral and political education that, in contrast to both Stephen Gordon's and Evelyn Hall's, intertwines an enthusiastic celebration of the pleasures and varieties of lesbi-queer sex (to which the novel's title alludes), with an awareness of the importance of communal responsibility.[153] The latter concern is, of course, core to lesbian, feminist, and queer activism. It is also, crucially, central to the moral vision of Victorian realism that has its roots in the communal vision of Part 2 of *The Pilgrim's Progress*. Waters foregrounds the proximity, even entanglement, of literary and political visions of progress. Her interweaving of realist conventions with lesbi-feminist-queer concerns constitutes her contribution to the tradition of lesbian progress fiction laid out by Radclyffe Hall and Jane Rule.

2
Love in the Shadows: The Same-Sex Marriage Debate and Beyond

1. Introduction

One of the issues that emerge from the previous discussion of lesbian progress novels is the subgenre's ambivalent relation to marriage. As Chapter 1 has shown, lesbian novelists who engage Bunyan and more generally Christian-inflected culture and literature do so in part in order to claim for their heroines a space for loving, thinking, and telling stories. For Radclyffe Hall writing *The Well of Loneliness*, that space is ultimately shut down because protagonist Stephen Gordon is unable to marry her lover. Indeed, Stephen's consciousness of that inability determines the novel's ending. For Jane Rule, in turn, the enabling lesbian space exists apart from marriage. In *Desert of the Heart*, her representation of the legitimacy of lesbian desire depends upon a critique of marriage as a political, religious, and cultural institution. Reading these two lesbian novels against *The Pilgrim's Progress* thus foregrounds two different approaches to not only literary but also social and political traditions: Hall is calling for the expansion, Rule for the rejection of those traditions. The contrast here reflects the ongoing tensions within literature and more generally within society regarding the representational politics of lesbian and more broadly queer desire.

These two very different positions achieve strained and, at times, implausible expression in the 'strange marriage' novels of gay and lesbian 1950s and 1960s pulp fiction. Ann Bannon's *Women in the Shadows* (1959), in particular, evinces the paradoxical demand that its main gay and lesbian characters not only uphold marriage as a cultural and personal good but that they regard marriage as the heteronormative means to a queer end: the socially stable vantage point from which to acknowledge and explore their same-sex desires. This configuration of marriage and desire is itself, however, anything but stable. In *Women in the Shadows* queer passions are not simply relegated to the shadows of marriage in order to be dismissed; from the shadows those passions also figure the lack, the want of desire inhabiting marriage. The relation, dynamic and potentially volatile, necessarily invites the doubled question of how marriage would further or efface queer desire. Stated another way, Bannon's 'strange marriage' novel may be understood as an early queer polemic *both for and against* marriage, analysis of which offers a compelling perspective on the current US same-sex marriage debate.

This debate, which began in earnest in the mid 1990s, draws on a distinctly American discourse of democracy, one in which marriage both as metaphor and legally recognized rite has determined people's access to social rights. So, for example, revolutionary figure Thomas Paine, in his capacity as the editor of *The Pennsylvania Magazine*, continually employed the marriage metaphor in order to explain the American colonies' need to break away from British rule: theirs was a bad marriage.[1] Of course, the political resonance and applicability of this metaphor varied among Colonial America's inhabitants, particularly across gender and racial divisions. Long after the founding of the United States, anti-miscegenation laws prevented whites and nonwhites from marrying, while within 'all-white' marriages, legally speaking, men 'covered' women; men in themselves represented the union with their wives. There was no legal recognition of slave marriages. In other words, '*What is marriage for*', as E. J. Graff observes, has been 'like most serious political or social questions ... a question about what it means to be fully human.'[2]

Given this history, it is unsurprising that marriage has figured prominently in US social justice struggles of the last sixty years. Against the broad cultural backdrop of the civil rights struggle and the sexual revolution, marriage was simultaneously and at times contradictorily understood as a vehicle for both racial equality and male domination. In the 1950s and 1960s civil rights leaders fought for the repeal of anti-miscegenation laws, while during the 1960s and 1970s second-wave feminists challenged the patriarchal oppression lodged within institutional marriage. The complexity of that oppression was in turn underscored by women of color who, both within and without the feminist movement, argued that race, together with class and gender, was a crucial axis for patriarchal exploitation. As George Chauncey has pointed out, 'the tenuous "security net" created in the United States in the twentieth century made access to many benefits contingent on employment or marriage'; within this social system marriage 'acquired a unique status . . . as the nexus for the allocation of a host of public and private benefits'.[3] Such a system works well for those who can imagine and enact (and so sustain the illusion of) employment and marriage as matters of individual choice rather than as markers of social limits or barriers; those who can not – more often than not, women, particularly women of color – occupy especially vulnerable positions.

Since the mid 1990s, lesbian and gay and queer activists have revisited the issue of marriage. Some have considered same-sex marriage *the* fundamental issue for gay men and lesbians; others have viewed same-sex marriage advocacy as inherently implicated in the discriminatory realities of a racist, classist, sexist, and heterosexist social system; still others have argued that the extension of same-sex marriage is one of many crucial steps in the struggle for any number of social groups, not just gay and lesbian couples. In this sense, the current same-sex marriage debate, not to mention the 'strange marriage' novels that precede it in literature, recalls a foundational and historically resonant and contentious national discourse in which the power of marriage is weighed against the importance of individual freedoms; the primacy of inalienable rights; the possibility, even the necessity, of divorce. As contemporary readers of US culture, we might well then turn to the marriage metaphor and ask, what happens when the vehicle for that metaphor gets upgraded? Does the expansion of marriage rights (and rites) to more citizens equal an expansion of democracy? And who is overlooked and relegated to the shadows of this metaphorical exchange? These are some of the questions of this chapter.

Thus, the current US same-sex marriage debate should properly be understood as consisting of several debates – both within and without LGBT and normative communities and cutting across national and international contexts. That is, there is necessarily a 'beyond' that must be considered when one speaks of the same-sex marriage debate: the complexities of human entanglements – the webs of affection and sex that exist within and without and across social and political categories – inevitably exceed dualistic arguments of 'for and against'; binary characterizations of marriage as a cultural good or a state mechanism for social control; or of the desire to enact it as a mark of either having socially 'made it' or having 'sold out'. In effect, same-sex marriage gestures toward, even as it defines itself against or shuts down the complex relations, those 'deserts of the heart', that perplex or elude or threaten not only individuals' but also cultural, medical, religious, and state models for viable human relations.

The same dynamic is at work in Ann Bannon's novel. Though written more than a half century ago, *Women in the Shadows* proves a fascinating text for considering the representational politics of the current US same-sex marriage debate.

2.   Marriage's shadows, Part 1: the gutting of queer desire in Ann Bannon's novel

Published during the late 1950s and early 1960s, Ann Bannon's Beebo Brinker novels – *Odd Girl Out* (1957), *I am a Woman* (1959), *Women in the Shadows* (1959), *Journey to a Woman* (1960), and *Beebo Brinker* (1962) – offer an example of how lesbian paperback originals (pbo's) simultaneously upheld and queered mainstream cultural values. That doubled process reflects what Jaye Zimet has termed the paradox of the 1950s cultural moment: 'straightlaced suburban sensibility at one extreme and postwar freedom, excitement, and sexual exploration at the other'.[4] As a result, while pbo publishers, wary of censorship and prosecution, insisted that lesbian characters' stories could not end happily, subversion of the mandated heteronormative plots, which typically exacted madness, heterosexuality, marriage, or death for lesbians, was still possible. Writers could resist the unhappy ending not only by drawing readers' attention elsewhere but also by queering the requisite move toward heteronormative closure. Bannon herself, in her 2001 introduction to the Beebo Brinker chronicles, notes this subversive potential within her fiction:

> I gave at least some of the stories a happy ending, sort of .... Bad things did happen that reflected the arrogant ignorance of the authorities, the contempt of conventional society, and the occasional desperation of the women of the times; modern readers may feel impatient with some of this now, but it was part of life back then. But still there was humor and there was love, in at least as good measure ...[5]

This potential was sustained by Bannon's readers, who could disregard the ending as the most important aspect of the storyline.[6] Written at a time when, as George Chauncey observes, there was neither a widespread LGBT movement nor any laws protecting LGBT people,[7] these works offered lesbian readers a chance, no matter how transitory, not only to engage a community of characters but also to join a virtual public whose sexual desires mirrored and validated their own.

This capacity on the part of both Bannon and her readers to resist the demands of heteronormative endings proves particularly resonant when one considers Bannon's five- novel series as a whole. In her foundational essay 'Zero Degree Deviancy: The Lesbian Novels in English', Catharine Stimpson writes that 'the lesbian writer who rejects both silence and excessive coding can claim the right to write for the public in exchange for adopting the narrative of damnation'.[8] Reading Bannon's fiction against Stimpson's observation, Suzanna Danuta Walters in turn argues that both 'through its use of the "low" genre of the pulp/romantic paperback' and 'through the complexity of its content and characterization', Bannon's fiction 'escapes the narrative of damnation'.[9] With respect to the first part of Walters' point, Bannon herself states, pbo's were 'not even a blip on the radar screens of literary critics'; discounted as serious writers, the authors of lesbian pulp experienced a kind of 'benign neglect' that allowed them to 'work in peace'.[10] What is also striking is the extent to which Bannon's characters not necessarily within individual novels themselves but over the series as a whole can also live and work in peace. As Walters explains,

> In producing a serial in which lesbian characters live, work, love, and grow old together, Bannon was implicitly challenging the prevailing belief that homosexual life was brief, episodic, and more often than not resulted in early death. By showing characters moving in both fictional time and space, as well as real time and space (the period of time in which she wrote the books) Bannon insisted on the continuity of lesbian love, while everything in her culture was speaking of its quick and ugly demise.[11]

The principal characters that reappear over the course of the series – Laura Landon, Beth Cullison, Beebo Brinker, and Jack Mann – may face trauma, danger and heartache, but they also realize love and passion, and after breakups they do not fade away into narrative oblivion. As Diane Hamer recognizes,

> In Bannon's novels, momentary happiness is *always* followed by further conflict, and the stories never really end. (Note that the fifth novel in the series is actually the first, chronologically.) ... [H]ere, the nature of desire, restless and insatiable, works against this compulsory closure. Instead of the perhaps more comforting endings conventional romance offers its readers, Bannon has captured accurately the contradictory experience of sexuality and desire in her recognition that sexual desire (heterosexual *or* lesbian) often works against the stability of monogamous coupling. The resolution that such coupling promises is only ever partial and exists primarily in fantasy.[12]

Thus, when considered not only individually but also as a whole, Bannon's five novels speak to the complexity of sexual desires, which exceed or resist the conventional signs of resolution, social as well as literary.

Ann Bannon's third novel, *Women in the Shadows*, proves itself to be an excellent example of the kind of mixture of convention and subversion that her novels in particular and lesbian pulp in general have afforded their readers. Like Artemis Smith's *The Third Sex* (1959) and James Colton's *Strange Marriage* (1965), *Women in the Shadows* offers readers a 'strange marriage' plot, one in which marriage itself facilitates a compromise that allows characters simultaneously to sustain their homosexuality and adhere to social norms.[13] By the end of Bannon's novel, not only are best friends Laura Landon, a lesbian, and Jack Mann, a gay man, married, they are also expecting a child. But for a few signal features, theirs may said to be an outcome that celebrates the 1950s [white] heteronormative family. This is a crucial qualification, as Laura and Jack's marriage is thematically bound to two other pairings, the 'shadows' of the novel's title, which undermine marriage's conventional semiotic power.

Laura's earlier relationship with the butch Beebo Brinker, who gives her name to Bannon's five-novel series, casts the primary shadow over Laura and Jack. Laura and Beebo, together with Beebo's dachshund Nix, may prove the untenable inversion, the *Nichts* (Nix) of the socially stable but utterly sexless union of Laura, Jack, and fetus. Laura and Jack's story, though, cannot be extricated from Laura and Beebo's.

Initially that doubling suggests the inadequacy of Laura and Beebo's relationship. Jack tells Beebo early on, 'I want a child';[14] a few pages later Beebo admits the same. Squeezing her dog, she says, 'I know how it feels. To want one. You just have to make do with what you've got.'[15] Beebo's resolve 'to make do' says something about her personal bravery and her strength; yet it also discloses her, as well as her relationship's position at the margins of various social plots: like Stephen Gordon before her, Beebo cannot marry her lover, nor can she give her a child. After two years together, Beebo has managed to give Laura 'a pretty good record' for Greenwich Village gay life; Laura, however, can only see 'the corpse of [their] romance'.[16] She writes in her diary, 'If I have to go on living with her I'll go crazy. But if I leave her – ? I'm afraid to think what will happen. Sometimes she's not rational. But what can I do? Where can I turn?'[17] Significantly, Laura reads the volatility and instability of the relationship as markers of individual rather than structural failings: for Laura they are integral not to a violent, intolerant society but rather to Beebo, specifically her gender presentation. Beebo the butch is dangerous. Laura is embarrassed by Beebo's 'freak[ish]' attire and 'sick' of her job as an elevator operator.[18] Beebo may confide to Nix, 'I'd sell my soul to be an honest-to-god male. I could marry Laura! I could marry her. Give her my name. Give her kids.' Even so, she recognizes, 'she wouldn't have me'.[19] Beebo is neither the lover Laura desires nor the man she could marry. While she has given Laura her name – her nickname for Laura is 'Bo-peep', whose first syllable repeats the last of 'Beebo' – the word play, the mark of endearment, in contrast to the 'Mrs Mann' that Jack can proffer, remains legally insignificant and illegible, and in its echoing of the nursery rhyme, it even seems childish.

While Beebo as butch and lesbian seemingly fails to measure up to stereotypical expectations regarding a woman's gender and sexuality, her relationship with Laura also throws a shadow over Laura's with Jack for another reason. The women's relationship reveals the homophobia and heterosexism, the Scylla and Charybdis of any 1950s lesbian pulp odyssey, of Laura and Jack's commitment to a narrative of desire predicated upon marriage. As Walters explains, Bannon's 'critique of the family comes through loud and clear, particularly in the way the marriage of Laura and Jack is handled. . . . [T]heir marriage can clearly be read as a reconstitution of the patriarchal family.'[20] Stated in slightly different terms, the couple embraces not only [white] middle-class heteronormative values, but also an accompanying complacent bigotry. So, for Jack and increasingly for Laura, 'the real world' is 'the *straight* world',[21] obtainable through marriage. Marriage for Jack entails 'a home . . . a place to rest in and be proud of, and a purpose in life';[22] after 'a lifetime of homosexual adventures', marriage makes him 'truly a man'.[23] For both of them, it is the key to feeling 'normal'.[24] Procreation in turn fills out their marriage plot. For Jack, 'A man needs a child . . . So does a woman. That's the whole reason for life. There is no other . . . We can't live our lives just for ourselves . . . Or we live them for nothing. We die, monuments to selfishness.'[25] Once pregnant (via artificial insemination), Laura finds that she is 'going to be a woman'.[26] She has avoided the fate of those 'pitiful old women in their men's oxfords and chopped-off hair, stumping around like lost souls, . . . living together, . . . ugly and fat and wrinkled . . . in a cheap walk-up with . . . a stinking cat.'[27] Such descriptions bear out Walters' observation of Bannon's fiction in general: it never permits readers 'to escape the realities of homophobia. Her world is one where passionate lesbian sexuality and culture exists side by side with the hardships of being gay in a repressive heterosexual society.'[28] Of course, one might well ask how the lack of children within a marriage or, implicitly, the begetting of children out of wedlock or the living and growing old with another lesbian and perhaps a pet or, for that matter, the various other combinations that rupture conventional gender and sexual expectations for forming families would necessarily signify 'selfishness'. One might also wonder what Laura was before marriage and expectant motherhood, if not a woman. And what about Jack? In other words, Laura and Jack's plans to marry and have a child do not so much quell their queer desires and gender dysphoria as provoke a series of questions about them.[29]

At the 'heart' of the series, *Women in the Shadows* is Bannon's most disturbing novel, largely because the novel participates in a gutting of lesbian narrative, a marginalization of the overarching lesbian storyline. Within the novel, queer passions not only are violently relegated to the shadows of the story but are also themselves linked to violence; for the series as a whole, as Christopher Nealon remarks,

> [r]eading this book is extremely painful: characters that retained hints of good humor in the two earlier books seem to have lost everything in their repertoires except cutting sarcasm, and most of them are bitterly, exuberantly alcoholic. Bannon depicts Beebo in particular as capable of murdering Laura out of jealousy, as capable of brutally assaulting her.[30]

Apparent from the outset, Laura's fear of Beebo's volatility is realized at various points in the novel, as in, for example, the disturbing moment that precipitates Laura's departure, when Beebo slams Laura's head repeatedly against the floor. Still, it is worth recognizing that Beebo reserves the heart-wrenching examples of her violence for herself and her beloved dog. In an attempt to keep Laura, she beats herself up and kills Nix, and claims that she has been attacked and raped and the dog murdered by a gang of young men. Beebo's violence reflects the social dispossession that defines her capacity to act. From this perspective, her claim that she has been sexually assaulted may be read as an attempt to disrupt and redeploy that conventional narrative of lesbian dispossession to her advantage. Beebo draws attention to that narrative as she explains why, after she has ostensibly been sexually assaulted, she will not go to either a doctor or a lawyer for help. Violence against lesbians, while expected – a 'sort of occupational hazard',[31] she tells Laura – remains socially insignificant: 'It's an old story … I don't know why it didn't happen to me years sooner. Nearly every butch I know gets it one way or another. Sooner or later they catch up with you.'[32] Beebo continues, 'Who's going to mourn for the lost virtue of a Lesbian? What lawyer is going to make a case for a poor queer gone wrong? Everybody will think I got what I deserved.'[33] Beebo's interest here is in garnering Laura's sympathy, in arousing Laura to define herself against 'everybody' and care for (and so remain with) Beebo. For a time, the strategy works. Importantly, however, the paradigmatic butch story of sexual violence and social indifference that Beebo calls forth is one enacted by the novel as a whole. By the end, the configuration of Jack, Laura, and baby-in-the-making has replaced that of Beebo, Laura, and Nix. 'I'm not in love with her now. Maybe I never was,' Laura tells Jack on the last page of the novel. 'But I respect her and I admire her.' 'Save yourself for me and the baby', he responds.[34] Laura and Jack have nixed Laura and Beebo's relationship – have relegated it to the unreality of *Nichts*, the nothingness of experience existing beyond the narratable boundaries of marriage.

That de-centering of lesbian story functions as a kind of narrative evisceration, which brings into focus the symbolic import of Beebo's killing of Nix. This death is especially troubling. Beebo has slit his belly open the length of his body, and her violence here is undeniable. Beebo is not, however, vicious and depraved in committing it; she is desperate. As the novel's opening underscores, she loves her dog, regards him as her child. In this, she belongs to a long line of lesbians, real and fictional, whose pets are integral to their lives.[35] (One thinks, for example, of Radclyffe Hall and her dogs and of Stephen Gordon and her horse, Raftery.) Beebo's is a crime of passion, a brutally symbolic act: the disemboweled Nix embodies her sacrifice of the reality of queer family for the possibility of a sustained relationship with Laura.

Nix's death insofar as it marks off the end of Beebo and Laura's relationship also functions as a metaphor for Laura and Jack's marriage, which lacks the sexual attraction – the animality – that characterizes Beebo's hold over Laura and the women's attraction to one another. Beebo offers Laura a mixture of passion and violence – what Amber Hollibaugh in another context has called those 'dangerous desires'[36] – that she finds deeply arousing. Beebo's anger invites Laura's sexual hunger, even after Laura has decided to leave her: 'Laura looked at her and found herself caught by Beebo's spell again. Beebo was born to lose her temper. She looked wonderful when she did. It exasperated Laura to feel a bare animal desire for her at times like this.'[37] Beebo's turbulence, while problematic, is likely a function of her answering, foolishly, as well as bravely, the violence around her. By contrast, Laura and Jack's relationship is filled with a kind of sexless calm. 'Jack, darling, I love you, but I don't love you with my body', says Laura in response to one of his proposals. 'I love you with my heart and soul but I could never let you make love to me.'

Jack agrees, 'I could never do it, either . . . If we married it would never be a physical union, you know that.'[38] The married couple offer each other reassurance rather than excitement. For Jack, the 'sweat and passion' of gay love can only lead to 'ashes and melancholy'. Laura's love, however, is 'steady and comforting'; it 'won't fail . . . no matter what'.[39] Following the conventions of heteronormativity, while still allowing for the recognition that both of them are gay, Jack and Laura's marriage serves as a 1950s version of 'don't ask, don't tell'.

While Walters argues for the subversive cast of the marriage – 'the fact remains that these are two committed homosexuals marrying each other and neither of them renounces their homosexuality for the marriage . . . In Bannon's world, the nuclear family is deconstructed and a new sort of homosexual hybrid is constructed in its place'[40] – it is important to recognize the severe limits placed on this subversive potential. Here George Chauncey's discussion of 1950s gay discretion proves helpful:

> So long as gay people remained 'discreet' and didn't tell people they were gay, most of their fellow workers and straight friends did not care to ask. Some gay people found it stressful to live a double life and difficult to keep their gay and straight social worlds separate, but given the draconian new laws of the postwar period, they simply had no choice. Indeed, to a degree that is difficult to grasp today, most gay people became extraordinarily adept at – and habituated to – doing so. Many even resented and avoided the drag queens, 'sissy men,' and butch lesbians who refused to conform publicly, sometimes blaming them for drawing attention to the gay world.[41]

In contrast to the passionate and volatile Beebo, Jack and Laura prove 'discreet'. Jack encourages Laura to have affairs, but she is to 'keep them very quiet' and to 'keep them out of the Village',[42] that quasi-allegorical space that already by the 1920s was known for its bohemian and homosexual demi-monde.[43] They then leave what Jack calls the 'rotten little prison' of the Village and settle into a comfortable one of their own, in a respectable midtown apartment one block from the Waldorf Astoria.[44] Here they become shadows of their former sexual selves, with their marriage a memorial to queer love. When she goes back to the Village for a fling with Beebo, Laura discovers that 'the exalted shivering passions of the past' have dwindled down to a love that is 'good and tender'.[45] Ironically, while this diminution into passionless intimacy marks the end of the women's relationship, it is also the emotional basis for marriage; 'unbearable tenderness' memorializes queer love and makes marriage with Jack and the impending reality of having his child possible and his kiss on her mouth 'right and wonderful'.[46]

In sum, with regard to the two pairings, the one relationship necessarily calls forth the other, and together they engender a series of mutually exclusive choices for narrative representation: reproduction or passion; sexual technology or sex; constancy or instability of relationship. Understood from the vantage point of these choices the significance of the novel's narrative arc is clear: Laura may have been the one initially to leave Beebo; ultimately, though, it is Beebo who can no longer consider Laura as her emotional and sexual partner. Heteronormativity – without the sex – is Laura's consolation prize. She gets Jack and with him a pregnancy via artificial insemination. Laura and Jack's marriage may meet with outward approval and support, and it may as a consequence prove viable over the long term. Yet, because the genre of pulp, and more specifically, the Beebo Brinker series as a whole, locates the heart of relationship in passion, in desire, Laura and Jack's marriage is curiously, oddly empty, with author Bannon's attempt to infuse 'their feelings for one another' with eroticism belying what 'could realistically have been expected'.[47] On so many levels and with Laura and Beebo's relationship acting as its doppelgänger, Laura and Jack's is a relationship without passion; without guts.

3.   Marriage's shadows, Part 2: marriage does not take a village

Bannon's strategy of juxtaposing marriage with shadow relationships in effect destabilizes marriage's function as a conventional sign of narrative resolution. While within *Women in the Shadows* Laura and Beebo's relationship offers the obvious counterpoint to Jack and Laura's, another married couple, Tris Robichon (Patsy Robinson) and her husband Milo, constitute the other shadow relationship in the novel. Like Laura and Beebo's, Tris/Patsy and Milo's relationship comments on Laura and Jack's; it, too, figures desire as elsewhere – as existing apart from marriage, though not solely to mark out marriage's lack of passion. Delineating the race privilege of 'the man', the Robinsons disrupt the Manns' expectation that marriage inevitably confer social respectability. Like Laura and Beebo, Tris/Patsy and Milo embody the novel's persistent questioning of marriage, particularly its capacity to engender a narrative that secures both personal fulfillment and social stability.

Though she appears only in this one novel and, as a character, seems more sketched than developed, Tris/Patsy especially embodies Bannon's most complex and wide-ranging critique of marriage. Her double name reflects her troubled position within a society in which white opposes black and heterosexual opposes homosexual. Conflicted about desiring women and about being black, she is Patsy, the patsy of a social and legal order that, barring interracial as well as same-sex sexual relationships, instates through marriage the barriers against race mixing and homosexuality. And she is Tris (as she is hereafter referred to), as in Tris-tan, a failed romantic heroine in the tradition of the tragic mulatta, whose interracial same-sex trysts attest to the pervasive sadness (*tris-tesse*) of the person who is invested in a socio-legal system that forbids them.

Within such a system, hybridity, whether racial (as in bi- or multi-racial-ness) or sexual (as in bisexuality or queer) appears as distorted otherness, at best mysterious, at worst diseased, and most certainly illusory. This is even true in the transgressive space of the Village, where Tris, who introduces herself as an Indian from New Dehli, runs a dance studio and where first Tris and Laura and then Tris and Beebo have most of their sexually charged encounters. So, the initial descriptions of Tris may suggest an appealing foreignness of her physical features: 'She was black-haired and her skin was the color of three parts cream and one part coffee. In such a setting her green eyes were amazing';[48] or again, '[h]er smile was as warm and luscious as ripe fruit in the sun'.[49] Such descriptions identify Tris as an exotic other, whose place within a race-based sexual hierarchy is open to negotiation. Her attempts at passing as Indian, however, only prove successful over the short term. The appearance of her dark-skinned husband, Milo, whom she has kept 'out of sight because she thinks he'd be a drag on her career',[50] identifies her as black and married. In contrast to Jack Mann's middle-class, white masculinity, which facilitates Laura's upward mobility, Milo's 'well-educated',[51] black maleness signals that even within the context of the bohemian and sexually permissive Village, Tris's attempts at passing are only ever out of place. Even as Milo's appearance 'protects' her, it also 'humiliate[s]' her.[52] It disrupts the illusion (for characters and readers alike) that she can escape easy racial and sexual categorization, and it projects her own ambivalence regarding lesbianism and blackness.

For Tris, it is not so much that race is her sexuality, as Nealon argues,[53] but rather the inverse: for her, lesbianism is a kind of blackness. In a moment of sexual panic, she tells Laura, 'If you force me to choose between black and white, I'm white ... I like men. More than women.'[54] Laura, however, does not force her. Instead, her attraction to Tris engenders a momentary image for their intimacy's potential to transform racial and sexual proscriptions. Lying on the beach with her, Laura can imagine Tris touching her; through the contact Tris's color would merge with Laura's: 'You'd have to touch me everywhere', Laura says, '... every corner of me, till we were both the same color. Then you'd be almost white and I'd be almost tan – and yet we'd be the same.'[55] Both women are struck by the 'strangeness' of the image,[56] which suggests that the intimacy of touch could engender a vision of equality capable of answering the fierce oppositions regarding race and sexuality, which govern their lives. In this it recalls Audre Lorde's assessment: 'Lesbians were probably the only Black and white women in New York City in the fifties who were making any real attempt to communicate with each other; we learned lessons from each other, the values of which were not lessened by what we did not learn.'[57] The image, though, is, fleeting; it only offers a trace of an alternative social vision, one that, as Bannon herself explains, was conceived 'awkwardly' and that 'in the absence of rigorous insight', she never develops.[58] Tris, then, is forced to choose not by Laura but periodically by Milo who 'lays down the law on the Lezzie stuff' and more generally by a larger society that, within an otherwise middle-class patriarchal landscape, has produced the Village as a space in which racial and sexual prohibitions can be temporarily suspended.[59] Tris may occupy most of the sexually graphic lesbian scenes in the novel; she does so, however, not as a lesbian so much as an 'un-lesbian' who is 'un-black'. The eroticized transgressor of racial categories, she recalls 'the figure of the mulatt[a]' who, as Siobhan Somerville writes, 'characteristically symbolizes both psychic and social dilemmas'.[60] 'Positioned as a vehicle for narrative conflict and tension'[61] Tris remains caught in the semiotic monstrosity of a neither-nor identity. After a tortured affair with her, Laura no longer reads her as an exotic other but rather as a 'sick' girl,[62] who can admit to neither her lesbian desires nor her African-American descent. Reminiscent of Beebo in her attempts to manipulate the social narratives of what it 'means' to be a lesbian, Tris can only achieve a mobility that is confined to racial and sexual indiscretion. She follows what Mary Dearborn has called the 'tragic mulatto trajectory, [which] demands that the mulatto woman desire a white lover and either die ... or return to the black community.'[63] Tris at the novel's end is claimed by Milo and fades from narrative view.

Tris's is the story of a never realizable, melancholy pursuit of sexual and emotional connection beyond a culture of marriage shaped by a racist and homophobic semiotic system. Tris may yearn for lesbian relationships, particularly ones that cross racial categories, but she remains deeply ambivalent about them. She can only see them in opposition to marriage and not as part of a larger intersectional vision of emotional, sexual, and racial interdependence in which marriage may or may not play a part. For her only marriage regulated by prohibitions against race mixing expresses a sustainable, if sorrowful relation between erotic choice and communal recognition. At the same time, Tris' story also proves an indictment of marriage, even while she cannot imagine any viable revision of or alternative to it. Accordingly, she laughingly dismisses the idea of a 'strange marriage'. Early on she asks Laura, 'Can you imagine two homosexuals getting married? Could anything be sillier? What would they do with each other?'[64] This comment, especially when read alongside the *'fort-da'* quality of her relationship with Milo, highlights not only the sexless-ness of Jack and Laura's 'strange marriage', but also the latter's race privilege. Like Milo and Tris, Jack and Laura may not have a passionate relationship; as a married couple they are, however, able to achieve a propriety that Milo and Tris never can. Tris's is a story about the foreclosure of the racial, sexual, and social possibilities of the Village.

What can readers of the marriage equality struggle learn from Bannon's *Women in the Shadows*, written some fifty years ago? There are two important points about the issue that the novel brings into focus. First, as in the novel, passion in the current debate is typically aligned with social chaos, while marriage is aligned with social order, specifically an order in which sex itself occupies a kind of discursive void. The novel's ending leaves us wondering queasily and uneasily *how* Jack and Laura are ever going to 'get some', and this closing down of the possibilities for sex suggests that as readers of the contemporary debate we need to think of this opposition between passion and sexless-ness. Sexual desire is at the eviscerated core of the novel; what are the implications of its occupying of the same position within the current debate? Second, as especially Tris's story indicates, marriage does not guarantee a narrative of either personal fulfillment or social agency. Marriage can discriminate – against those who are not allowed to enter into it and even against those who are. So, the same-sex marriage debate needs to be lodged within a larger discussion of interdependence and intimacy, one that allows us to imagine the validity of many different kinds of family formations, structured across not only categories of gender and sexuality but also, for example, categories of race, class, age, and citizenship. These are the lessons to be learned from *Women in the Shadows*, if not simply same-sex marriages but also a variety of family arrangements are to be recognized for their value and dignity.

4. The 1980s: shaping the same-sex marriage debate

Importantly, the lessons that come to us from the reading of Bannon's fiction can also be gleaned from the developments of the 1980s that laid the groundwork for the widespread struggle for same-sex marriage recognition beginning in the mid 1990s. As George Chauncey has observed, this struggle was shaped by three crucial developments of the 1980s: a growing acceptance of gay men and lesbians in some parts of the country, the AIDS crisis, and the lesbian baby boom.[65]

In terms of acceptance, the 1980s witnessed the growth of gay and lesbian cultural institutions; it was also during the 1980s that some private companies and local and state governments began articulating policies and passing ordinances and laws protecting people irrespective of their sexual orientation. Some municipalities and states challenged sodomy laws, and some prohibited employment and housing discrimination. Writing this almost a quarter of a century later, I still feel that mixture of dread, nervousness, and incredulity that life in the 1980s held for me as a 'woman in the shadows', a young lesbian who, depending on situation and location, could be categorized as either pervert or citizen. My experiences after coming out in the early 1980s are hardly atypical, even for LGBTQ people inhabiting as I did for most of that period the rather privileged and protected sphere of academia. I was harassed and beaten up and lost a job or two because of my sexual orientation. As a graduate student I was dismissed from the university's infirmary for the same reason, even though I was suffering from a back injury that had left me barely able to walk. What, then, was the thrill I experienced when I discovered after consulting an American Civil Liberties Union (ACLU) lawyer that the landlady who was threatening to evict me because I was engaging in 'homosexual' sex would not be able to do so; my state of residence, New Jersey, had just passed a law forbidding housing discrimination on the basis of sexual orientation. In 1985 only a handful of states could guarantee as much; I have loved the Garden State ever since. Yet, this was also the decade of the infamous *Bowers v. Hardwick* (1986), in which the Supreme Court 'upheld the nation's sodomy laws' and, in so doing, 'gave the opponents of gay rights carte blanche to ... justify everything from excluding gays from the military to removing children from the homes of lesbian mothers'.[66] When it came to civil protections, gay men and lesbians did see gains during the 1980s; importantly, though, these gains were often only experienced in select arenas and in certain parts of the country (such as the Northeast and the West Coast), and they typically affected gay men and lesbians *as individuals*.

By contrast, the AIDS crisis and lesbian baby boom both foregrounded gay men's and lesbians' relation to family. For gay men especially, the AIDS crisis left many experiencing the profound, painful, and costly disjunction between private and local recognition of one's relationship by friends and acquaintances, on the one hand, and public and institutional disregard and invisibility, on the other hand. As Chauncey explains, 'By 1988, seven years into the epidemic, 82,000 Americans had been diagnosed with AIDS, and 46,000 had already died.... Couples whose relationships were fully acknowledged and respected by their friends suddenly had to deal with powerful institutions – hospitals, funeral homes, and state agencies – that refused to recognize them at all.'[67] Not to be overlooked here is the institution of the family: partners and friends charged with carrying out the wishes of those ill with the disease could easily be overruled by biological family, even when the latter had been estranged from and their views ran counter to those of their ill family members. The crisis also disclosed in dramatic and painful terms the limits of the US healthcare system, in which employment and marital status were (and have continued to be) the most important factors in determining individuals' access to insurance. Pointedly, within the context of gay families, the crisis disclosed the inability of gay men to provide health insurance for their ailing partners.

The AIDS crisis and with it the death of so many young people had a profound impact on the gay men's relation to community, friendship, and partnership. As Chauncey writes, the crisis led to 'many more venues for the formation of friendships and ties to the larger community'. Such groups as Queer Nation, ACT UP, and the Gay Men's Health Crisis (GMHC), offered a fearless and unapologetic insistence on the viability and validity of life at the social margins: they pushed back against widespread stereotypes that pathologized gay people. Through AIDS awareness and education and through national outing/coming-out campaigns, these groups took on the demonization of sex, particularly queer sex, and they offered critical networks for support and outreach: 'AIDS service and activist organizations had a dramatic effect on the social organization of gay life ... The response to AIDS ... simultaneously multiplied and strengthened the diverse forms of sociability and communal solidarity that had already developed and further reinforced the importance of relationships.'[68] One manifestation of that heightened awareness of relationships' importance was the upsurge in support for gay marriage. The AIDS epidemic pushed many same-sex partners to advocate for the recognition of their relationships as examples of what Evan Wolfson in his thoughtful consideration of marriage, *Why*

Marriage Matters, has called 'the loving union of companionship, commitment, and caring between equal partners that we think of today'.[69] More broadly, AIDS brought into focus and politicized models of human interdependence, intimacy, and family beyond those generated by heteronormative marriage. The struggles for both same-sex marriage and the legal recognition of family formations configured differently from the two-spouse model have common roots in the AIDS crisis.

These struggles also have an origin in the lesbian baby boom of the 1980s. Centered on parts of the country in which gayness in general and gay parents in particular were tolerated, perhaps even accepted, the boom represented the decision by an increasing number of lesbian couples to have children, either via artificial insemination, adoption, or sex with a male friend. Even in these areas, throughout the 1970s and 1980s and indeed into the 1990s, courts in custody battles ruled against the parental rights of lesbians and gay men who while married had had children. Whether explicitly or implicitly, and particularly when read against the presumed heterosexuality of the other parental party, homosexuality often proved a ground in legal judgments that deemed lesbian and gay parents unfit to raise their children. The lesbian baby boom, in turn, brought into focus a set of differently inflected questions – differently inflected because the women raising those children had not only as their private but also as their legal starting point the understanding that children were and would continue to be growing up in lesbian-headed households. Beginning in the mid-1980s some states began to open up second-parent adoptions for lesbian and gay parents; by recognizing the non-biological parent's legal status as parent, such adoptions offered gay and lesbian families a much needed protection that could counter or at least hamper homophobic biases and practices within the legal system and society at large. Whether or not couples had been able to secure them, such adoptions proved especially important in instances when either the biological parent died or the couple's relationship ended. As Chauncey explains, the dramatic increase in lesbian-headed families 'raised novel issues with which the courts had to grapple. Most commonly, the courts had to decide where to place a child when its biological mother died and one of her relatives contested the right of her surviving partner, the child's second mother, to continue to have a relationship with the child.'[70] Couples' separation also posed problems: 'Equally vexing issues were raised when two women separated after one of them had given birth to a child whom both of them had raised. Since the women's relationship had no legal standing and the second mother had no legal relationship to the child, the usual rules governing custody disputes during a divorce did not apply.'[71] The same-sex marriage push should be understood in terms of such cases. The lesbian baby boom engendered a drive on the part of organizations such as Lambda Legal Defense and Gay and Lesbian Advocates and Defenders (GLAD) to shore up the rights and protections for gay and lesbian families. Such crucial work had as one of its consequences the realization of same-sex marriage as a desirable political goal. Advocating for the right to marry could be a way of securing parental recognition and stabilizing the lives of the children within lesbian- and gay-headed households.

Yet, it is important to recognize that, as in the case of the AIDS crisis, the lesbian baby boom also facilitated the formation of other family structures, alternatives to the cultural ideal of the couple with children that same-sex marriage advocates would simultaneously re-inscribe and expand. In this regard, lesbian writer and pro-sex activist Dorothy Allison's 1999 essay 'Mama and Mom and Dad and Son' comes immediately to mind. Allison's family consists of her son, Wolf, her partner and Wolf's biological mother, Alix, and Dan, Wolf's biological father and a gay man. Together they constitute what Allison calls 'our own design of a happy family: mama and mom and dad and son'.[72] They live together and, as she explains, '[w]hen we can manage it, we all go to his school functions together, and our boy cheerfully introduces us to his friends, blithely unaware that his three parents are not the norm'.[73]

In contrast to the lesbian or gay couple with two parents, Allison's family, consisting of three parents and a child, faces very real limits when it come to the legal capacity of all of the adults to represent and care for their son. Further, while there is no intrinsic reason for reading Allison's family in opposition to the two-parent household, it is important to recognize that such readings do take place, within not only lesbian and gay contexts but also larger heteronormative contexts. Especially troubling is the resistance to her family that she experiences from gay men and lesbians. She explains:

> We have already rewritten our wills and named each other as guardians should anything happen. We're exploring what it will mean to have all of us recognized legally as Wolf's parents, something that appears to be even more difficult than have me adopt while Alix retains her rights as Wolf's birth mother. The adoption process seems to be based on the idea that there is no birth father to claim the rights that I have assumed. But along with our shared sense of humor goes a hard-nosed pragmatism. If it were necessary to keep Wolf safe, either of us would happily marry Dan, but it is less the law than everyday

life that concerns me: people who stare at us because they cannot quite categorize us as easily as they would like, gay men who sneer at what they read as our heterosexual guise, lesbians who get angry when we bring 'male energy' into women-only situations, or even the mailman, who simply wants to know who belongs to this household after all.[74]

Allison knows that both she and Alix would readily marry Dan, if doing so would secure their son's safety. Though not quite in the same manner as for normal-seeking characters Jack and Laura in Bannon's 1950s lesbian pulp, 'strange marriage' proves to be an imperfect but potentially important legal protection for queer families at the turn of the twentieth century. In Allison's case 'strange marriage' could not secure the legal rights and visibility of all three adults as parents. Nor could it answer the indignities of everyday acts of bigotry on the part of gay men and lesbians. 'Strange marriage' would also discursively eviscerate the importance that BDSM culture holds for her, within her political activism, her fiction and essay writing, and her imaginative, emotional, and sexual life.

Allison's story of family gestures toward the divisiveness across LGBT communities – one that has often pitted normative gay and lesbian couples against other queers enacting their necessary and vital forms of intimacy. This divisiveness is a feature of the same-sex marriage debate.

5.   The 1990s: normalizing gayness and the 'maelstrom of sex'

Both literary analysis of *Women in the Shadows* and historical analysis of key developments of the 1980s point to the importance not only of recognizing the social and political power of sexual desire but also of de-stigmatizing non-normative sexualities and sexual practices. Further, like the range of relationships existing within Bannon's novel, both the AIDS crisis and the lesbian baby boom have thrown into relief the various kinds of family formation that, standing beyond the pale of marriage, are in need of legal recognition. Yet, the lessons to be learned from these contexts have at times been shunted aside, relegated to the shadows of same-sex marriage advocacy. Some proponents of gay marriage have perpetuated what Michael Warner has called a culture of sexual shame; they have reduced the push for the recognition of a range of kinds of family and relationship to one calling for the legalization of same-sex marriage. Such a strategy reflects not only the failure of a broad-based queer political vision and divisiveness across queer communities, but also the inevitable cost of attempting to enfold queer politics within the political mainstream. Theirs may be understood as adopting a kind of political pragmatism (and in this sense conservatism), one that seeks to find commonality with a host of government policies for which marriage has functioned as a figure for individual empowerment and state fiscal responsibility; at least in part, the same-sex marriage debate needs to be read in terms of this ideological engagement.

In this regard, one might well consider Andrew Sullivan's 1995 'Argument about Homosexuality', *Virtually Normal*, which offers one of the most rhetorically savvy calls for same-sex marriage, alongside welfare reforms put in place during the 1990s and the early years of the new century. Marriage, for Sullivan, maintains the privileged social status of married couples; it reaffirms the nuclear family as the social ideal; and, importantly, it protects couples from the potentially destructive power of sex. In these instances, Sullivan argues, the gay couple is no different than the heterosexual couple:

> Society ... has good reasons to extend legal advantages to heterosexuals who choose the formal sanction of marriage over simply living together. They make a deeper commitment to one another and to society; in exchange, society extends certain benefits to them. *Marriage provides an anchor, if an arbitrary and often weak one, in the maelstrom of sex and relations to which we are all prone.* It provides a mechanism for emotional stability and economic security. We rig the law in its favor not because we disparage all forms of relationship other than the nuclear family, but because we recognize that not to promote marriage would be to ask too much of human virtue.[75]

What is problematic here is, of course, that Sullivan's argument for gay marriage happens at the expense of many, many people who do not regard marriage as either a personal goal or an expression of human worth or *the* organizing feature of a just society.

Marriage may be a cultural ideal for some, but, one must remember, it is an ideal with a particular history of exclusion reverberating across categories of religion, race, class, gender, and sexual divides. For example, as George Chauncey has explained, 'The vision of a male-headed and – dominated household may no longer structure the law of marriage itself, but it continues to structure many of the social insurance or welfare programs put in place over the course of the twentieth century.'[76] So, the welfare reforms passed during both the Clinton and George W. Bush administrations either implicitly or explicitly linked individuals' capacity to support themselves and their families to their marital status: of course, households with two working adults are much more likely to be able to succeed economically than families headed by single parents. While by extending this logic one might readily recognize the benefits of invoking expansive models of family or kinship (such as Dorothy Allison's own family model), since 'three or four' adults, as Judith Stacey has argued, 'might prove better yet', government officials have remained ideologically committed (wed?) to the marriage metaphor.[77] What is striking is the touting of marriage as one of the positive 'goods' yielded by welfare reform – a 'good' that could in turn function as a 'solution' to the overburdened welfare system. In other words, in times of economic crisis, marriage is invoked as an asset: the married couple becomes a legitimate symbol of national resilience. For Mattie Richardson, this kind of logic is indicative of the 'compulsory heterosexuality put into policy and practice' and aimed disproportionately at poor black women.[78] The marriage workshops introduced under the Bush administration in particular are indicative of this redirected state attention from policies waging war on poverty to policies attempting to curtail welfare programs:[79] the rhetoric of personal and government accountability accompanying this shift has obscured how cutbacks in welfare benefits have left single mothers and their children increasingly vulnerable.[80]

For both welfare reformers in the Clinton and Bush administrations and Sullivan, marriage is the answer to emotional and economic crises. It is also, importantly, the answer to sexual disorder, where, among other things, disorder may be read as poverty, pathology, passion, and dysphoria. In this regard, Sullivan's metaphoric rendering of sex is striking. He invokes that standard Christian trope for the believer's battle against temptation, the storm-tossed ship: in this case it is marriage that proves to be the 'anchor' that will keep him from the powerful chaos of sex, that vortex of ineluctable fluids that would swallow him up, anchor and all. Ann Bannon's Jack and Laura might agree, but the metaphor as figured proves inadequate to describe the intersections of race, class, gender, and sexuality that structure Beebo's and Tris's sexual desire. For them, the metaphor needs to be inverted and reconstituted. Again, it is not sex but rather prejudices that cast marriage as the only legitimate form of social and moral anchor against which Tris and Beebo must struggle. To varying degrees racism, homophobia, and heterosexism configure the trials of the queer odyssey in pulp fiction and beyond. They produce the ineluctable Charybdis that not only Beebo and Tris but also LGBTQ people in general and even now necessarily confront.

Contemplating the connection between mid 1990s politics and Bannon's pulp fiction, Jennifer Levin writes of Beebo and the other main characters,

> Confined though they were to consuming weak booze, bad coffee, and stale deli sandwiches in that eternally underground West Village of the queer mind and heart, they could not help but fall, time and again, deeply into lust and love. ('L for Love', Beebo says, 'L for Lust . . . L for Let's – let's'. Go, girl.) Yes, these outcasts suffered horribly; but they also *triumphed*.
>
> As some of us prepare, in our clumsy and varied artists' ways, to uncustomarily enter political battle against terrible odds, it is important to remember that. Beebo liked her wine and she liked her women and she liked her suits and ties. But having a place at somebody else's straight 'respectable' table meant nothing to her . . . [81]

This reading of the political significance of Beebo's passion throws into relief the importance of understanding Sullivan's equation of sex with chaos in terms of not simply the question of sex but also the issue of political equality.

In *The Trouble with Normal: Sex, Politics, and the Ethics of Queer Life*, Michael Warner offers an extended analysis of how same-sex marriage is not 'about' equality. In a direct response to Sullivan, Warner asserts,

> marriage, not just *straight* marriage . . . sanctifies some couples at the expense of others. It is selective legitimacy. . . . To a couple that gets married, marriage just looks ennobling . . . Stand outside it for a second and you see the implication: if you don't have it, you and your relations are less worthy. Without this corollary effect, marriage would not be able to endow anybody's life with significance. The ennobling and the demeaning go together. Marriage does one only by virtue of the other. Marriage, in short, discriminates. [82]

Warner's critique of Sullivan's same-sex marriage argument discloses how the latter turns on a definition of marriage as the moral foundation of family and state, a definition that in turn permits the state's (immoral) penalization of those who are not married. For Warner, the legitimization of the gay couple through marriage happens at the expense of a renewed de-legitimization of other gay and queer relations and of sex acts not directly linked to the production and maintenance of the two-parent family. And that de-legitimization plays out differently, according to the gender, class, sexual, and racial dynamics of the people affected. Within the United States, marriage's exclusionary power depends largely on its legal linkage to family, on the one hand, and to basic social rights constructed as 'benefits' (such as citizenship and health care), on the other hand. As John D'Emilio has so eloquently argued in his essay 'Capitalism and Gay Identity', marriage's status as a trope for social harmony depends largely on its socially divisive reach within a capitalist society that does not extend basic rights to its citizens who exist beyond the *chuppa* of marriage.[83] In the name of marriage, the state can erase or, borrowing Sullivan's phrase, relegate other relations to a juridical 'maelstrom of sex'.

Writing in 2000 in response to Canada's decision to recognize same-sex marriages, Jane Rule makes a similar point regarding the policing capacity of the state:

> To be forced back into the heterosexual cage of coupledom is not a step forward but a step back into state-imposed definitions of relationship. With all that we have learned, we should be helping our heterosexual brothers and sisters out of their state-defined prisons, not volunteering to join them there.[84]

Marriage, when viewed in this light, is a far cry from what Evan Wolfson has termed 'the loving union of companionship, commitment, and caring between equal partners that we think of today'.[85] Stated another way, an expanded, gay-inclusive definition of marriage has depended in part on a politics of sexual policing and shaming that turns on the notion of two complementary genders and, further, disregards various class- and race-based understandings of the relations among sex, family, and community.[86] Ironically, the inclusive definition has entailed a narrowed understanding of and diminished tolerance for sex itself.

Seen from this perspective, Sullivan's same-sex marriage position in *Virtually Normal* recalls the gutting of passion in *Women in the Shadows*. It also shuts down any meaningful discussion of the relation between sexual expression and such terms as 'commitment', 'fidelity', and 'integrity', a relation that at very least is complex, mutable, and multivalent. His discussion collapses 'sex' into 'sexual identity', as if the variety of sexual expression were something positioned fundamentally outside of marriage – as if sex that is public or non-procreative; that involves toys, role-playing, or fantasy; or only one person, for example, cannot exist inside or be conducive to marriage.[87] Yet, it can. Marriage, indeed, is often facilitated and sustained through the very forms of sexual activity that the debate has marked out as suspect, illicit.

Let me illustrate this point by way of personal anecdote. In the summer of 1982, my parents, sister, and I were living in three different countries: my parents had just moved to the United States; I was in West Germany, where we had lived for most of my childhood; my sister was in the United Kingdom. In July I heard from my sister that she was planning to marry her English fiancé and that soon, given UK visa restrictions. She explained further, my parents' work situation would not allow them to travel; could I possibly attend her wedding? Of course, I said yes, even though at twenty I was a lesbian with no personal investment in marriage, little cash, and less savings. So I dubbed a porn movie. Two days' worth of lip-synching gave me money enough to buy the bus ticket and attend my sister's wedding; I was her best man. How does this story about a little dissident lip service on behalf of 'family values' complicate conventional notions of sexual integrity? At times the talking points of the same-sex marriage debate have assumed divisions between heterosexual and gay or, again, between the 'good' sexual subject and the 'bad'. In the process, discussions have obscured how very complex the issue of sexual expression is. As Douglas Crimp writes, 'This is not a debate between so-called ordinary homosexuals and a marginal group of sex radicals. Nor is it a debate about monogamy versus promiscuity. These false oppositions denigrate the culture all gay people have made.'[88] The 'good' sexual subject is not so distinguishable from the 'bad'.

Sullivan's apologia for gay tolerance ends with a self-admitted moment of homophobia. He argues that the cessation of public discrimination against gays and lesbians will result in a re-inscription of gender norms. Sullivan describes his own struggle to come to terms with his own gayness. He details how he first

> developed mannerisms, small ways in which I could express myself, tiny revolts of personal space – a speech affectation, a ridiculous piece of clothing – that were, in retrospect, attempts to communicate something in code which could not be communicated in language. In this homosexual archness there was, of course, much pain. And it came as no surprise that once I had become more open about my homosexuality, these mannerisms declined. Once I found the strength to be myself, I had no need to act myself. So my clothes became progressively more regular and slovenly; I lost interest in drama; my writing moved from fiction to journalism; my speech actually became less affected.[89]

His journey toward self-acceptance is marked by the move from affectation to authenticity, from fiction to fact. His comfort level is achieved once he effaces the distinction between sex and gender and delight-edly recovers his own 'nature' as gender normative. He is, he discovers, assimilable; he is 'virtually normal'.

Sullivan's argument is, of course, not the definitive one for same-sex marriage, though it was one of the most prominent and widely circulated and discussed in the mid 1990s. I have chosen it from among many com-pelling examples because of its capacity to alienate potential advocates across queer communities. In this regard, we might also take issue with queer rebuttals such as Warner's, which categorically dismiss marriage advocacy. It is only when same-sex marriage becomes '*the* queer issue' – when, in effect, it is put forth at the expense of other queer issues – that it loses its connection to a politics of inclusion. It is under these conditions that Michael Warner's critique of marriage resonates most strongly. As Judith Butler cautions,

> No doubt, marriage and same-sex domestic partnerships should cer-tainly be available as options, but to install either as a model for sexual legitimacy is precisely to constrain the sociality of the body in acceptable ways. In light of seriously damaging judicial decisions against second parent adoptions in recent years, it is crucial to expand our notions of kinship beyond the heterosexual frame. It would be a mistake, however, to reduce kinship to family, or to assume that all sustained community and friendship ties are extrapolations of kin relations.
>
> ... [T]hose who live outside the conjugal frame or maintain modes of social organization for sexuality that are neither monogamous nor quasi-marital are more and more considered unreal, and their loves and losses less than 'true' loves and 'true' losses. The derealization of this domain of human intimacy and sociality works by denying reality and truth to the relations at issue.[90]

Same-sex marriage advocates cannot afford to conspire in the perpetua-tion of such a 'derealization', to which they themselves are vulnerable.

Religious institutions and political organizations invested in defining marriage in terms of 'one man and one woman' often work to semioti-cally dismiss LGBTQ people as human beings in general, irrespective of their position on same-sex marriage. So, for example, the US Conference of Catholic Bishops' 23 November 2003 statement, 'Between Man and Woman: Questions and Answers about Marriage and Same-Sex Unions', reaffirms the Church's position that marriage is a 'union of a man and a woman'. As a 'personal relationship with public significance', it 'makes a unique and essential contribution to the common good'. Because of this, '[t]he state rightly recognizes [it] as a public institution in its laws'. Further, because

> [t]he legal recognition of marriage, including the benefits associated with it, is not only about personal commitment, but also about the social commitment that husband and wife make to the well-being of society, [i]t would be wrong to redefine marriage for the sake of providing benefits to those who cannot rightfully enter into marriage.[91]

This statement sustains the derealization of LGBTQ people, particularly same-sex couples, and reasserts Church teachings that marriage defined as heterosexual union is the only natural and healthy form of sexual relationship.

This representation of gay couples as pretenders to marriage also, of course, reverberates across fundamentalist-inflected mainstream political discourse, one of the best examples of which is President Bush's 20 January 2004 State of the Union address. In a speech in which he mentions the words 'terrorist(s)' or 'terrorism' sixteen times, the president speaks of the government's need to defend 'the unseen pillars of civilization': 'families and schools and religious congregations'.[92] Bush's rhetorical strategy here is to efface the gay couple (not to mention family) as either a social or a political unit and, concomitantly insist that gay individuals be understood solely within the framework of moral failure. The country, he argues, 'must defend the sanctity of marriage', even as '[t]he same moral tradition that defines marriage also teaches that each individual has dignity and value in God's sight'.[93] The recognition of same-sex marriage would amount to a sanctioning of sexual terrorism, with gay and lesbian couples, in a metaphor that works to undercut itself, cast as so many benighted (morally blind) latter-day Samsons, seeking to topple those pillars of civilization. Homosexuality may be treated with a kind of benign social tolerance only to the extent that it is understood to be God's problem.

Such examples of gay and lesbian couples' derealization within not only conservative and fundamentalist frameworks but also the political mainstream underscore the need for proponents of same-sex marriage to recognize the limitations of marriage advocacy and the need to support alternate forms of queer activism. In other words, the marriage debate is part of a larger struggle for the social validation and political recognition of a variety of forms of human interdependence, intimacy, and family beyond those generated by heteronormative marriage. Mab Segrest's essay 'Hawai'ian Sovereignty/Gay Marriage: *Ka Huliau*' turns on this assumption. Recasting Paine's metaphor, she argues,

> the wedding vow – *to have and to hold, for better or worse, richer or poorer, in sickness and in health* – is a social contract for everybody. If the legislature does not protect the rights of workers to safe jobs with decent pay, or provide healthcare and insurance for everyone, or protect the most vulnerable among us such as women and children on public assistance, then all our relationships suffer.[94]

The significance of that 'wedding vow' resonates across American history. We think, for example, of Segrest's moving reading: the struggle for same-sex marriage has 'inherited the legacy of [the] struggle against slavery and the "badges of slavery" '.[95] We also think of Evan Wolfson's:

> The freedom-to-marry movement's connection to this country's previous civil rights struggles, then, is about much more than just parallels or analogies. The abolitionist and suffrage movements of the nineteenth century and the racial equality and women's movements of the twentieth century are more than just shining moral moments. They are the wellsprings from which much righteousness in our nation flows, and from which companion social justice movements, including ours, draw.[96]

I am writing this chapter in late 2008; currently there are two states, Massachusetts (since May 2004) and Connecticut (since November 2008), that allow same-sex marriage. (Beginning in June of that same year, California, too, had allowed it; the passage of Proposition 8 in November, however, effectually barred further same-sex marriages.[97]) Access to marriage may answer any number of important, poignant, and powerful needs. We might consider the dilemma of the same-sex couple with children, where one partner has no legal claim to her family, and the horrific refusal of a hospital to allow a gay man to administer the medical wishes of his dying partner. Then there are also, as Wolfson underscores, 'the important *intangible* protections to couples and their children' that marriage affords.[98] Importantly, though, not every gay/lesbian couple that might wish to marry in Connecticut or Massachusetts will do so. GLAD's recently released document 'A Brief Q&A for Couples About Marriage for Same-Sex Couples in Connecticut', reminds us of a number of constraints regarding adoption, immigration, military policy, and health insurance that might make marriage inadvisable. So, for example:

> Nearly all international adoptions will be unavailable;
> For bi-national couples getting married will not help the immigration status of the non-citizen and in fact may be harmful;
> Getting married violates the military's 'Don't Ask, Don't Tell' policy;
> Getting married may not guarantee your access to spousal health insurance benefits.[99]

Moreover, because the 1996 federal Defense of Marriage Act (DOMA) defines marriage as only between a man and a woman, 'for all federal purposes . . . , same-sex married couples will not have access to the 1138 federal provisions that pertain to marriage'.[100] Reading these very real limits alongside Laura and Jack's 'strange marriage' in *Women in the Shadows*, we must necessarily confront the gutting of the marriage metaphor: *even* in those states where same-sex marriage is possible, gay and lesbian couples face so many restrictions affecting their recognition and protection that they are left 'less' married – and so relegated to the shadows of – their heterosexual counterparts. Disproportionately vulnerable to the damaging effects of these restrictions are the poor, the elderly, transgender people, people of color, and non citizens. Stated in slightly different terms, the marriage struggle brings into focus a much wider range of issues that are in need of reform if marriage equality is to be realized. Within its limits, same-sex marriage is a social justice issue. A social justice vision requires recognizing the need to look and advocate beyond those limits.

6.   Thinking beyond marriage

Core to such a vision is an awareness of the need to offer families, households, and relationships legal and economic recognition irrespective of their marital status. The 26 July 2006 activist document 'Beyond Same-Sex Marriage: A New Strategic Vision for All Our Families and Relationships' articulates this vision. Written by a number of LGBT and allied 'activists, scholars, educators, writers, artists, lawyers, journalists, and community organizers', including Lisa Duggan, Amber Hollibaugh, Surina Khan, Richard Kim, Ana Oliviera, Suzanne Pharr, and Kendall Thomas,[101] 'Beyond Same-Sex Marriage' argues for 'securing governmental and private institutional recognition of diverse kinds of partnerships, households, kinship relationships and families'.[102] Even as a majority of

US households fall outside the cultural ideal of the nuclear family, the many other kinds of relationships that, on the one hand, are so very recognizable but, on the other hand, have not been deemed worthy of state support, remain without the benefits of economic and legal recognition. The marriage equality struggle, then, is part of a much larger movement to stabilize the variety of US households. These households include not only same-sex couples, but also the following: siblings and/or friends who are living together; elderly partners or friends who take care of each other; two or more interdependent adults who may or may not be sexually involved with each other; extended families comprised of citizens and non-citizens; blended families; relationships that involve and perhaps center on medical caretaking; relatives or friends who are raising children to whom they may or may not be biologically related. These are just some of the types of relationships that are in need of social respect and economic support, a need that, it must be said, has only grown more urgent and apparent in the last few years of historic economic hardship.[103] As the authors of 'Beyond Same-Sex Marriage' observe, 'marriage should be *one of many avenues* through which households, families, partners, and kinship relationships can gain access to the support of a caring civil society'.[104]

Such a society understands interdependence not only as part of the foundational ethos for any social justice vision but also as a cultural value for sustaining and a practical measure for defining families, households, and relationships. Recently, with this in mind I asked students in my LGBT course to imagine the following situation: A person has three individuals with whom she in intimately engaged, whom she thinks of as comprising her household. They are a long-term partner with whom she lives, a lover with whom she does not live but whom she sees regularly, and a best friend with whose medical caretaking she is involved on a daily basis. By marrying, the person can offer one of these members of her household health and economic benefits. Whom should she choose? The question, which I asked midway through the semester, carried through to the end. It unsettled the class, much as it continues to unsettle me – and not because the choice is so very obvious; it is not. As one student revisiting the issue wrote in her final exam, the point is that one should not be forced to choose. 'A caring civil society' understands that families, households, and relationships are comprised of people who look after and love each other and who, accordingly, are worthy of social respect and economic and legal support. This is the lesson of the AIDS crisis; this is the lesson of the lesbian baby boom. This is also the lesson of Ann Bannon's *Women in the Shadows*.

'[Y]ou can't play around with love as if it were a bargain basement special',[105] Beebo tells Laura near the novel's end. These words ring true not only for Laura in her 'strange marriage' to Jack, but also for twenty-first-century readers of lesbian pulp. What is more, for those of us who contemplate marriage equality as part of a larger social justice movement, Beebo's words voice the ethical call that would move any number of relationships – those wide-ranging examples of 'love in the shadows' – into the light of legal and economic recognition and support.

3
Reading for Fantasy in 'Rip Van Winkle' and *The Farewell Symphony*

fantasies are hungrier than bodies[1]

Reality, I think, is too small for most of us, but we don't get a choice about it[2]

1. Introduction

Chapter 2 considered the need to move beyond the US same-sex marriage debate. That debate has at times participated in what Judith Butler has called the 'derealization' of any number of people,[3] including those whose gender and sexual yearnings exist beyond the normalizing pale of gender (male vs. female) and sexual (hetero vs. homo) binaries. Chapter 3 analyzes how such groups of people erased from the debate have had a long-standing (if at times ghostly) presence in American culture. Further, through its reading of two texts, Washington Irving's 'Rip Van Winkle' (1819–20) and Edmund White's *The Farewell Symphony* (1997), the chapter suggests a pedagogical strategy for recovering and reclaiming such groups. In general, this chapter explores how particular expressions of gender and sexuality threaten narratives of normative sexuality and are consequently repudiated or rendered unintelligible – are outlawed to cultural lacunae, epistemological 'deserts of the heart'.

Specifically, this chapter begins by considering a difficulty that I have encountered in the American lesbian, gay, bisexual, and transgender (LGBT) studies classroom. My students are in general quite supportive of the right to claim a sexual identity. They tend to think of sexualities and genders in terms of identity categories, categories that are socially intelligible and sustainable, giving the illusion of stability. Thinking of people in terms of identity categories allows for (some) gay and lesbian representation within narratives of normative sexuality.

There are, of course, problems with this mode of thinking about gender, sex, and sexuality – problems that extend far beyond classroom discussions. Thomas Piontek makes this point with regard to the 1980s:

> Because the assertion of identity always depends on the exclusion of difference, the consolidation of a unified gay and lesbian identity required the policing of that identity's boundaries, which resulted in the exclusion of any number of groups that did not fit this new 'ethnic' model – the so-called fringe elements of 'the gay community', including drag queens, leatherdykes, and butch-femme couples.... What made this exclusion particularly distressing, of course, was the fact that this time around those doing the policing were gay men and lesbians.[4]

Some twenty years later such policing still continues. Within the limits posited by identity category thinking, queer struggles risk being reduced to complacent discussions of inclusion/inclusiveness. So, for example, writer David Leavitt, in a 2005 article on gay bookstores, dismisses the identity issue as settled, passé, and he celebrates a post-gay present: lesbian and gay fiction is now available in mainstream bookstores – it can 'be found anywhere'.[5] He concludes:

> Once it was revolutionary to publish a gay novel, or open a gay bookshop, but now the time may be upon us when the revolutionary thing to do is to retire the category altogether. I'm for stepping into the post-gay future – which is why, every time I go into a Borders, I move a few books from the gay fiction shelf to the general fiction section, restoring them to their rightful place in the alphabetical and promiscuous flow of literature.[6]

His use of the word 'promiscuous' notwithstanding, Leavitt speaks to the mainstreaming of gay and lesbian literature, without acknowledging the very troubling ways in which LGBT desires are continually marginalized, punished, excised.

Within the framework of identity categories, queer desire and political struggle have come to be represented by the same-sex marriage push. There are, of course, urgent and pressing reasons for lesbians and gay men to work toward legalizing same-sex marriage. Yet, part of that work involves a de-politicized argument: marriage should be read not as a political institution but as an expression of personal choice.[7] What is not questioned is the controlling or policing of sexuality via marriage and still less the uneasiness with which sexual expressions not ideologically linked to marriage are regarded.

A similar de-politicization can be seen in the feminist movement. Alexandra Jacobs makes this point, in a review of the 2005 edition of the feminist classic *Our Bodies, Our Selves*. She traces the text's successive de-radicalization, which has resulted in what she tellingly terms the book's newest 'makeover'. Regarding this version's authors, she remarks, they are 'far more pro-wedlock than their foremothers'.[8]

Because the call for an expansion of rights for women, lesbians, gay men, and transgendered people depends on a widespread acknowledgement and acceptance of 'legitimate' categories of gender and sexual acts, desires, and identities,[9] it is worth underscoring here that any number of those acts, desires, and identities are not readily articulable or intelligible within conventional frameworks for thinking about gender and sexuality. They rather exist beyond the pale of legitimacy, within the space of fantasy or, perhaps, along the borders of fantasy and reality.

Talking about gender and sexual fantasies is difficult. As Dorothy Allison has remarked:

> It's unnerving to talk about how our sexual imaginations really function, even if our sexual desires are nowhere near those black leather and chrome scenarios our social magistrates would love to outlaw. For feminists, it often seems dangerous to acknowledge the sexual imagination at all. The sexual is unpredictable, irrational, sneaky, and far-reaching. Worse still, it is completely resistant to simple legalisms or clear philosophical categories. Most sexual imagery does not have one interpretation but a range of multilevel impacts depending on context, personal taste, and hidden symbolism.[10]

It is no wonder, then, that the topic of fantasy has both sparked fierce debates and been met with equally determined silences. How is it possible for a lesbian to have fantasies about being a boy who is having sex with a woman? Or, again, how is it possible for a straight man to fantasize about having sex with another man or, again, imagine himself as part of the girl-on-girl sex scene that he is watching?[11] What happens if these fantasies occur while the given individuals [lesbian; heterosexual man] are having sex with their particular [lesbian; heterosexual woman] partner? Is the one partner merely using the other? Beyond being a potentially disruptive one for the partners' respective identity categories or pronominal matrices, is the fantasy (along with the sexual pleasure that it brings), even when mutually engaged in, to be read as an act of betrayal, not only on the level of individual relationship but also on the levels of gender and sexual identity; a betrayal that exceeds the grammars of gender, sex, and sexuality? Or is it, after all, the commitment to identity categories that does the betraying, exacts the loss, so that gender and sexual behaviors not in accordance with those categories are labelled perverse or shameful or simply, or ruthlessly, left unacknowledged?[12] To summarize this dilemma in queer aphoristic terms, all marriage and no play makes Jane a dull boy – or, perhaps, no boy at all.[13]

There is value, then, in recognizing Jane in her various gendered and sexed parts. Pedagogically and culturally, that value lies in reading for fantasy: that is, broadening the definition of humanity to include acts, desires, and identities that become visible through fantasy. One's personhood, more particularly one's sexual personhood, is not confined to a given gender identity category. Further, one's sexual desires or sex acts that are not [typically] represented as part of a narrative of normative sexuality are not, because of that absence, themselves non-existent or immoral or perverse – that is, an indictment of the person as a whole.

In order to explore how particular expressions of gender and sexuality threaten narratives of normative sexuality (and are consequently repudiated or outlawed or rendered unintelligible), I would like to engage contemporary discussions of melancholia, especially those of Judith Butler regarding fantasy and melancholy gender. There is, as Mari Ruti observes, a long literary tradition of understanding sadness as a 'site of a special kind of truth or knowledge'.[14] I am interested in exploring this site for the insights it can offer for two American literary texts: the first Washington Irving's early nineteenth-century classic, 'Rip Van Winkle'; the second Edmund White's late twentieth-century novel, *The Farewell Symphony*. For this purpose I am defining melancholia not as a pathological condition but rather, following Gayle Salamon, 'as a collective response of a community to the conditions of psychic loss when that loss is culturally unrecognized and mourning is disallowed or disavowed'.[15] In offering a close reading of the two texts, I seek first, with 'Rip Van Winkle', to explore an epistemological framework that, on the one hand, identifies, legitimizes – and even names as 'American' – certain expressions of gender and sexuality, while, on the other hand, repudiating and relegating to the realm of melancholy fantasy others.[16] Written circa a half century before the constitution of sexual identity categories but after some two centuries of Puritan interrogation and regulation of sexuality, this iconic text of American literature teaches readers to read culture, in this case particularly the links between gender and sexuality and fantasy and reality that express Americanness, in terms of fixed narrative patterns, deviations from which result in non-narratable textual moments and non-liveable gender identities. Second, turning my attention to *The Farewell Symphony*, I wish to show how White's novel, particularly on the issues of fantasy and gender melancholy, challenges the ways of knowing gender and sexuality that 'Rip Van Winkle' offers. This novel, I argue, proves a key text for the praxis of a queer pedagogy – what in this chapter I specifically call reading for fantasy – which pushes students beyond viewing gender and sexuality merely in terms of identity categories.

2. 'Rip Van Winkle', fantasy, and melancholy gender

Washington Irving is widely regarded as the father of American literature.[17] This paternity, which contrasts sharply with the writer's own life-long bachelor status during a time when bachelors were considered 'idle and sexually suspect',[18] rests largely on the literary importance of *The Sketch Book*. *The Sketch Book* begins with an epigraph from *The Anatomy of Melancholy* (1621), written by another life-long bachelor, Oxford scholar Robert Burton:

> I have no wife nor children, good or bad, to provide for. A mere spectator of other men's fortunes and adventures, and how they play their parts; which methinks are diversely presented unto me, as from a common theatre or scene.[19]

With this passage Burton offers a partial explanation for his melancholy. It derives from his remove from a world of marriage and children, a remove figured as a lack: as a writer he is only a 'mere spectator' of life.[20] Yet, reading the passage as an epigraph to *The Sketch Book*, one finds that the passage suggests a different expression of melancholy: the fantasy of Irving's inversion of the above relation between literary and sexual reproduction, so that the former proves central and the latter marginal to the understanding of his own masculinity. That is, the passage reflects Irving's desire that literary composition be recognized 'as an alternative to marriage'.[21] More specifically, it suggests Irving's yearning to attain what Michael Warner terms 'a generational continuity', engendered by neither sexual reproduction nor heterosexuality's ideological function as a vehicle for familial and communal memory: a queer kind of paternity that is 'social and public rather than merely private and familial' and that is fundamentally homosocial in its focus.[22] Such a fantasy is at the center of *The Sketch Book*'s most well-known tale, 'Rip Van Winkle'.

'Rip Van Winkle' tells the story of an indolent but affable character, Rip, who, living in a sleepy village in upstate New York's Catskill region, habitually escapes work and his shrewish wife. So he retreats to the village inn, where he passes his time with like-minded men in lazy conversation. For complete quiet – well beyond the upbraidings of his wife – Rip goes off into the mountains. On one such adventure he encounters a strange, silent man, a quaint Dutchman wearing clothes from an earlier time when the Dutch first explored the Hudson River Valley. The man leads Rip up the mountain, where they come upon a group of similarly dressed men, who are wordlessly playing ninepins and drinking. Rip begins to drink as well and soon falls asleep. When he awakes and returns to the village, he finds that he has been gone not simply for a day but for some twenty years. In the interim his wife has passed away and his children grown up; his village has expanded into a bustling town; and America itself has become a state independent of England. If initially confused and met with villagers' skepticism, the now-old Rip is soon enough welcomed back as a living monument both to the historic past of the pre-Revolutionary era, perceived as simple and slow paced, and to an (inarticulable) yearning for a queer mythic past, understood as a foreclosed reality.

Washington Irving's tale, then, turns on the importance of a melancholy nostalgia for the making of not only individual lives but also communal and national identities. Following Freud's definition of melancholia, this condition indicates a subject's resistance to loss, an inability 'to discard its lost loves,' held onto 'with the kind of faithfulness that contradicts reason and logic'.[23] As such, it 'provides the subject an indirect means of sheltering objects that it considers so precious that their loss seems inconceivable.'[24] Rip himself yearns to return to a life that he arguably never had: a life free from the tyranny of both colonial rule and gender norms, themselves consolidated and enforced through heterosexuality. Within the story, then, Dame Van Winkle, functioning allegorically as the embodiment of 'the tyrant Britannia of the late colonial era,'[25] is the enforcer of these norms. Her shrewishness discloses not simply the story's participation in the comic (and misogynist) literary tradition of the 'unnatural' defiant woman but, more importantly, that tradition's function as a means of foreclosing the possibility of recognizing and articulating male transgression of heterosexual gender norms, norms regulated primarily through marriage. In other words, Dame Van Winkle's outbursts should be understood as comic discursive distractions for a nascent American scene: they are projections (and inversions) of lazy Rip's repeated defiance of village norms of heterosexual masculinity. For while his love of ease is shared by other men in the tranquil village, including its patriarch, Nicholas Vedder, Rip finds 'doing family duty, and keeping his farm in order ... impossible.'[26] A 'simple, good-natured fellow', Rip has 'inherited ... but little of the martial character of his ancestors.'[27] His 'meekness of spirit' and his 'insuperable aversion to all kinds of profitable labour' have their discursive distraction in 'the ... shrew[ ] at home', on whom the villagers 'lay all the blame.'[28] By comparison, silence – or near silence – marks his retreat into all-male companionship. He is most content in the company of other men, who, like him, retreat to Nicholas Vedder's inn, where they prefer 'talking list-lessly over village gossip, or telling endless sleepy stories about nothing' to either work or expressive language.[29] So Rip – the trope of the hen-pecked husband notwithstanding – flees heterosexually-imposed gender norms as much as his wife when he takes himself to the inn or, more effectively, into the mountains. Rip longs for the wild[er]ness beyond the village. The woods and mountains demarcate the space for his desire to play, not work or, again, demarcate a landscape that configures his desire, specifically, the relations among gender, sexuality, and labor that constitute that desire, as unproductive, un-reproductive, and useless.[30] The mountains especially, whose 'hood of grey *vapours* about their summits' suggests not only mists but also melancholy,[31] recall the circling 'vapour' of Nicholas Vedder's pipe and function as objective correlatives to his all-male fantasy life.[32] (See Figure 3.1.) That life, despite Rip's status as 'a great favourite among all the good wives',[33] is neither sustainable within the confines of the village reality nor articulable within the limits of village speech.

Rip's subsequent entrance into the all-male world of the anachronistic Dutchmen may be understood in terms of Judith Butler's discussion of fantasy. In her book *Undoing Gender*, Butler explains that fantasy

> is part of the articulation of the possible; it moves us beyond what is merely actual and present into a realm of possibility, the not yet actu-alized or the not actualizable. The struggle to survive is not really separable from the cultural life of fantasy, and the foreclosure of fantasy – through censorship, degradation, or other means – is one strategy for providing for the social death of persons. Fantasy is not the opposite of reality; it is what reality forecloses, and, as a result, it defines the limits of reality, constituting it as its constitutive outside.[34]

Rip's time with the men – his playing, drinking, and falling into a twenty-year sleep in their midst – has been foreclosed by the reality of village

Figure 3.1: *Rip Van Winkle and His Companions at the Inn Door of Nicholas Vedder* (1839), by John Quidor (1801–1881), Oil on canvas, 68.9 × 86.68 cm (27.5 × 34.125 in.), Museum of Fine Arts, Boston. Gift of Martha C. Karolik for the M. and M. Karolik Collection of American Paintings, 1815–1865. 48.469. Photograph © 2009 Museum of Fine Arts, Boston.

life. Since in contrast to the home, the woods and mountains make up his space to desire a differently gendered economic landscape, they in effect constitute the place beyond the limits of reality. In Ruti's terms, 'under the spell of melancholia', Rip 'no longer loves in "real" time';[35] instead, '*unconsciously* scrambl[ing] to one of the highest parts of the Kaatskill mountains',[36] he 'embraces a mythical conception of a loving connection that transcends the boundaries of tangible space and experience'.[37]

   This message – that nature offers a retreat from the framework of village life – is in turn taken up by the next generation of American artists. One thinks, for example, of the wild, forest covered and mist shrouded mountains of Thomas Cole's Hudson River paintings (Figures 3.2 and 3.3). Writing in 1830, Cole's dear friend, the poet William Cullen Bryant,

Figure 3.2:   *Clove, Catskill Mountains* (1827) by Thomas Cole (1801–1848), Oil on canvas, 63.5 × 83.8 cm (25 × 33 in.), New Britain Museum of Art. Photograph © 2009 New Museum of Art.

begins his discussion of the landscape depicted in Figure 3.3 by quoting Irving:

> Irving, who has made these mountains the scene of one of his most popular tales, thus describes their aspect, as viewed from the river and its banks: –
> ' ... sometimes ... [the Catskills] will gather a hood of gray vapours about their summits, which, in the last rays of the setting sun, will glow and light up like a crown of glory'.
> The traveller, as he looks from the shore of the river to the broad woody sides of this mighty mountain range, turns his eye from a scene rich with cultivation, populous with human beings, and ringing with the sounds of human toil, to one of primeval forest ... a wide sylvan wilderness ... [38]

That the passage incorporates a direct quote from the opening of Irving's story serves to underscore that for Irving, as for the writers and painters following him, the linkage between melancholy yearning and landscape – indeed, the former's inscription within the latter – is a vital

Figure 3.3:   *View of the Round-Top in the Catskill Mountains* (1827) by Thomas Cole (1801–1848), Oil on panel, 47.31 × 64.45 cm (18.625 × 25.375 in.), Museum of Fine Arts, Boston. Gift of Martha C. Karolik for the M. and M. Karolik Collection of American Paintings, 1815–1865. 47.1200. Photograph © 2009 Museum of Fine Arts, Boston.

focus for artistic composition, as well as, perhaps, a sign of artistic legacy. Like Irving's Rip, Bryant's traveller and Cole's implied viewing subject find that nature answers the desire to retreat from 'a scene ... populous with human beings, and ringing with the sounds of human toil' – to one marked out from the conventions of time and space.[39]

If the wooded mountains are Rip's space to desire, it is important to recognize here how the significance or the social legitimacy of that space is itself delimited, first by the strangeness of the men and second by the function of landscape within American culture as the *locus* for unintelligibility, fantasy, and gender melancholy.[40] The Dutchmen, with their 'strange, uncouth, lacklustre countenances', cause Rip's 'heart [to] turn[ ] within him, and his knees [to] sm[i]te together'. How is Rip to think of them, and how, in turn, are we to think of Rip among them? Though Rip 'obey[s]' them,[41] the space that they occupy constitutes what, according to Butler, 'reality forecloses'. Susan Sontag, in her essay 'Melancholy Objects', writes, 'The American landscape has always seemed too varied, immense, mysterious, fugitive to lend itself to scientism.' She continues, quoting from Henry James's *The American Scene*, published in 1907: ' "The *il*legible word, accordingly, the great inscrutable answer to questions, hangs in the vast American sky ... as something fantastic and *abracadabrant*, belonging to no known language ..." '.[42] In other words, when Rip escapes into the woods and finds himself amongst the quaint Dutchmen, he in effect enters another world, 'natural', in that it consists of nature, but also denaturalized, 'unnatural', in that it exists beyond the borders of the village and turns on a different kind of gendered economy, which he experiences as a 'strange and incomprehensible ... unknown'.[43] This unknown lacks the village's reality grid – the clear linkage between gender and heterosexuality. What, after all, does one call a heterosexual man who desires only the company of other men? The village's particular patterns of gender and sexual life do not allow a modern audience readily to name this space beyond calling it fantasy or to identify Rip, beyond calling him queer.

If Rip's place among the men must be understood 'in excess of the real',[44] it is nonetheless important to note that, in contrast to his running away from his wife and work, Rip does not try to escape from the men. Their economy of same-sex play – marked by ninepins, drinking, and silence – grants him a sleep that both 'the labour of the farm and the clamour of his wife' do not permit. The men's silence here is of particular importance. It suggests that Rip's interaction with the men cannot be articulated, and so legitimized through language. He cannot exist with them within the bounds of the communicable. Important, too, is the following description: Rip notes that the men have the 'gravest faces'; theirs is 'the most melancholy party of pleasure he had ever witnessed'.[45] Much like their silence, their melancholy denotes the impossibility of living beyond the exigencies of a gendered heterosexual reality. In *The Psychic Life of Power*, Butler explores this relation between melancholy and gender. She writes, 'In opposition to a conception of sexuality which is said to "express" a gender, gender itself [may be] understood to be composed of precisely what remains inarticulate in sexuality.'[46] Gender may be termed a form of melancholy; gender is 'both the refusal of grief and the incorporation of loss, a miming of the death it cannot mourn'.[47] For Ruti, this is Butler's central insight: 'melancholia lends silent expression to an impossible love that we are not even necessarily aware of. ... Love is lost, in a sense, before we have had a chance to experience it as love.'[48]

By the end of the nineteenth century that loss of a love that dared not speak its name would be known as homosexuality. Written some fifty years before the formulation of sexual identity categories, Irving's story offers no such euphemism.[49] Within the realm of Rip's fantasy, the companionate men remain enthralled in a loss that Rip himself cannot name – cannot even recognize as a loss. In an analysis of the relation between utopian discourse and 'America', Lauren Berlant writes,

> the experience of 'the nation' as nation is primarily a symbolic one – communicated through the subject's understanding that certain spatial and temporal experiences reflect, perform, and/or affirm her/his citizenship – the spatial and temporal ambiguity of 'utopia' has the effect of masking the implications of political activity and power relations in American civil life.[50]

For Rip and his fellow villagers, his twenty-year sleep, his mythic experience of time and space, functions in this way: as a testimony to his, as well as the villagers', Americanness. Berlant continues by asking, 'If the "meaning" of nation is its utopian "promise", then is America utopia incarnate, the already-realized fulfilment of the assurance of universal sovereignty whose history is the unfolding of its national being-brought-to-perfection?'[51] Irving's text, engaged in a discourse of fantasy and melancholy gender, produces a slightly different question, focused on the mythic past: if the 'meaning' of nation is its yearning, then is America engendered by melancholy, the unrealized possibility of a queer past, of an American paradise not so much lost as foreclosed?[52]

   Speaking of how homosexuality occupies this kind of narrative void, Butler observes,

> To the extent that homosexual attachments remain unacknowledged within normative heterosexuality, they are not merely constituted as desires which emerge and subsequently become prohibited; rather, these desires are proscribed from the start ... This is, then, less a *refusal* to grieve ... than a pre-emption of grief performed by the absence of cultural conventions for avowing the loss of homosexual love. And this absence produces a culture of heterosexual melancholy, one which can be read in the hyperbolic identifications by which mundane heterosexual masculinity and femininity confirm themselves. The straight man *becomes* (mimes, cites, appropriates, assumes the status of) the man he 'never' loved and 'never' grieved ... It is in this sense, then, that what is most apparently performed as gender is the sign and symptom of a pervasive disavowal.[53]

   The link between the consolidation of gender norms and this disavowal becomes apparent when Rip, upon awakening from his twenty-year sleep, returns to the village, which, during his absence, has experienced the Revolutionary War and undergone a demographic shift. Gone is the village's 'accustomed phlegm and drowsy tranquillity'.[54] Gone, too, are the shrewish protestations of Dame Van Winkle. The village – now 'busy, bustling, and disputatious' – itself has taken over her role as regulator of gender norms. Yet, within this space, Rip finds himself welcomed and even celebrated: he is 'reverenced as one of the patriarchs of the village, and a chronicle of the old times "before the war" '.[55] That is, an aged Rip, now too old to work, achieves a queer paternity: he functions as a figure of melancholy nostalgia for the villagers. He not only recalls an earlier time, when the village itself held to a slower pace but also incorporates an idleness that has no space within the lives of men of (re)productive age. Foremost in its hold over them is, however, his 'story',[56] 'even among those who pretended to doubt the reality of it'.[57] Rip's story is a particularly American story, one in which national transformation – the making of a national reality – lies encoded within gender politics.[58] Rip returns to a village whose 'country had thrown off the yoke of old England – [so] that ... he [is] now a free citizen of the United States'.[59] Like Rip, on whom 'the changes of states and empires made but little impression',[60] the other men in the village prove wary of the 'despotism' of 'petticoat government'.[61] So, the narrator concludes, 'it is a common wish of all hen-pecked husbands in the neighbourhood, ... that they might have a quieting draught out of Rip Van Winkle's flagon'.[62] Rip's desire to escape into an all-male world that lies unobtainable, beyond the spatial and temporal borders of village reality, confirms for the village its 'culture of heterosexual melancholy'. This, ultimately, is the pull of Irving's iconic text: its capacity to signal for characters and readers alike that particularly American fantasy – to return to a home that is never considered as such.

3. The Farewell Symphony: 'vitriol and impudence'[63]

> Homosexualism is a *symphony* running through a marvelous range of psychic keys, with many high and heroic ... harmonies; but constantly relapsing to base and *fantastic* discords![64]

> Call us *hopeful melancholics*, but we think that a depathologized and politicized melancholia offers resources for surviving into the future precisely because of melancholia's greedy (and heart-stretching) conservation of loss.[65]

The equation at work in Washington Irving's tale – the rigid demarcation between fantasy and reality that in turn produces the village's melancholy – is present in any number of literary texts. I have chosen to consider 'Rip Van Winkle' because in it we find the equation engendering a kind of Americanness or American character that disavows queer desire. How very different is Edmund White's 1997 novel, *The Farewell Symphony*, whose timeframe, covering the 1960s to 1990s, also spans a series of 'nation-building events' – most notably, the Civil Rights Movement, the sexual revolution, the women's movement, gay liberation, and the AIDS crisis. Where Rip and his narrator have no language available to them for the desire to exist apart from institutionalized heterosexuality, *The Farewell Symphony*'s narrator-protagonist can frankly recount his range of queer sexual experiences – from shit scenes to anonymous club sex to S/M role playing to masturbation, celibacy, and heterosexual sex – and divest them of the moral stigmas of sordidness and shame. Within the novel sex – various, intense, frequent, and promiscuous – is a visible and uncompromising condition of humanity.

Like 'Rip Van Winkle', White's novel explores the boundary between fantasy and reality, and this on the level of both story and genre. His narrator-protagonist early on remarks of his sexual fantasies, 'My fantasies are memories as accurate as I can make them of past lovers and what they did to me. These days I find myself fucking the dead most of the time.'[66] With the phrase 'fucking the dead', the aging narrator-protagonist reminds readers that while death is the ultimate barrier between fantasy and reality, it also proves the malleability of this border: for isn't it fantasy, after all, which keeps alive the memory of those whom we've lost? Making this point in slightly different terms, Ruti observes,

> as human beings we do not always know how to meet the future unless we are familiar with how the past makes itself present in our psyches. To look to the past is therefore not merely to confront what is dead (although this can be a part of it, as an act of farewell to something that has been outlived), but also to discover our potential in what is 'already living' within us.[67]

For White, fantasy actualizes that potential, evincing what David L. Eng and David Kazanjian have termed the 'counterintuitive' creativity of loss.[68] His novel incorporates 'melancholia's insights without succumbing to the pull of sadness'.[69] Thus, the phrase 'fucking the dead' reveals one of White's discursive aims: to incorporate into his textual body accounts of the loss of past lovers, even those whom he proves unable to mourn. The latter, centering on the AIDS-related death of his lover, Brice, indeed generates the telling that is the novel itself:

> Everything I'd lived through in the last five years had changed me – whitened my hair, made me a fat, sleepy old man, matured me, finally, but also emptied me out. I met Brice five years before he died – but I wonder whether I'll have the courage to tell his story in this book.[70]

After the opening pages, Brice appears only fleetingly in this fictional chronicle. He becomes the genius spectre hovering over, haunting the novel.[71] Within the terms of Butler's discussion of gender melancholy, the narrator-protagonist's persona may well be understood in relation to the loss of his lover, who is both the impetus and the limit of his storytelling.

Yet, even if one argues that *The Farewell Symphony* is the site of the lover's absence, it is perhaps more profoundly the place in which writer Edmund White explores the questions articulated by Judith Butler in *Undoing Gender*, ' ... who counts as human ... what makes for a grievable life?'[72] Taking its title from Haydn's 'Farewell Symphony',[73] White's novel offers a philosophical and political meditation that, like Butler's work, responds to 'moralistic America',[74] with its widespread refusal to mourn the loss of queer lives – a refusal apparent in activist Larry Kramer's dismissive response to the novel.[75] In this sense *The Farewell Symphony*, like Irving's early nineteenth-century short story, raises the refusal to mourn to a national issue, one affecting Americans as a collective and a legislative body. But unlike Irving's work, White's pays tribute to gay and queer lives that, not grieved, are rather typically written off as monstrous, aberrant, perverse, or grieved only once they have been sanitized of their sexuality – a tribute incorporated into his textual body. Such tribute may be understood in terms of David L. Eng and Shinhee Han's work on melancholia with respect to Asian Americans: within the context of a dominant culture that not only discounts the meaning of those lives lost but also overlooks the existence of the lives themselves, melancholia functions as an ethically and politically charged act of resistance.[76] Thus, *The Farewell Symphony* may be located within a tradition of activist art that addresses the racism, sexism, and homophobia that in the 1980s (and of course since then) fuelled the AIDS crisis in the United States and elsewhere. (See Figure 3.4.) So one reads of the 'artistically fertile and brilliant' New York scene of the late 1970s; of the 'enormous gay parades of dykes in work boots and drag queens' whom

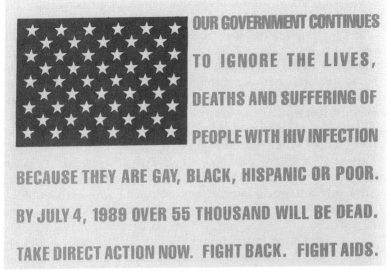

Figure 3.4:   *American Flag* (1989) by Richard Deagle, Tom Starace, and Joe Wollin. Subway advertising poster, silkscreen, 27.9 × 36.85 cm (11 × 14.5 in.), also used as T-shirt.

'the public saw'; and of those they did not – the 'doughy clarinettist scuttling . . . to lunch with a lesbian musicologist . . . , or the Asian teenage woman holding hands with her Puerto Rican girlfriend in the park late at night'.[77] One reads of the friendships with Joshua and Eddie, fiction-alized versions of the Renaissance scholar David Kalstone, who died of AIDS in the mid 1980s, and of James Merrill, the pre-eminent American poet. And one reads of casual acquaintanceships, such as the one with a gay couple who perform a tea ceremony for the narrator, Brice, and Brice's brother; within a year, the narrator remarks, two of those partic-ipants were dead; or the one with the guy at the gym, who '[coming] down with something the doctors couldn't diagnose . . . just seemed to deflate in front of our eyes'.[78] The stories of those lives mix with the narrator's own in a kind of sexual and textual metamorphosis, produc-ing a hybrid corpus that is part *Bildungsroman*, *roman á clef*, sex manual, activist tract, cultural history, and philosophical memoir. That is, with this tribute the boundaries between fiction and reality prove permeable, porous.

At one point in the novel, White's narrator-protagonist remarks, ' . . . I [have] realized that whereas gay life is always aberrant, there's not a moment of straight life, no matter how bizarre or melodramatic, that isn't cosily familiar, that can't be associated with a song lyric or a movie or a poem'.[79] While blanket statements such as this one are necessarily problematic – since who's to say, among other things, that what goes on between a man and woman's sheets is always 'straight' – the basic contrast is an important one: heterosexuality is culturally highly narratable; homosexuality is not. Pushing the point further, I would say that queerness, that is, acts or desires that exist apart from identity categories, gender or sexual, resists ready interpretation; eludes cultural shorthand; is often lodged within discourse's melancholy lacunae.

Queerness, in effect, turns on – moves along, occupies, and genders or sexualizes – the realm of fantasy. So, returning to Butler's discussion, we find that fantasy 'challenge[s] the contingent limits of what will and will not be called reality. Fantasy is what allows us to imagine ourselves and others otherwise ... '.[80]

Fantasy's metamorphic relation to the real can be clearly seen in *The Farewell Symphony*. For example, at one point the narrator-protagonist recounts his desire to be raped:

> I wanted to be treated brutally ...
>
> I made an effort to understand that what for me was no idle if persistent fantasy constituted a real danger for women – but the effort failed, since the minute I contemplated, soberly, disapprovingly, the idea (or the image) of rape, I immediately became aroused.[81]

Here the protagonist, in recognizing his desire, acknowledges that rape exists simultaneously in different realms: that of sadomasochism (S/M) and that of reality. Within the former, the fantasy of his being raped excites him. 'The key word to understanding S/M is *fantasy*', observes Pat Califia. ' ... A sadomasochist is well aware that a role adopted during a scene is not appropriate during other interactions and that a fantasy role is of the sum total of [his] being.'[82] As Gayle Rubin elaborates, 'S/M fantasy does involve images of coercion and sexual activities that may appear violent to outsiders.' S/M itself, however, 'is not a form of violence, but is rather a type of ritual and contractual sex play whose aficionados go to great lengths in order to do it and to ensure the safety and enjoyment of one another'.[83] By contrast, within reality, rape is obviously 'a real danger' especially 'for women'.

Thus, the moment in the novel, with its distinction between reality and fantasy, proves a crucial one. It reminds readers of how violence is a constitutive element of reality or, if one will, a constitutive element of the fantasy that is called 'reality'. As Laura Kipnis in her essay 'Fantasy in America' remarks,

> Mainstream culture constructs elaborate fantasies about what it purports it's not – subcultural, foreign, pornographic, violent – which propel, and are enacted in, these highly publicized rituals of control and punishment, policing and mastery. ... The overarching fantasy is that the powerfully monstrous bad thing is somewhere else, that it can be caged, and most crucially, that it's 'other'. Violence isn't here, it's *there*.[84]

In other words, returning to the moment in White's text, one finds that, beyond inviting us to consider whether the protagonist's fantasy is aberrant if it does not harm anyone – if it is accompanied by an awareness of 'real danger' –, the moment foregrounds the violence of a reality that conflates sex and violence. If this blurring serves to justify (and proleptically 'naturalize') the policing of sex acts within reality, one recognizes from White's passage that sexual fantasy challenges the epistemological limits of reality; challenges the conflation of sex and violence itself.[85]

Throughout the novel the protagonist's fantasies push back the conventional limits for narrating reality. In contrast to 'Rip Van Winkle', *The Farewell Symphony* directly challenges a configuration of desire whose relations among gender, sexuality, and labor define that desire as useless and therefore perverse. So, in another example that reflects what Rubin terms the 'highly negotiated nature of most S/M encounters',[86] White's narrator-protagonist offers the following interpretation of a three-way BDSM scene:

> I was dating a handsome little slave from Kentucky who was always looking for new thrills ... I stripped my slave naked and tied him up in one room and then, as prearranged, I buzzed Leonard in. ... When we went into the bedroom all my slave could see in the half light was a six-foot-four sadist with a hard-on and leathers, his face cast in shadow by the bill of his motorcycle cap. The slave moaned and came before Leonard even touched him.
>
> What he couldn't see was that this was Leonard ... This was the warm, smiling genial Leonard who encouraged Billy to learn Schubert and Schumann, who gave dinner parties for all men at which the guests would linger till dawn, discussing life, love, art, money, morality. He wasn't competitive, he loved nurturing other people's talents, he'd learned, all on his own, the arts of life ... [87]

Much as the narrator's musings during his rape fantasy indicate a realm of pleasure that de-naturalizes reality and so calls it into question, the terminology of BDSM – in this case the particular reference to 'slave' – indicates an erotic context in which, according to Rubin, 'a man can be overpowered, restrained, tormented, and penetrated, *and yet* retain his masculinity, desirability, and subjectivity'.[88] Following Eng and Han, one might say that in this scene fantasy's facilitation of sexual pleasure discloses the national melancholia for a country whose discourse of inclusion depends on a series of exclusions: on strategic erasures and a widespread forgetting of various racial, sexual, and gender minorities. The scene resists the conventional metaphorical hold that 'usefulness' exercises over desire and, in so doing, exposes the reality of American slavery: its location within the metaphorical domain of 'usefulness', with the term 'slave' recalling a particularly wrenching fact of American history.[89] How, then, can the term's resuscitation within this sexual context effect the perverse validation of social abjection, dehumaniza-tion? What happens when sexual fantasy takes up and de-historicizes the language of abjection? What happens when that language signals con-sensual acts of pleasure? Shouldn't the pleasure then be understood as existing both apart from a dehumanizing historical reality and along the boundary between fantasy and reality – especially a reality that has habit-ually made of violence a constitutive element; a reality often constituted through the exclusion of all kinds of people not considered fully human, including those who engage in or *even think of* non-normative sexual behaviors?[90] Doesn't the language of abjection within the context of sexual fantasy signal the possibility of transforming – metamorphosing – the damage of an historical reality?[91]

This is the reading that I find particularly important for the above excerpt, for the description of the 'slave' orgasming at the *sight* of the top Leonard – that is, at the recognition of Leonard's embodiment of the possibility of pleasure – is followed by a paragraph characterizing Leonard 'in reality'. What is it that makes Leonard identifiably 'human'? Is it his love of the arts, his cultivation, his 'nurturing, but not his sexual fantasies? Following Ann Pellegrini and Janet R. Jakobsen's terminology, is it his 'making sex' here that makes him less human?[92] Or is it that the two-paragraph description of him – with its juxtaposition of fantasy and reality – reminds us that our humanity, with its 'terrible vulnerability',[93] turns not on reality *per se* but on the promise of acceptance – which we attempt to realize if only in our fantasies? As Butler observes, '[fantasy] establishes the possible in excess of the real; it points elsewhere, and when it is embodied, it brings the elsewhere home'.[94]

4. Conclusion: a reader's valediction forbidding mourning[95]

Literature belongs to the dispossessed[96]

To do something very common, in my own way[97]

So the question presents itself, how *at home* with fantasy are we, as readers of American literature and, more broadly, cultural texts, including the corporeal texts of our own lives? As the discussions of 'Rip Van Winkle' and *The Farewell Symphony* show, American fiction, even realistic fiction, turns on (or, more accurately, turns *on* and *off*) fantasy, and as readers we find that our own interpretive *pleasure* consists in recognizing, engaging, and re-visioning those narrative mechanisms that either curtail or permit fantasy's representation. Reading for fantasy requires that we read against or across culture. So our reading pleasure is politically charged: it depends upon our ability both to recognize and challenge the cultural investment in stable identity categories; it necessitates a suspension of reality or, better said, 'reality'. Reading for fantasy leads us out of that everyday commitment to stable identity categories, and in so doing it transforms us; it educates us. It leads us to appreciate the permeable and therefore vitalizing relation between fantasy and the real. Edmund White remarks in his essay 'The Personal is Political: Queer Fiction and Criticism', 'A book exists only when a living mind re-creates it, and that re-creation comes into being only through the full imaginative participation of a particular sensibility.'[98] Like the book that comes into *being* through the *doing* of reading, so, too, do gender and sexuality. Through reading for fantasy we recognize ourselves *in part* – not wholly – but in parts, gendered and sexual parts that often find no context for visibility or acknowledgment or respect or pleasure within narratives of normative sexuality. Reading for fantasy provides us with a way out of identity category thinking, which, even if it expands gender norms, still leaves us feeling incomplete. Reading for fantasy enables us to expand our definitions of humanity and, in so doing, to recognize is our 'terrible vulnerability'. Reading for fantasy is our way through the melancholy landscape of gender and sexual possibility.

4
Remaking Gendered Systems of Story: Sexual Violence in *Bastard Out of Carolina* and *The Way the Crow Flies*

> [T]rue speaking is not solely an expression of creative power; it is an act of resistance, a political gesture that challenges politics of domination that would render us nameless and voiceless.[1]

1. Introduction

Whereas Chapter 3 considered 'reading for renewal', Chapter 4 is concerned with 'writing for renewal'. Specifically, this chapter explores the links between violence, lesbian identity, and intellectual creativity. It does so through an analysis of two novels: Dorothy Allison's *Bastard Out of Carolina* (1992) and Anne-Marie MacDonald's *The Way the Crow Flies* (2003).[2]

I begin with two personal memories. The first of these is an image, much of which is captured in Figure 4.1: I am a skinny teenage girl with reddish-blonde hair. Feet planted shoulder-width apart, I'm dressed in boys' pants – plaid; it was the seventies, after all – and a t-shirt. Around my neck is a strap, which holds an alto sax. The reed is inches from my mouth. I am fingering the keys. The horn reaches my crotch and then bends, the bell facing up and slightly out. For this younger me, who does not yet have the words to articulate my gender and sexuality, the sax is an extension of myself: it's the big snake, my strap-on, the imaginary, imagined, and imaginative body. It allows me to sing.

The next memory takes the form of an anecdote, set some ten years later and thousands of miles away. Now in my mid twenties, I am walking with my girlfriend toward a movie theater where a lesbian film is playing. Some fifteen feet from the entrance a group of young men is standing. They are harassing anyone entering the theater. My girlfriend and

Figure 4.1: My mother and I, circa 1976.

I approach, buy our tickets, and are then pushed and shoved. We are called 'dyke' and 'faggot'. Silently we make our way past the men. We are determined to see the film. It's a love story. With sex.

Even though such interactions should be recognized for the complex cultural productions that they are, I cannot help experiencing (and remembering) the harassment on a deeply personal level. What was it that tipped the young men off that we were lesbians? Was it how she or I was dressed? Was it the shortness of my hair or the length of hers? Was it that we were walking together; that we were going to see a lesbian film? What makes that 'it' matter? After all, I can still feel that mid-eighties hunger, the deep need that propelled us from documentaries to the slowly growing number of independent films in order to see lesbian stories, ones with women having sex; ones that had a happy ending. Isn't that the 'it' that counts? In my story it is.

Such memories tell us something about the profound impact and daily importance of art in the lives of lesbians, who so often do not have a ready socio-cultural framework or the language to recognize and affirm themselves and their desires. For lesbians, who can so suddenly find themselves the would-be victims of violence at once random and deliberate,[3] art can function as a site of visibility and truth-telling, and as a means of resisting a culture that exacts their erasure.[4]

Lesbian writer Dorothy Allison has written extensively about her early absorption in books. When she was a young girl, literature afforded her an escape from the violence of everyday life and, crucially, a context for recognizing and validating her sexual fantasies and desires. Growing up poor, white, and southern in the 1950s and 1960s, Allison writes that before the Women's Movement, being a lesbian meant having 'to have the most dangerous addiction, risk the greatest loss, defy the most terrible consequences. The moon was not sufficient, and too many of us hated ourselves and feared our desire.'[5] Even as a child she knew that she could not express her attraction for other girls. A vague collective yet very real 'they' would 'beat me up and leave me, fuck me up and hate me. I'd wind up in a mental hospital, never get a job, have to be supported by the family for the rest of time, and anyway, never, never amount to anything.'[6]

For Allison, it was science fiction especially that opened up the possibility of an alternative world or worlds to the one in which she lived. Of her teenage fascination with the genre Allison observes, 'Justice happened in those books – justice, revenge, vindication, female bonding, sex – and what seemed to me a more humane, compassionate philosophy of life.'[7] The women in those stories 'read like dykes to me. They even had sex, real sex, without symbolic shrouding'.[8] So, she continues,

> I was conditioned to suspend my disbelief with science fiction, and that meant I could imagine myself in the books. But it was still a big jump from my tentative and careful fantasies to imagining the sexual adventures of those marvelous heroines. That I began to do it at all I credit to the power of the really gifted science fiction writers who gave me worlds in which little girls did not have to confront the horrors of my everyday life.[9]

Science fiction taught Allison that there were other narrative possibilities for lesbian desire: '... for me, the hidden message was clear. It didn't have to be the way everybody said it was. It could be different. You might be able to have sex with plants or intelligent waterfalls or friendly machines – or women – and not have it be a social or moral catastrophe. Once out, that's a secret that could change everything, and has.'[10]

That is the secret at work in her novel *Bastard Out of Carolina*, as well as in the more recent *The Way the Crow Flies* by Ann-Marie MacDonald.

This chapter considers both texts within the context of art's expressive and transformative relation to lesbians who as children have experienced sexual abuse.[11] Both novels may be understood as *Bildungsromanen* that, on the levels of story and narrative construction, explore how art allows the lesbian protagonists, beginning in their childhood, to tell the truth of their abuse and so lay claim to a validating sense of their sexual pleasure, sexuality, and identity. By focusing on the cultural contexts that the two young characters occupy, the novels reveal their necessarily politically resonant role as works of art. They expose and critique the hegemonic power of heteronormativity, which at best remains benignly indifferent and at worst violently opposed to the girls' lesbianism. In so doing, they dispel cultural narratives of gender, sex, and sexuality – what Suzanna Danuta Walters has called the narratives of determinism – that, so often haunted by the spectre of homophobia, read lesbianism as a traumatic extension of sexual violence.[12] As Allison writes in her essay 'Believing in Literature', 'we are the ones they make fiction of – we queer and disenfranchised and female – and we have the right to demand our full, nasty, complicated lives, if only to justify all the times our reality has been stolen, mismade, and dishonored',[13] and exiled to the 'deserts of the heart'. Both Allison and MacDonald exercise that right.

2. *Bastard Out of Carolina*: illusion, violence, and middle-class gender norms

There is a moment in Virginia Woolf's novel *To the Lighthouse* when Mrs Ramsay, the heroine, contemplating the marriage of a young couple, Minta Doyle and Paul Rayley, reveals her awareness of the distinction between love and marriage. That the latter would fully express the former – that marriage would necessarily be 'about' love (or, that love, for that matter, would necessarily lead to marriage) – is for Mrs Ramsay an 'illusion'. The subject of the novel is indeed love, but it is love of life in all its emotional complexity that *To the Lighthouse* celebrates. That marriage would necessarily 'mean' love (or that love's trajectory would inevitably include marriage) is a dream that only Minta and Paul, Woolf's 'glittering eyed' lovers, could possibly sustain.[14]

How very different is the story that Dorothy Allison tells about 'glittering' eyes. Written more than six decades later and set not in Cornwall, England, but in Greenville, South Carolina, Dorothy Allison's novel explores the anger lurking in those eyes. While like Woolf's, Allison's work explores the emotional complexity of love, it also scrutinizes marriage as a cultural ideal and reveals the violent damage that inability to live up to that ideal can cause. Specifically, Allison's novel traces the coming-of-age of Bone Boatwright, who as a young child finds herself the victim of repeated sexual abuse at the hands of her stepfather, the 'glittering'-eyed Glen.[15] Eventually, after he has raped her, Bone finds herself abandoned by her mother, Anney, as well. Anney, whose eyes are ultimately as 'glittery' as those of the husband who violates her daughter,[16] also makes the mistake of Woolf's lovers: she loses herself in the illusion of marriage. At novel's end, Glen and Anney's failure to realize a narrative of marital bliss leaves them running away from Bone, the character who for both embodies that failure. Written, according to Allison, for 'girls who had had experiences like those recounted in the book'.[17] *Bastard Out of Carolina* offers those girls – and readers in general – a powerful example of the transformative capacity of storytelling: to recount the hard truths of sexual violence in order to validate, dignify, and heal the lives of those abused.

Told by Bone herself, *Bastard Out of Carolina* is a novel about the power of personal narrative to engage and re-shape familial and social meaning. The story focuses up front on Bone's status as a socially marginal figure, by illustrating the difference between the narrative patterns of, on the one hand, her family, who, as white trash, exist apart from class, race, and gender norms and, on the other hand, those narrative patterns of the state, implicitly white middle-class, patriarchal, and heteronormative. The novel begins with Bone explaining the origins of her name. Registered as Ruth Anne, she is called 'Bone' from the moment the Boatwrights bring her home from the hospital and her Uncle Earle assesses her as 'no bigger than a knucklebone'.[18] The name sticks, and, within the context of her family, serves not only as an effective indicator of her toughness and her Boatwrightness, but, too, of a vulnerability that her family recognizes and is willing to honor and protect. How very different is her reception within the local legal system. Bone recounts that neither her aunt nor grandmother, who took care of her registration, 'could write very clearly, and they hadn't bothered to discuss how Anne would be spelled, so it wound up spelled three different ways on the form – Ann, Anne, and Anna'.[19] Nor can the aunt and grandmother agree on the last name of a father whom they regard as only biologically incidental to Bone's arrival in the world. The vagaries of spelling aside, the issue of Bone's last name – the absence of a father who can be legally and socially validated – serves to solidify her outcast social status: she is 'certified a bastard by the state of South Carolina'.[20]

Author Dorothy Allison has remarked of herself, 'There's no division separating my identities as a lesbian writer and as a working-class writer and as a pervert in this society.'[21] I am reading Bone's nascent lesbian sexuality analogously: it is inextricable from her working-class tough-ness, which is apparent to her family from the time she is a little girl. Significantly, hers is a gender and sexual identity that underscores her belonging within a family that subverts the neat middle-class divisions of male and female, masculine and feminine. So, for example, her Aunt Alma remarks early on that Bone's stubbornness makes her, 'just like her mama ... Just like her aunts, just like a Boatwright ... '.[22] Or, again, her cousin Butch explains, ' ... you got a man-type part of you. Rock-hard and nasty and immune to harm. But hell, Boatwright women come out that way sometimes.'[23] Because of her toughness, which might be read within a specifically lesbian context as the toughness of a young femme, she has Butch's respect; for the same reason she also, significantly, is met with tenderness by the women she loves. In a moment of mother–daughter intimacy, her mother, Anney, again calls attention to Bone's obduracy: ' "You are so stubborn". Her fingers trailed lightly across my brow, smoothing back a few loose strands of hair. "Even more stubborn than your mama, I think" '.[24] Within the Boatwright family, Bone soon learns that being tough is a reason for being loved.

In contrast to the Boatwrights' appreciation of Bone's toughness is her stepfather Daddy Glen's disgust with it. His uneasiness, discomfort, and antipathy vis-à-vis Bone are all apparent from the time he marries Anney: ' "You are hard as bone, the stubbornest child on the planet!" Daddy Glen told me. "Cold as death, mean as a snake, and twice as twisty" '.[25] As the novel's recurring off rhyme suggests, the anger that Glen Wad-dell exhibits toward her is rooted in his un-sated hunger to inhabit the narrative of American and more specifically the Waddell family dream of realizing middle-class consumerism and gender norms.

As narrator, Bone relentlessly demonstrates the consequences of Glen's investment in those norms. She juxtaposes extended descriptions of the tract houses he rents for his family – shabby imitations of his broth-ers' well-tended suburban homes – and the rickety older houses with porches that the Boatwrights all inhabit.[26] Glen's investment pushes him to devalue the life he has made with Anney and, more broadly, the Boatwrights as a whole. Boatwright women work for pay along with the men to support the family. Glen can only read this gender config-uration as a sign of social failure, since it contrasts with the divisions in his parents' and brothers' families: 'His own mama had never held a job in her life, and Daryl and James both spoke badly of women who would leave their children to "work outside the home" '.[27] The brothers brand Anney and the girls as 'Just like any nigger trash'.[28] Glen echoes this assessment. He refers to the Boatwrights in general as 'that trash'.[29] His classist, as well as racist, investment does not allow him to recognize what Bone's narrative so clearly demonstrates: the discursive and cultural richness of that trash.

Bone readily makes the connection between Glen's hunger for [white] middle-class acquisition and his anger toward her. As she notes after one visit to a Waddell household,

> replaying in my head two separate movie images; Daddy Glen screaming at me, his neck bright red with rage, and the other, impossible vision just by it, Daddy Glen at *his* daddy's house with his head hanging down and his mouth so soft spit shone on the lower lip.[30]

In her social illegitimacy, which encompasses her class-, race-, and gender-marked Boatwright toughness and her 'certified ... bastard' status,[31] Bone embodies her stepfather's distance from bourgeois propriety – an engendering that not only upsets his notion of social norms but destabilizes his own sense of masculinity.

The first example of Glen's cultural impotence – as a progenitor of middle-class family values and male offspring – significantly is linked to his first violation of his stepdaughter. She becomes the literalized metaphor of his fear of a failed bourgeois manhood. So, for example, while Anney is in the hospital for the delivery of their baby, Glen, waiting outside in the car, along with Bone and her baby sister, Reese, attempts to reassure himself with the happy dream of his masculinity, much as he has done for the entirety of Anney's pregnancy:

> Glen was like a boy about the baby, grinning and boasting and putting his palms flat on Mama's stomach every chance he could to feel his son kick. His son – he never even entertained the notion Mama might deliver a girl. No, this would be his boy, Glen was sure ...'. My boy's gonna look like the best of me and Anney', he told everyone insistently, as if by saying it often enough he could make it so.[32]

In the car, Glen returns to this narrative of the generative and normatively gendered middle-class family, with his actions simultaneously exposing his uncertain relation to that narrative: his desire to inhabit it and his fear of failing to do so; his hunger and his anger. Bone describes the moment:

> It made me afraid, his big hand between my legs and his eyes glittering in the dim light. He started talking again, telling me Mama was

going to be all right, that he loved me, that we were all going to be so happy. Happy. His hand was hard, the ridge of his wristbone pushing in and hurting me. I looked straight ahead through the windshield, too afraid to cry, or shake, or wiggle, to afraid to move at all.

He kept saying, 'It's gonna be all right'.[33]

Both the molestation and accompanying verbal repetition signal Glen's attempt to comfort himself and his awareness that things might *not* be all right. As a social outsider, Bone is an example of that possibility, and significantly Glen unleashes his violence against her, even before he learns that his baby has died and that Anney will not be able to have any more children.

As in the above scene, so throughout the novel: Bone signals for Glen the illusory and elusive narrative of happily living out a [white] middle-class coupledom in which he and also, importantly, Anney are invested. Bone's role here intensifies with the repeated molestation and the emergence of Anney's complicity. Regarding the latter, Anney's language, after one particularly violent episode that lands Bone in the hospital, is eerily reminiscent of Glen's own in the scene described above. Bone recalls her mother's words:

I love him. . . . Sometimes I hate myself, but I love him. I love him'.

I looked up. Mama's eyes were deep and glittery . . . 'I've just wanted it to be all right', she whispered. 'For so long, I've just hoped and prayed, dreamed and pretended. I've hung on, just hung on.'[34]

Anney and Glen cannot imagine a narrative framework that would allow them to live together *and* keep Bone safe.

Both parents' refusal to abandon narrative expectations that are directly damaging to Bone ultimately leads to their double violation of her: Glen's raping and Anney's abandonment of Bone. So, near the novel's end, Glen screams at her:

'You're the one. You're the reason. [Anney] loves me, I know it. But it's you, you're the one gets in the way. You make me crazy and you make her ashamed, ashamed of you and ashamed of loving me. It ain't right . . .

'You little cunt!' . . .

'*You!*' he cursed, and it echoed in my head. '*You goddam little bastard!*'[35]

Glen's rape of Bone, prefigured by the above outburst, discloses incest abuse's function. It is the violent means of imposing a rigid gender order, one in which the bond between mother and daughter must not possibly serve to signify their love for each other but rather necessarily reflect Glen's authority. As the child who is a cultural outsider many times over – in terms of her illegitimacy, her white trash class, and her tough adolescent dykishness – Bone proves threatening to Glen. In this sense, it is Bone's potential for signaling a counter order – a narrative of lesbianism – that threatens the rupture of his gendered narrative illusion – a rupture that, tellingly, neither he nor Anney, who joins him in his post-rape flight south, can bear to face.[36]

3.   Bone's queer storytelling: resistance, ambivalence, and 'look[ing] at it from the other side'[37]

Bone answers Daddy Glen's abuse and Anney's betrayal through her own complex narrative strategies. When Glen beats her, she thinks of the 'bone in [her] head ... cradling [her] brain'.[38] In effect, she thinks of her capacity to respond to him through the power of her mind. Bone's storytelling takes place on three different levels and is aimed at three different audiences: first, there are the horror stories she tells her cousins; then there are the sexual fantasies she tells herself; finally, there is the autobiography that is *Bastard* itself and whose audience is the novel's readership. All three allow her to encode and recontextualize her experiences of Glen's violence and Anney's complicity, as well as her complicated feelings toward them.

The first of these offers Bone her most obvious and straightforward claim to an autonomous personal voice. If 'All the Boatwrights told stories, it was one of the things we were known for',[39] Bone proves exceptional in her ability to enthrall her cousins:

> My cousins loved my stories ... My stories were full of boys and girls gruesomely raped and murdered, babies cooked in pots of boiling beans, vampires and soldiers and long razor-sharp knives. Witches cut off the heads of children and grown-ups. Gangs of women rode in on motorcycles and set fire to people's houses.... I got to be very popular as a baby-sitter; everyone was quiet and well-behaved while I told stories, their eyes fixed on my face in a way that made me feel like one of my own witches casting a spell.[40]

Through storytelling, Bone wields a narrative authority that allows her to represent but also, significantly, control images of violence. Perhaps more importantly, her ability enables her to cultivate a temporary community for herself and her cousins, which, in contrast to the violent uncertainty that typifies life with Daddy Glen, is characterized by imaginative engagement.

Sexual fantasy is Bone's second means of narratively resisting and redefining her experiences of abuse. She answers the question hovering over her memory of Glen's violation of her outside the hospital with a 'daydream' and her own sexual pleasure:

> Sex. Was that what Daddy Glen had been doing to me in the parking lot? Was it what I had started doing to myself whenever I was alone in the afternoons? I would imagine being tied up and put in a haystack while someone set the dry stale straw ablaze. I would picture it perfectly while rocking on my hand. The daydream was about struggling to get free while the fire burned hotter and closer.... I orgasmed on my hand to the dream of fire.[41]

In this, the novel's earliest description of her masturbating, Bone exercises the narrative control and satisfaction that marks her storytelling.

Her later fantasies, however, are much more complicated in their production and effect. They reflect the struggle for a sexual agency that she, as an adolescent lesbian who is increasingly populating her erotic landscape with elements of public danger, does not yet possess:

> My fantasies got more violent and more complicated as Daddy Glen continued to beat me ...
>
> I was ashamed of myself for the things I thought about when I put my hands between my legs, more ashamed for masturbating to the fantasy of being beaten than for being beaten in the first place. I lived in a world of shame. I hid my bruises as if they were evidence of crimes I had committed ...
>
> Yet it was only in my fantasies with people watching me that I was able to defy Daddy Glen. Only there that I had my pride. I loved those fantasies, even though I was sure they were a terrible thing. They had to be; they were self-centered and they made me have shuddering orgasms. In them, I was very special. I was triumphant, important. I was not ashamed. There was no heroism possible in the real beatings. There was just being beaten until I was covered with snot and misery.[42]

Bone's relation to her fantasies is ambivalent. She experiences them as pleasurable, and she sees that with them she can 'defy' Glen, not least by inscribing and reconfiguring her mother's incapacity to intervene. Nonetheless, she also finds them harmful – indeed, more harmful than even his violence. Her understanding of sex remains caught in a conventional web of meaning that intertwines sexual pleasure with sexual shame and, in so doing, emphasizes the perversity of her pleasure rather than the perversity of her abuse.[43]

Significantly, the adolescent Bone's self-condemnation here mirrors more than the grip of normative gender values over her. Bone's reductive dismissal of her experience of sexual pleasure to a dirty little secret also reflects the kind of vilification that author Dorothy Allison herself encountered during and subsequent to the 1982 Barnard Conference on Sexuality,[44] what Allison herself has called 'the Barnard Sex Scandal'.[45] As Allison recalled in a 1993 interview, ' . . . I was picketed and leafleted and pilloried by Women Against Pornography as a proponent of childhood sexual abuse. Because I was writing about it.'[46] Allison's work on child sexual abuse and, more importantly, her insistence on the distinction between that abuse and an adult sexuality that included S/M practices provoked a kind of queer panic for certain conference participants. Bitter debates, key to what have come to be known as the lesbian sex wars,[47] erupted, pitting pro-sex activists, including Allison, against feminists who argued that engagement in various forms of sexual role-playing could only be interpreted as degrading.[48] The latter group's assessment of course turned on a very narrow – white middle-class and vanilla sex – definition of lesbianism that remained prominent within lesbian feminist literary contexts well into the 1990s when *Bastard* first appeared. Indeed, when the novel was published in 1992, it was not considered 'lesbian enough' to be eligible for the Lambda Lesbian Fiction Award.[49] As Dorothy Allison remarked in the 1993 interview, 'you can't be a real lesbian if you do things that the rest of us don't approve of. . . . [T]his controversy is about a community defining itself for its own purposes . . .'[50] Whether within the realm of late twentieth-century culture debates or *Bastard*'s southern 1950s working-class setting, lesbianism cannot apparently be permitted to include dangerous sexual fantasies; nor can it go unnamed, even though, in the case of Bone, that lesbianism is 'named' in that it is grounded in so many aspects of her tough, white trash, and sexualized life.[51]

Finally, apart from her own as well as 1980s and 1990s lesbian feminism's ambivalence, Bone's sexual fantasies serve, on the level of novel construction, as a paradigm for storymaking, especially for the making of stories about socially marginalized people. Reminiscent of 'contrary instincts', Alice Walker's trope for African-American women's creativity,[52] Bone's imagined scenarios encode the harshness of life with

Daddy Glen, her complicated emotions toward the mother who 'witnesses' that life,[53] and the pleasure that can be experienced despite and through the texture of that life. Accordingly, the fantasies signal the third and final example of Bone's narrative resistance, the storytelling that is the novel itself. As Vincent King has observed, Bone is

> 'not even thirteen years old' at the end of the novel, but she is *at least* seventeen when she tells a story called *Bastard Out of Carolina*. In the years following the end of the novel, she transforms herself from a Boatwright to a storywright, from the victim of a story into the author of one. In effect, then, she renames herself by writing a story that forces the reader to reevaluate names such as 'bastard', 'poor white trash', and 'ugly'.[54]

If her experience of growing up within the context of both Daddy Glen's household and the Boatwright family proves the stuff of her narration, it is her lesbian aunt, Raylene, who serves as that narration's catalyst and as Bone's literary role model. When her enraged adolescent niece tries to blame her white trash origins for her difficulty of grappling with her mother's continued involvement with Daddy Glen, Aunt Raylene urges her to '[m]ake up a story where you have to ... [l]ook at it from the other side for a while. Maybe you won't be glaring at people so much.'[55] Adopting a narrative perspective 'from the other side' means primarily acknowledging the complexity that characterizes Bone's relation to her mother. One of the most influential and certainly the most stable figure in her life, Raylene warns Bone not to repeat her own mistake: 'Bone, no woman can stand to choose between her baby and her lover, between her child and her husband. I made the woman I loved choose.... It just about killed her. It just about killed me.'[56]

Bone as autobiographer learns from her aunt and allows multiple perspectives to pattern her storytelling. Bone's narrative strategy turns on the aesthetic and ethical pivot of 'not choos[ing]'. In this, Bone's narrative economy may be understood as the discursive version of her aunt's relation to the world around her. Raylene lives along the river. Salvaging the trash that her neighbors discard, she makes her living by cleaning, repairing, and eventually selling it: her goods, then, are simultaneously useless and useful, one thing *and* the other. By refusing to choose, by keeping multiple perspectives in play, Bone asserts a kind of authority that contrasts directly with Daddy Glen's assertion of power. Whereas Daddy Glen and ultimately Anney herself cannot imagine a world of emotional complexity – one in which Anney could want both to live with him *and* to keep her daughter safe from him – this is precisely the kind of world that Bone as autobiographer engenders. Bone asks, 'Who had Mama been ... before I was born? ... Would I be as strong as she had been, as hungry for love, as desperate, determined, and ashamed?'[57] The novel's final lines offer an answer: 'I was who I was going to be, someone like [Raylene], like Mama ... I wrapped my fingers in Raylene's and watched the night close in around us.'[58] As autobiographer, Bone achieves a queer authority: one that inscribes rather than shuts down within a larger narrative structure the narrative perspectives that have betrayed her.[59] *Bastard* questions Anney's and Glen's exclusionary choices about which stories of family, class, and love to inhabit.

This narrative complexity not only brings into focus the link between her parents' illusionary investment in middle-class gender norms and the abuse they exact. It also allows Bone to tell her own story that, while marked by specifics of stigma, violence, and pain that resemble her mother's, is fed by her own experiences of sexual pleasure and emotional intimacy, however ambivalently understood. Wresting that pleasure and intimacy away from conventional meanings of shame and laying claim to its rightness is ultimately beyond narrator Bone's power; this is the implied gesture of the novel, the inchoate promise of the ending, and as such it belongs more nearly to Allison herself. This gesture is not unlike Allison's own real-life desire – indeed, it is perhaps an extension of it – to comfort and reassure her own abused adolescent self:

> I have an ambition to be my own adolescent fantasy, to realize the science fiction fable and go back to that girl I was. I want to appear out of a moonlit lotus, find her twelve years old on a hardwood floor, reach down and take her hands, pull her up and tell her the story she has not yet lived. My life, her life, the life of a lesbian who learned the worth and price of sex. I want to call her Little Sister and laugh in a voice she will recognize. Say, sex is delicious. Sex is power. Never pretend that you do not want power in your life. Sex.
>
> I'm going to get there somehow, swing my hair and promise my younger self that the struggle will be worth it.
>
> 'Girl', I want to say to her. 'Hang on, honey. You are going to like it. It is going to be worth the price, worth the struggle. Child', I want to say, 'you are going to be happy.'[60]

4. *The Way the Crow Flies*: failed narrative upkeep and queer reading practices

As in *Bastard Out of Carolina*, so in *The Way the Crow Flies*: sexual abuse is linked to heteronormativity and not to either sexual or gender fantasy.

While the settings, class markers, and focal points in the two novels differ significantly – the one, concentrating on a particular family, takes place in working-class Greenville, South Carolina, in the 1950s and early 1960s; the other, in epic fashion linking family events to Cold War espionage, spans Canadian military, middle-class, and, later, urban artsy locales between the 1960s and 1980s – the protagonists of both novels come to understand the importance of reading against narratives of personal happiness at the center of which is marriage.

MacDonald's 2003 novel begins with a post-World War II encomium to marriage. The opening chapter, titled 'Many-Splendoured Things', identifies marriage as the key to personal and national optimism and integrity for Canadians in 1962:

> The sun came out after the war and our world went Technicolor. Everyone had the same idea. Let's get married. Let's have kids. Let's be the ones who do it right.[61]

In their investment in the marriage ideal, Jack and Mimi McCarthy remain blind to the violation that their nine-year-old daughter, Madeleine, along with some of her classmates, suffers at the hands of her teacher, Mr March, whose name, like that of Jo March in *Little Women* or the title of George Eliot novel *Middlemarch*, tellingly gestures toward the progress narrative. Highlighting this narrative fallout, the novel exposes how a paternalistic accounting of nurture and safety, whether focused on the micro level of family or the macro one of nation, could sustain as part of its narrative economy betrayal, duplicity, violation, and even murder. As MacDonald herself remarked in a 2003 interview regarding the novel, 'I wanted to kill people with sunshine.' She continues, 'This is about the world of good dads'[62] – and its failures.

Recounting its lesbian heroine's quest for emotional wholeness, the novel offers a transformative response to her experience of sexual abuse. That response begins with the novel's title. The phrase 'the way the crow flies' might be read as a trope for artistic composition. Importantly, the phrase is not 'the way the crow flies', which generally suggests an impossible-to-realize straightness … or progress. MacDonald's title implies something different. Much as crows are known to collect or cache bright, shiny objects, writers are often invited into the creative process by a recurring image, sound, texture, or feeling.[63] So, returning to MacDonald's work, one might ask, *what is* the way that a crow flies, and how is that way related to the novel's structure? As the title signals, the novel offers a possibility for recognizing and making meaning that is distinct from a paternalistic progress narrative. Structured around the piecing together and disclosure of stories that a paternalistic model has either demonized or withheld, the novel insists on the integrity of these stories and the insight and oversight that they offer. Like the nests that the crows in the novel build in air-raid sirens that rarely sound, descriptions of which both bracket and punctuate MacDonald's storytelling, the stories themselves are the stuff of memory, more specifically of memory as a repository or vehicle for personal and political salvation. Much as memory has proven to be a key organizing principal for the way crows fly, so too memory impels the novel's storytelling. That is, like 'the way the crow flies', the novel's narrative structure insists on the efficacy of personal memory and also, particularly for a Canadian readership attuned to the phrase '*je me souviens*', of national memory.[64] For MacDonald, the power of memory resides in its capacity to witness and answer; to record and so dignify stories that exist apart from a gender-based (as well as race- and class-based) cultural narrative norm.

From the beginning, the novel sets up Mimi and Jack McCarthy as an ideal 1960s Canadian couple. He is handsome; she is beautiful. He is Anglo; she is Acadian. He is a successful RCAF officer; she is an organized and efficient homemaker. With their two children, Madeleine and Mike, the McCarthys' family life offers a microcosm of national harmony and stability. There is a ready exchange between the two spheres: if state concerns are central to Wing Commander McCarthy, based at Centralia, Ontario air force station, family concerns are central to the state. Both equations of exchange are apparent in Jack and Mimi's relation to stories. So, for example, a young Madeleine asks her mother to recount 'The Story of Mimi and Jack'. It is a love story, with World War II serving as its backdrop: 'Once upon a time there was a little Acadian nurse called Mimi, and a handsome young air force officer named Jack...'.[65] Within this formulation it is Jack and Mimi's falling in love as much as Jack's RCAF appointment that is a response to enemy aggression. And it is in turn the family storymaking that finds its mirror in the gendered reading materials and practices in national circulation during the 1960s. Thus, at home, while Jack follows the Cuban Missile Crisis by reading the newspaper, Mimi looks to the Canadian ladies' magazine *Chatelaine* for tips on how to avoid facial wrinkles. The McCarthys' reality, paternalistic and dichotomously gendered, depends upon an economy of storymaking in which 'Pattern is a matter of upkeep. Otherwise the weave relaxes back to threads ... Repeat or the story will fall.'[66]

On both the macro and micro levels, in the cases of both Cold War espionage and Madeleine's sexual abuse – two loosely intertwined storylines

connected through the murder of Madeleine's classmate, Claire – the
McCarthys fail in their narrative upkeep. Despite the warning embodied in their surname,[67] they do not recognize – they remain blind to –
the possibility that a male authority figure might not embody trust and
security but rather duplicity and violation.

So Jack, whom Mimi praises as the 'nice Papa' and 'the nicest Papa
in the world',[68] and who stands in sharp contrast to *Bastard*'s Daddy
Glen, fails to realize that the pattern of paternalistic protection can also
prove harmful: that there can be casualties of war during the ostensi-
ble peacetime of the Cold War and that the most immediate casualties
would be a culturally queer family. Jack initially does not see how the
disappearance and presumed murder of one friend, engineer and Nazi
work camp survivor Henry Froelich, and the wrongful imprisonment of
Henry's adopted sixteen-year-old son, Ricky, a *Métis* (a person of mixed
Indian and European, usually French, ancestry), on murder and sexual
abuse charges, could be part of an allied intelligence cover-up hiding
the involvement of former Nazi war criminals in the US space program.
Nor can he imagine that his other friend, his former World War II flight
instructor, counter-intelligence agent Simon Crawford, would facilitate
that cover-up by manipulating Jack. Once he does recognize these plot
lines and his own involvement in them, he finds intelligence interests
pitted against testifying on Ricky's behalf. His moral struggle symbolized
by his own impaired eyesight, Jack chooses to turn away from helping
the teenager; by failing to provide the alibi that would prove the boy's
innocence, Jack seals the cover-up. The eventual moral fallout for Jack
is not simply disillusionment regarding counter-intelligence work; it is
a profound sense of betrayal and loss. As a military officer, Jack special-
izes in cost–benefit analysis, yet he comes to realize that the betrayal of
and by friends cannot be justified under any circumstances, the space
race and, more generally, the Cold War notwithstanding. He is forced
to recognize the treachery of fathers, real and symbolic, beginning with
himself. In his failure to witness, Jack, as the Froelichs' name suggests,
has lost the possibility of being happy (*fröhlich*) within a paternalistic narrative. Jack knows that fathers are supposed to protect children.
While unaware of the specific features of Ricky's prison life – the rape
and psychological abuse that he suffers during his incarceration – Jack is
nonetheless haunted by his moral entanglement in the harm that befalls
the boy.

The epic sweep of such developments might be read as an artistic failing in the novel: the storyline of Cold War deception might be dismissed
as overly complicated, forced; so extravagant that it distracts from the

novel's narrative concern with Madeleine and her experience of sexual abuse. Perhaps this kind of reading, a mistaken one, I believe, explains why, in contrast to MacDonald's acclaimed first novel, *Fall on Your Knees*, published in 1996, *The Way the Crow Flies* has been critically overlooked. A richer reading recognizes MacDonald's intertwining of the two storylines as strategic; as an example of what I will call narrative intersectionality. That intersectionality reflects the structural implications of abuse. Local, individual actions, no matter how muffled or overlooked, and no matter the particular patterns of gender, race, and sex, and sexuality involved, have large-scale moral, political, and narrative consequences, for any number of peoples across constellations of gender, race, sex, and sexuality. This is an epic sweep well worth recognizing. MacDonald's Cold War storyline throws into relief the betrayal of which Jack is never aware: his daughter's abuse at the hands of her teacher, Mr March. 'Here, little girl, feel my muscle – that's it – squeeze it, it's strong', Mr March says to her. The narrator continues, representing the experience of sexual abuse as a kind of narrative blank spot within Madeleine's memory. 'It's rubber, there is a smell. Blank it out or you'll throw up.'[69] If Madeleine's dissociation may be understood as a survival strategy, the narrator's characterization of a subsequent moment in which rape goes undetected, underscores the necessity of that strategy, since no adult figure recognizes what Mr March is doing to the girls: 'You would never know by looking at his face that he has his hand up a little girl's dress. Madeleine doesn't think of it as "my dress". It's as though she's seeing the plaid pleats from the level of her hem – there are her bare legs, and a man's grey sleeve up between them as if she were a puppet. It stings.'[70] The abuse is in effect a loose narrative thread from which Madeleine the puppet dangles.

There is a poignant irony that the McCarthys' narrative upkeep vis-à-vis Madeleine tends to discourage her tomboyishness, one of the crucial aspects of her life that enables her to deal with the sexual abuse. Madeleine draws comfort from reading stories, most notably *Tom Sawyer*, which offer her the possibility of gendering herself differently. She actively imagines herself as a boy:

If you believe hard enough, is it possible to enter the world of a book? If you pray to God for a miracle, can He transport you to St. Petersburg, Florida, long ago? Set you down by the Mississippi in a pair of tattered overalls, as a boy? Madeleine squeezes her eyes shut and prays ... Have faith. Keep reading, and when you wake up in the morning, perhaps the miracle will have occurred ... [71]

In part, security for Madeleine means reading herself as a boy. Yet, it is precisely this gendered reading practice that her mother polices. Early in the novel when Madeleine asks her parents what a dyke is, it is Mimi who responds, 'It's a woman who's sick in the head', and who then asks, 'Where did you hear that word?'[72] That Madeleine has come across the term in *Time* magazine is itself disturbing, for, in the McCarthys' world, news magazines are read by men, not women.

Perhaps the saddest example of Mimi's failure to distinguish between sexual perversion and her daughter's emerging lesbianism occurs when she discovers blood on her daughter's underwear after Mr March has raped her. Mimi assumes that Madeleine has hurt herself by falling on her brother's bike:

> Mimi sighs and says, 'Madeleine, did you take your brother's bike again without asking?" Madeleine nods yes – I'm not lying, I have taken his bike a couple of times without asking. 'And you hurt yourself on the crossbar.'
>
> ...'*Écoute bien.* I've said I don't want you riding boys' bikes, not your brother's, not anyone's do you understand why now? Next time you find blood on your panties, *ma p'tite*, you have to tell Maman.' ... 'Because that's part of growing up.'
>
> ...'A few years from now you'll bleed a little bit once every month, and that's how God prepares your body so that one day you can get married and have babies.'
>
> ...
>
> 'I don't want to get married.'
>
> Maman winks and sings, 'Someday, My Prince Will Come'.[73]

For Mimi, it is Madeleine's emerging boyish lesbian self that proves disturbing and potentially harmful. Intent on measuring her daughter's coming of age in terms of Disney's version of Snow White, she cannot conceive that the threat to her daughter's happiness is not gender non-normativity but rather gender violence.

Urging her daughter toward stereotypical feminine roles through a combination of gentle firmness and shaming, Mimi in effect pushes Madeleine's queer desires to the margins of family life. Interestingly, though, it is at those margins that Madeleine, together with her older brother, Mike, begins to explore narrative patterns in which gender transgression and heterosexuality are not pitted against each other. So at bedtime a nightmare-plagued Madeleine induces Mike to pretend that she is a boy:

> 'Let's say I'm a boy.'
> 'Yeah, but you aren't.'
> 'Yeah, but let's say.'
> 'Well...'
> 'Yeah, and my name is Mike, I mean Mitch, okay? And I'm really a boy.'
> 'You're stunned.'
> 'Pretend I'm really your brother, okay?'
> 'Mitch?'
> 'Yes Mike?'
> 'No, I mean are you sure you want your name to be Mitch?'
> 'What should it be?'
> '...Robert.'
> 'Okay.'
>
> He doesn't say anything for a while and Madeleine figures he has fallen asleep. Then he whispers, 'Hey Rob?'
> 'Yeah?' Her voice feels slightly different...
> 'What do you think of Marsha Woodley?'
> Madeleine is so embarrassed she wants to squeal ... but she remembers she is Rob. 'Gee, Mike. I don't know. Why?'
> 'Do you think she's ... You know. Special?'
> 'Yeah, that's what I think.'
> ...
> ... She falls asleep and has no nightmares. Rob never has nightmares.[74]

In the liminal space of bedtime, Madeleine can be a boy who is a girl, a gender role that allows her not to have the nightmares with which the abuse has left her. Importantly, too, her role as such actually allows her brother to explore his own heterosexual desire, in voicing his adolescent crush on their babysitter.

5. Madeleine the artist: image, memory, story

For Madeleine, it is easier to articulate a sense of shame and fault by confessing to a gender transgression than by trying to articulate the abuse for which she has no language. The other little girls who, as part of Mr March's 'exercise group', are made to stay after school, most notably

Claire, Grace, and Marjorie, are also at a loss. Three-quarters of the novel is taken up with describing the girls' year with Mr March, which culminates in Claire's murder – the murder for which Madeleine's neighbor Ricky Froelich is wrongfully convicted. The final quarter of the novel follows a thirty-something Madeleine's journey into memory. The narrator captures the struggle of this remembering:

> Sexual violation turns all children into the same child ... Children heal quickly, so that, like a tree growing up around an axe, the child grows up healthy until, with time, the embedded thing begins to rust and seep and the idea of extracting it is worse than the thought of dying from it slowly ... Once pleasure and poison have entwined, how to separate them?[75]

As for *Bastard Out of Carolina's* Bone, so for Madeleine: the experiences of sexual abuse and sexual pleasure have become entangled and have become so because of a lack of consent. While Bone achieves this consent in part through her fantasies and more wholly through her agency as narrator, Madeleine the adult achieves consent through the power of memory, specifically through the power of memory as a creative medium. For Madeleine the adult, a successful comedian, recollecting (as well as re-collecting) the trauma becomes itself an aesthetic act, a kind of artistic performance. Starting as images, Madeleine's memories gradually unfold into a narrative that, reflecting the overall structure of the novel itself, pieces together the experiences of abuse and Claire's murder.

Madeleine's incorporation of childhood trauma into her comedy is readily evident. While her writing team is called the 'After-Threes', encoding the memory of Mr March's 'exercise group', one of her most popular impersonations is Maurice, a character that, necessitating her donning a fat suit, recalls Mr March himself. Yet, for all the incorporation of these memorials to an unexplored past, Madeleine only begins to confront and recognize the signs of abuse that pattern her life once they begin to disrupt the narrative routine of her adult world: fugue states that abruptly curtail her comedy performances, and, most importantly, the recurring appearance of a yellow smear that sends her driving off the road.[76]

Similar to the crows that, from their nests atop the air-raid sirens in Centralia, notice details of their surroundings, Madeleine begins to understand the overlooked year – the year of childhood abuse and murder – by teasing out the meaning of the smear and by recognizing that, as an adult, she now needs 'to bear witness' to the rape she experienced as a nine-year-old. As the narrator remarks, 'Some things are difficult to see straight on. They can only be glimpsed by looking away, caught by the corner of the eye.'[77] From the remove (crow's nest?) of time, Madeleine remembers her rape. When her therapist asks what she would do if she were able to revisit that moment, Madeleine answers, 'I would watch.'[78] She explains to her therapist:

> *Mum, Dad. Watch me.* ''Cause I can't change it. But at least, if I watched it, she wouldn't have to be alone.'
> 'Who wouldn't?'
> 'Madeleine. Me.'[79]

Reminiscent of Bone, who, in her sexual fantasies, imagines people watching her atop a burning haystack, Madeleine imagines her adult self – stand-in for the parents who, despite all their love and care, never noticed or knew – watching her child self.

As a witness Madeleine achieves what Jack and Mimi earlier could not. Her role resonates across her relationships with both of them. She becomes the stand-in not only for the parents who never recognized that she was being abused but also for Jack alone, who failed to testify for Ricky Froelich. As such, she achieves a doubled narrative authority – over both the story of her own sexuality and the story of Claire's murder. So, for example, once she remembers the rape, Madeleine confronts the tired link between trauma and lesbianism. She correctly predicts her mother's response to hearing of the abuse: 'So that's why you're the way you are'.[80] And, importantly, she severs that link: her sexuality is 'Something so precious and individual, put down to a crime, an obscenity ... No'.[81] Her therapist reinforces the distinction: 'If surviving sexual abuse were a recipe for homosexuality, the world would be a much gayer place.'[82] Separating certain stories from each other also engenders a counterpuntal narrative movement threading other storylines together. It is with this re-crafting of narrative possibilities that Madeleine the adult can address the helplessness not only of her nine-year-old self but also of her abused classmates and her wrongly accused neighbor. Thus, the memory of her rape pushes Madeleine to probe further – to uncover those other narrative threads of the past that are '[h]iding in plain sight'.[83]

Madeleine's narrative strategy for uncovering the circumstances of Claire's murder turns on 'listen[ing] to the children'.[84] She must remember and re-member those accounts that, overlooked by the adults at the time, were provided by her classmates and fellow abuse victims, Marjorie and Grace. When Madeleine reads the court transcript, which includes their statements, she finds that their salient testimony comes from pictures that are not a part of the evidence – pictures that the girls made for class shortly after Claire's disappearance. Through a series of metonymic connections, Madeleine translates these drawings into words and story. So, for example, when Madeleine reads the police description of Claire's recovered body – 'the body was covered by reeds, I should say bulrushes ...'[85] – she thinks of 'Moses among the bulrushes',[86] and then retrieves the title of Marjorie's picture, 'Moses among the Cattails'.[87] So, too, the 'yellow smear' that propelled her to recover the memories of her own abuse reappears as 'a yellow orb tattooed inside her lids',[88] when she tries to recall the picture that Grace drew on that day. It then transforms into an image of 'a storm of yellow butterflies',[89] recalling for Madeleine both the pattern on Claire's underwear and the subject of Grace's drawing. Linking both Marjorie's and Grace's picture to the scene of the murder, Madeleine arrives at the 'truth [that] was always there ... [and] far sadder than anything she has imagined'.[90] Impelled by a series of evolving phrases and images, the narrative she creates tells the story that the pictures encode: the two girls have murdered Claire; perhaps re-enacting the rituals of Mr March's 'exercise group', they have strangled their classmate.

Significantly, the 'truth' is lodged not in a court document but rather in the story that Madeleine has crafted from memory and imagination. Storytelling rather than legal process proves the vehicle for uncovering, discerning, and answering the overlooked and untold experiences of gender and sexual violation.

6. Conclusion

The final section of *The Way the Crow Flies* begins with a passage that insists on the importance of storytelling:

> When stories are not told, we risk losing our way. Lies trip us up ... Time shatters and, though we strain to follow the pieces like pebbles through the forest, we are led farther and farther astray. Stories are replaced by evidence.... We forget the consolation of the common thread – the way events are stained with the dye of stories older than the facts themselves. We lose our memory. This can make a person ill. This can make a world ill.[91]

In MacDonald's novel, as well as in Allison's, the lesbian protagonist works to attain a sense of wholeness by uncovering and telling her stories of childhood abuse. In the process she exposes how the illnesses of 'a person' and 'a world' depend upon a widespread silencing of and tolerance for sexual violence. Both practices are attributable at least in part to the enforcement of gender norms through social systems of story that readily blur the lines between desire and abuse. Madeleine and Bone's stories reread and challenge, exceed and exist beyond these norms. Through their making of narratives that piece together – formally re-member – the images of their violation, both protagonists lay claim to an authority otherwise denied them. Their making of narrative is an act of cultural truth-telling that foregrounds art as an epistemological battleground in the struggle 'to think' social change.

Underpinning that action is an implicit belief in the possibility of a discerning, empathetic community that is dearly held if impossible to realize. Allison writes in her essay 'Public Silence, Private Terror':

The hardest lesson I have learned in the last few years is how powerful is my own desire to hang onto a shared sense of feminist community where it is safe to talk about dangerous subjects like sex, and how hopeless is the desire. Even within what I have thought of as my own community, and worse, within the tighter community of my friends and lovers, I have never *felt* safe. I have never *been* safe, and that is only partly because everyone else is just as fearful as I am. None of us is safe because we have not tried to make each other safe. We have never even recognized the fearfulness of the territory. We have addressed violence and exploitation and heterosexual assumptions without first establishing the understanding that for each of us, desire is unique and necessary and simply terrifying. Without that understanding, and the compassion and empathy that must be part of it, I do not know how to avoid those acts of betrayal. But it is one thing for me to confront my own fear of those different from me – whether they are women of color, middle-class women, or heterosexuals – and entirely another to demand of other feminists that we begin again with this understanding. Yet that is exactly what I want to do.[92]

And that is what Allison and MacDonald both demand of their readers.

For anyone for whom consent has proven a vexed issue – and here I am thinking primarily but not exclusively of one's gender socialization (but also of the effect of one's race, class, ethnicity, and religion, for example) – for anyone whose understanding of sexuality and sex has been linked to a sense of shame, dirtiness, or disenfranchisement, narratives of desire and violence risk becoming conflated.[93] How much more so is this the case for those who as children have experienced the traumatic entanglement of pleasure and abuse. The narrative task of the writers is in part this: to recall and record the entanglement but also, through narrative patterning, to distinguish between the two. 'Sex' is not the dirty word here. As Allison, recalling that deep need for truth-telling that impelled the writing of *Bastard*, writes,

> I found myself thinking ... that telling the truth was what feminist writers were supposed to do. That telling the truth – your side of it anyway, knowing that there were truths other than your own – was a moral act, a courageous act, an act of rebellion that would encourage other such acts.... I knew that what I wanted to do as a lesbian and a feminist writer was to remake the world into a place where the truth would be hallowed, not held in contempt, where silence would be impossible.[94]

Allison and MacDonald, along with their storytelling heroines, Bone and Madeleine, accomplish just that. They retrieve and re-contexualize memories of gender and sexual abuse, and in so doing question the stigma attached to experiences of sexual pleasure and fantasy. For lesbian readers especially, their stories offer narrative patterns that hold out the promise of happy endings. Those stories reveal art's powerful capacity to validate and inspire transformative acts of lesbian self-authorship.

5
Trussed/Trust/Dressed in Translation

[I]t is only through existing in the mode of translation, constant translation, that we stand a chance of producing a multicultural understanding of women or, indeed, of society.[1]

The monster ... is where we come to know ourselves as never-human, as always between humanness and monstrosity.[2]

Girls will be boys and boys will be girls
It's a mixed up muddled up shook up world except for Lola
La-la-la-la Lola[3]

1. Introduction

In his study of constructions of monstrosity within contemporary American popular culture, Edward J. Ingebretsen examines the critical role that monsters play in defining the borders of human community. He writes,

> Monsters are created, and fear exploited, not only by cinema and other industries of commercial mayhem, but equally in the more mundane places where fear occurs as a by-product of social intimacy. ... Monsters warn; they provide public shows of differing kinds; they redefine boundaries that have become frayed. In sum, monsters help a community reinterpret itself.[4]

Monsters are useful cultural others. They fascinate. They are a discursive necessity. For both individual and community they engender a doubled act of attraction–repulsion. So, we may regard the monster and say, 'while there is a resemblance between us and it, we are not like *it* after all'.

116

As Ingebretsen explains, such a pattern of identification and rejection depends not only on understanding the monster as 'awful and perverse' but also as 'desirable':

> the stories we tell about monsters are sexy, in literal ways – that is, the stories are *about* sex, however much this fact is disguised from view (sometimes the erotic charge is heightened by making the monster sexless or unsexy, at least in conventional ways – and thus, in a word, deviant.[5]

Through this pattern, which reflects a larger, cultural preoccupation with gender, sex, and sexuality as prime sites of cultural transgression, individual and community order themselves, creating the *appearance* of a stable and coherent identity. Existing apart from but within punitive reach of them are those monstrous others: the sexual perverts, the gender deviants.

Such a dynamic necessarily raises the issue of how to make space within language to live one's life and not feel monstrous, particularly when one's imaginings of gender, sex, and sexuality are not those of the norm – reside in the 'deserts of the heart'. This question, hovering over Chapters 1 and 2, has directed Chapter 3 and Chapter 4's respective explorations of reading and writing strategies for the engendering of queer agency. This final chapter considers translation in a similar vein. Specifically, how can translation, which I am defining broadly to include the equations within, between, or among languages, function as a vehicle for recognizing and opening up systems of interpretation that do not stigmatize gender and sexual variability but rather accord their expressions dignity and respect? As these questions suggest, this is a chapter about how translation, as both a linguistic operation and a metaphor, offers an empowering context for considering transgressive constructions of genders, sexes, and sexualities.

Translation is a linguistic operation that embodies a doubled and contradictory purpose. In its dynamic movement, translation is neither simply a vehicle for cultural propriety nor an agent for social change. In this neither-nor state it proves itself a figure of linguistic monstrosity that, as the root meaning of that word suggests, is something marvellous that serves also as a portent or warning. That is, monstrous translation – what Walter Benjamin in his discussion of poet Friedrich Hölderlin's literal translations of Sophocles refers to as '*monströse Beispiele solcher Wörtlichkeit*' ('monstrous examples of such literalness') – is deeply implicated in the making of human community and that community's understanding of humanity.[6] Translation exposes the cultural codes whereby people identify communities of meaning and their inhabitants. In so doing it serves as a gatekeeper, at times not simply of language but of larger cultural, national, and political values toward which one gestures with words such as 'purity' and 'truth'. This is because translation is selective; by definition it involves loss. Drawing from multiple possible meanings, translation marks one or perhaps a few as culturally appropriate; idiomatically fluent or proper; worthy of national/international transmission and circulation. Yet, this very engagement with a variety of meanings reveals translation's other potential to destabilize cultural norms and to undo stigma through an act of linguistic empathy that introduces and integrates into language and, more broadly, society meanings that, departing from those norms, might be labelled comic or odd or, more disturbingly, foreign or wrong. That is, apart from potentially consolidating norms, translation facilitates the questioning of those norms, as perhaps Benjamin would have it, in the name of a higher Truth.[7] This latter capacity is especially important when one considers translation's figurative power *vis-à-vis* transgressive genders, sexes, and sexualities. With regard to these axes of identity, monstrous translation proves a crucial figure of agency for queer bodies, which inhabit interstices of meaning between norms for gender, sex, and sexuality.

In order to examine this relation between translation and such transgressive bodies I turn to literature, which provides readers with a necessarily sympathetic and expansive context for considering the power of language to shape reality or, indeed, multiple realities. Literature, in both its written and filmic versions, moves one to recognize that meaning, more pointedly, definitions of personhood, can exceed cultural prescriptions. That is, print and cinematic texts help one acknowledge the interconnections among real and desired bodies; among those deemed monstrous and those embraced as fully human. Three works come immediately to mind: Mary Shelley's Gothic horror novel, *Frankenstein* (1818; 1831), Franz Kafka's frightening tale of alienation *The Metamorphosis* (1912/1915), and Pedro Almodóvar's zany melodrama *All About My Mother* (1999). All offer important insights into translation's capacity to refigure meaning – to reorient understanding of queer bodies so that monstrosity is aligned with rather than placed in opposition to humanity.

Kafka's and Shelley's text represent monstrosity on very different scales, and their representations of the relation between translation and gender differ markedly. In Kafka, claustrophobia saturates both setting and language. The confining domestic setting finds its linguistic counterpart in the impossibility of translation: the protagonist passively adheres to a system of language that renders his sexual desires shameful and unspeakable. In Shelley, something of the inverse holds: in terms of setting and drama, the scale of the story is epic, with the main character's humanity, as Judith Halberstam points out, 'immutable and ineffable'.[8] In contrast to Kafka's, Shelley's multilingual protagonist has an abundance of linguistic resources, but it is his refusal to trust in translation (specifically that embodiment of translation, Frankenstein's creation) that produces monstrosity.

By contrast, Pedro Almodóvar's *All About My Mother* early on asks its audience to understand sex, gender, and sexuality in terms of a proliferation of translations. Translation is itself a performative act whose constructed 'naturalness' can be readily exposed. The Spanish film incorporates and refigures Tennessee Williams' play *A Streetcar Named Desire* and the 1950 Bette Davis film *All About Eve*, two mid-twentieth-century American texts against which Almodóvar's contemporary heroine, Manuela, defines herself and more particularly sexual technologies, gender performativity, motherhood, and family. With translation acting as its critical *leitfigur*, Almodóvar's film celebrates the cultural production of gendered and sexual subjects that Kafka's and Shelley's earlier work deem monstrous.

2. Trussed in (the lack of) translation: Franz Kafka's *Metamorphosis*

Kafka's *Metamorphosis*, or, as it is titled in the original German, *Die Verwandlung*, would at first appear to be an unlikely text with which to examine the power of translation to refigure queer bodies as socially viable and recognizably human. Because Kafka's protagonist Gregor Samsa remains trapped within a system of meaning that vilifies him, translation would seem not a potentially empowering figure but rather one implicated in the marking of his status as monstrous within family and community. Yet, if access to translation's other capacity to challenge and undo cultural stigma proves impossible for Gregor, it remains nonetheless available to the reader who, empathizing with him, can call into question translation's capacity to codify and legitimate cultural intolerance within language. For this reason, I wish to begin by recounting my own experiences of reading of *Metamorphosis*.

In my professional writing I have returned again and again to this story first because of what it, like Shelley's novel, tells me about the making of community largely through the violent exercise of prejudice: the rejection of individuals or whole categories of human beings, who because of their race, class, gender, or sexuality, for example, are labelled as 'monstrous'. In that novella, Gregor Samsa, the dutiful son of a conformist and fearful family and, more broadly, of an intolerant and policing society, awakes one morning from 'unsettling dreams' to find himself transformed[9] – translated? – into *'ein ungeheures Ungeziefer'*, a 'monstrous vermin'.[10] No longer able to go to work and so provide for his family, he proves valueless to them. So Gregor awakens neither useful nor presentable; he is hidden away and re-gendered as an 'it'.[11] This process of dehumanization ultimately leads to his death, which the family only barely acknowledges and then as a source of relief.

The essays that I have written on Kafka's text have focused on a moment near the end of part two of this three-part text, when the bug-like Gregor sits atop his one prized possession, a magazine picture of a woman in furs, in order to prevent his mother and sister from taking it from his room. (At this point in the story they have removed most of Gregor's personal effects; that is, they have nearly succeeded in depersonalizing his room.) Kafka writes that Gregor's 'hot' and 'stick[y]' body 'completely covered' the picture.[12] I have argued that this sexually charged image of Gregor pressed against the picture, which recalls various late nineteenth-century medical discussions of aberrant sexualities, crystallizes his outcast status for his family. Here, Gregor embodies multiple socially destabilizing subjectivities: the masturbator and thus, potentially, the homosexual, subjectivities further intensified by the fin-de-siècle Viennese linkages among sexual excess, Jewish maleness, and feminization.[13] Stated slightly differently, encapsulating his devolution from a 'he' to an 'it',[14] Gregor's image mirrors translation's function of social policing. A primary burden of language – any language – is the burden not simply of what it leaves unsaid but what it renders unspeakable. While the reader may recognize the intertextual references in this as well as other moments in the novella and, in so doing, access alternative literary, racial, religious, and sexological discourses that help one produce an ironic or comic interpretation of an otherwise seemingly claustrophobic scenario, the same may not be said of Gregor. Within the context of his family and, more broadly, his society, both highly committed to sexual and gender (and, inevitably, racial) policing, his desires are surrounded by shame and silence; by rhetorical indirection. Gregor has no potential way out. He remains trussed in stigmatizing discourse.

This disturbing conclusion helps me understand why I have read *The Metamorphosis* and specifically this moment so often. Doing so locates my intellectual work within the context of recovery: the return to and revision of that critical moment in interpretation when one's system for making meaning proves inadequate to the task. Specifically, my interpretation of Kafka's *Metamorphosis* resonates with the memory of my sixteen-year-old self who read the novella for the first time. That initial reading triggered a crisis for me regarding my gender and sexuality, and, much as trauma inevitably leads to transformation or in Kafka's terms metamorphosis or again, following the German title, 'transfiguration',[15] it constituted my intellectual coming out as a queer interpreter of texts. Analyzing that initial response now enables me to identify translation as a potentially powerful figure for answering the equation of monstrosity in which Gregor proves trapped, aligning gender and sexual variability not with stigma but rather with dignity and respect.

I remember that first time. It was a late October Sunday morning in 1978 in Munich. I was lying naked on my bed and staring at my body: at my ribs and my hips. I loved how the bones jutted out; how there was no fat on my belly. My shoulders, I knew, were broader than my hips, and I could feel the wisps of down above my lip. This was the body that I wanted: small maybe, but hard, angular; a body that was, in 1970s parlance, androgynous. That morning, as I looked at my body and thought about the boy-girl that I knew I was, I had just finished reading Kafka's novella in German. My first thoughts about the book as a parable of gender intolerance are inseparable in my mind from the sound of my Austrian mother's voice as she called to me to get up. The German of her words sustained the German of Kafka's – in effect animated his words for me: '*Steh auf, und zieh dich anständig an*', my mother called to me. '*Wir kriegen Gäste, und du mußt präsentabel sein.*' ('Get up and get dressed. We're having guests, and you need to be proper, presentable.') I remember thinking, 'Oh, *no*, I am Gregor Samsa.' Hearing my mother's words while I lay stretched out on my bed and looking at my body, I initially identified with the trapped Gregor. In retrospect, I recognize that I was enacting a composite image of the opening of *The Metamorphosis* when Gregor awakens and finds himself a bug and that moment when mother and sister espy him atop the picture of the woman in furs. I might say, generally, that like so many teenagers, I often felt uncomfortable greeting my parents' friends: I read their disappointment in me, a disappointment that exposed and amplified my parents' own: the failed girl who could look so lovely *wenn nur* ... *if only* ... Specifically, though, the moment encoded for me an awakening into a consciousness of a troubled reality and, more pointedly, the horror of feeling my own queer desires – desires of pressing my own hot sticky belly against ... another woman, another woman speaking German, but if not another woman, then a text such as Kafka's, which choreographed Gregor's own desire. My desires at first seemed like his, trapped by language, with no cultural, epistemological, or imaginative way out of being figured as anything but monstrous. Initially in this moment, then, my mother's German confirmed my gender and sexual otherness.

Of course, one's relation to one's mother tongue and mother's tongue is necessarily complex, infused with feelings of guilt and debt, as Gayatri Spivak observes.[16] As someone who grew up speaking German and English and, most often, an unabashedly monstrous *Mischung* of both, I do not mean to suggest that German and more generally things Austrian were the source of my gender troubles.[17] American culture is herein implicated as well, though I cannot say that as a teenager I had much awareness of this. English is the language of McCarthyism, whose 'witch hunts' relied on the crossings of anti-Semitic and homophobic discourses, crossings that proved serviceable to the United States' Cold War espionage, in which my father participated during his more than forty years of counter-intelligence work. Still, my own life has necessarily linked German to the burden of personal and cultural history, a history that roots the struggle to understand and articulate gender and sexual variance in the recognition and rupture of the silence surrounding the anti-Semitism of the oft-idealized, nostalgically embraced *fin-de-siècle* Hapsburg Empire, in which the Jewish Kafka grew up, and, more immediately, the anti-Semitism of the Third Reich, particularly of its most notorious and unintelligible embodiment, *'l'univers concentrationnaire'*:[18] 'a universe apart, totally cut off, the weird kingdom of an unlikely fatality'.[19]

Within this historical context, the linkage between 'Jew' and 'homosexual' functions, as Janet R. Jakobsen proposes, as a 'complicitous' relation, facilitating 'a process for thinking about how to subvert the network of power that ties together anti-Semitic, antihomosexual, and white supremacist discourses'.[20] That the act of translation might itself be a part of that relation, serving as an imaginative force for subverting the intertwined discourses of gender, sexual, and racial abjection that propelled the Nazi project of systematic large-scale human annihilation cannot be overstated. One thinks, for example, of the 'Canto of Ulysses' chapter in Primo Levi's *Se questo è un uomo* (*Survival in Auschwitz*), in which Auschwitz prisoner Levi hungers to remember and translate the canto from Dante's *Inferno* into French for his fellow prisoner Jean. As the Italian title indicates (and the English title obscures), the memoir's overriding preoccupation is with the human condition and, more pointedly, with the gendered question of what it means to be a be a man (*uomo*); it is in the 'Canto',[21] through the process of what one might term a homo-erotics of translation, that Levi restores a gendered sense of humanity – a particular literary construction of masculinity – to himself and Jean.[22] Near the end of the chapter, in a temporal dislocation that mirrors the linguistic dislocation of his imperfect translation of Dante, the memoirist Levi writes, 'I would give today's soup to know how to connect "the like on any day" to the [canto's] last lines'.[23] Levi's expression of desire here – the need to answer the urgency of translation in order to affirm one's gendered and raced humanity – anticipates by nearly a half century Judith Butler's metaphor for the call for cultural translation to increase the possibilities of gender intelligibility: 'Some people have asked me what is the use of increasing possibilities of gender. I tend to answer: Possibility is not a luxury; *it is as crucial as bread.*'[24]

Returning to my own story, I find that Levi's and Butler's words help me understand the intense urgency of my own struggle for gender intelligibility when I first read Kafka some thirty years ago. Within my teenage mind, configurations of language, race, gender, and sexuality only offered an attenuated field of signification: while German came metaphorically to stand for my sense of gender and sexual otherness, English and things American offered a figurative escape insofar as they encoded my relation to German, Austria, and, above all, my mother. Emily Apter's remarks on the relation between ethics and translation come to mind here:

> The simple act of putting one's mouth and breath in different positions in order to produce the sounds of a language not one's own effects a shift from bodily to ethical semiosis. And though it is a truism, it must be said that the experience of being lost in translation affords great insight into the ultimate impossibility of ever being truly understood – even among speakers of a common language.[25]

As reductive as the logic behind the reasoning was, the language of English, as well as American cultural narratives, came to stand for my refusal to live a life 'lost in translation': English, which I spoke more fluently than the German that has always given voice to my emotional life, came to encode my rejection of the label of 'monstrous vermin' and the affirmation of my desire to *'steh auf'* ('stand up') for another woman. The complex realization with regard to my bilingualism was the recognition of the power of translation, that neither-nor linguistic monstrosity, to figure my identity. Translation could allow me to view my nascent lesbianism in humanizing terms.

Stated slightly differently, this moment, in which my mother's words triggered a reading of Kafka's text as a parable of gender and sexual intolerance and of violence raised to the levels of family and nation that confirmed my own gender and sexual otherness, produced a counter interpretive movement, or what I, tongue in cheek, will call a counter intelligence. I recognize now that my mother spoke her anxious and urgent words for both herself and my father. She articulated – and in effect translated – his requirement that our behavior, including gender expression, conform to the narrow set of expectations at work in the US military community in which we lived. Given this relation, it was clearly also possible for translation to effect meaning in other ways, such as through rupture, redirection, and subversion; through a discourse that could counter or reverse the stigma of gender and sexual otherness; pointedly, through a discourse that encoded in my lesbianism the love of my mother's voice. Thus, while Kafka's story forecloses for Gregor the potential of translation to function as a sign of possibilities beyond the male–female divide of a heteronormative order, my own reading of *Metamorphosis*, rooted in the experience of hearing my mother's voice, has actually facilitated a recognition of this potential. So it is that translation has become a crucial metaphor that, offering me a way of thinking myself out of a sense of gender and sexual shame, links my lesbianism and boy-girl identity to my bilingualism, with its everyday *monströse Mischung* of language and history, and facilitates my understanding of my sexuality and gender as part of a larger transnational story of violence, race, and desire, and tongue-on-tongue-in-cheek identity.

3. (The refusal to) trust in translation: Mary Shelley's *Frankenstein*

While reading *Metamorphosis* has taught me to understand Gregor's as well as my own monstrous gender and sexual desires in terms of the figure of translation, another text, written some one hundred years before Kafka's, details the importance of that figure for another, embodied monster. As many critics have pointed out,[26] Mary Shelley's Gothic novel turns on characters' awareness of the power of reading for understanding oneself and one's relation to society and, importantly, for questioning and possibly redefining that relation. All the major characters in *Frankenstein* remark on their access to education, especially the learning of languages, and the monster in particular recounts how reading literature in translation proves the cornerstone of his education.

Recognizing the metaphoric importance of translation for confronting and undoing the cultural imputation of monstrosity offers an intriguing way into analyzing representations of sexual and gendered otherness in Mary Shelley's *Frankenstein*. Like the novel's 'relationship between sexual reproduction and social subject-production' which, as Gayatri Spivak argues, 'remains problematic', the tension between the monster's constructed sex and his fully human desires, which he confirms through the act of reading in translation, 'constitutes [his] greatest strength'.[27] Stated another way, tethered to the figure of translation, the question that Judith Butler poses early in *Bodies That Matter* hovers over Shelley's novel from beginning to end: 'What challenge does that excluded and abjected realm produce to a symbolic hegemony that might force a radical rearticulation of what qualifies as bodies that matter, ways of living that count as "life", lives worth protecting, lives worth saving, lives worth grieving?'[28] That is, the monster in *Frankenstein* is never fully credibly monstrous; rather, he is, '*not human*', as Judith Halberstam has observed, 'because he lacks the proper body'.[29] He embodies scientist Victor Frankenstein's translation of his sexual technology into human life – a translation in whose human viability, crucially, Victor refuses to trust. Despite the push of Victor's – and, to a certain extent, frame narrator Walton's – account to identify the monster in terms of abject horror, the text as a whole resists such an othering interpretation. Instead, Shelley's novel aligns that traditionally feminine space, domesticity, with gender, sex, and race non-normativity (and so, with the monster). A key though overlooked mediating term for this linkage is the figure of translation, which the monster himself, in his lived paradox, his constructed nature, personifies.

Shelley's cautionary tale as a whole consists of a series of accounts. The frame narrative told by Walton, a sea captain and explorer, is comprised of letters addressed to his sister, Margaret, in England. Within those letters he records the life story of Victor Frankenstein, who first rejects his family and community because he is immersed in creating 'a new species ... many happy and excellent natures [that] would owe their being to [him]'.[30] Then, when the monster that he creates, whom he refers to as both an 'it' and a 'he', and who, as many critics have noted, occupies a feminine subject position,[31] fails to live up to his gendered expectations of that 'excellent nature[ ]', Victor rejects him too. Victor's story details his idyllic upbringing in Geneva, his immersion in his scientific studies at university, his isolated creation of the monster, and their subsequent pattern of flight and pursuit, along with its destructive effects. Victor may begin life surrounded by a loving family and friends, but he ends life with almost everyone whom he has ever cared for dead, and with their deaths directly linked to his abandonment of the monster. Victor's story in turn contains most, though not all, of the monster's own. This account, in which the monster recalls awaking into consciousness, his desire for human intimacy, the learning to speak and read born of that desire, his growing awareness of his alienation from both creator and community, and his consequent decision to exact revenge by killing the people closest to Victor, occupies the center of the novel and the heart of Victor's story. Contrary to what Marc A. Rubinstein has referred to as 'concentric circles',[32] the narrative structure of the novel is actually disruptive, as, for example, in the novel's final pages, when narrative frame and heart collide. Leaning over Victor's corpse and 'seem[ing] to forget [Walton's] presence', the monster offers a final soliloquy to Victor, 'generous and self-devoted being'.[33] As Judith Halberstam has argued, Shelley's disruption of the hierarchy of narratives that she has set out effects a monstrous form, whereby 'the sum of the novel's parts exceeds the whole'.[34] Like the Gothic genre to which it belongs, the novel itself manifests 'a hybrid form, a stitched body of distorted textuality'.[35]

Throughout, whether it is Walton or Victor or the monster, each narrator is highly aware of language – more particularly, the learning of languages – as the primary vehicle for identifying and consolidating one's position within private and public spheres: specifically, for furthering education; for exercising 'dominion ... over elemental foes' (1831);[36] for facilitating 'enterprise' (1831);[37] for making community; and for creating intimacy. Accordingly, throughout their various accounts, the three characters consistently draw attention to the language that they are speaking.

So, for example, Walton details how, on first meeting Frankenstein, the latter addresses him 'in English, although with a foreign accent'.[38] A few pages earlier, Walton writes his sister that at fourteen, 'I perceived the necessity of becoming acquainted with more languages than that of my native country.'[39] Walton yearns for a linguistic mastery that Victor himself possesses, 'for the dominion' he could then 'acquire and transmit over the elemental foes of our race' (1831).[40] Raised by a sister who has 'been tutored and refined by books and retirement from the world' (1831),[41] he also realizes, though, the elusiveness of this desire: 'Now I am twenty-eight, and am in reality more illiterate than many school-boys of fifteen.'[42] Walton's limited education may well speak to English class barriers; in any event, it also aligns him with England's feminine domestic sphere, more particularly the sister for whom a limited education is gender appropriate.

Victor, in turn, defines himself apart from the constraints of class and, at least figuratively, the restrictions of gender that Walton experiences. Describing himself at fifteen, he notes that, in addition to his native French, he had knowledge of several other languages: 'I was busily employed in learning languages; Latin was already familiar to me, and I began to read some of the easiest Greek authors without the help of a lexicon. I also perfectly understood English and German.'[43] Later, after creating and then abandoning the monster, Victor, along with his best friend, Clerval, studies 'Persian, Arabic, and Hebrew'.[44] While it is unclear whether Walton knows any language other than English, it seems likely that Victor has recounted his life story in the accented English with which he initially addresses Walton. In any event, it is obvious that Victor in his familiarity with so many languages serves as the idealized, imperialist, and impossible role model for Walton. In Judith Butler's terms, Victor is the 'unitary subject': he is

> the one who knows already what it is, who enters the conversation the same way as it exits, who fails to put its own epistemological certainties at risk in the encounter with the other, and so stays in place, guards its place, and becomes an emblem for property and territory, *refusing self-transformation, ironically, in the name of the subject.*[45]

Linguistic power – the *possession* of languages – is a key feature of Victor's Promethean appeal and, problematically, his abjectifying capacity.

From this perspective, the monster's relation to language may well be understood in terms of *dispossession*. Like Victor, the monster speaks French, but significantly he learns it not from the 'creator' who abandons him shortly after his 'birth', but by overhearing and mimicking the loving and close-knit French émigré DeLacey family that has fled to Germany. Having discovered Victor's journal, the monster realizes that his creator will never love him: 'the minutest description of my odious and loathsome person is given, in language which painted your own horrors, and rendered mine ineffaceable. I sickened as I read.'[46] For the monster, the revulsion that Victor describes in his journal is in turn written on his own body: his body literalizes (and renders inescapable) Victor's language. As Susan Stryker writes of the violent gendering that is one's birth into subjectivity, 'Phallogocentric language . . . is the scalpel that defines our flesh.'[47] Within the novel the monster remains nameless because Victor refuses to recognize in him a viable and viably gendered personhood; the monster is monstrous because Victor calls him so.[48]

Thus, the monster's tragedy results from Victor's linguistic authority, the power of his language to define the monster's entrapment within a reality in which intimacy proves impossible. All three characters – Walton, Victor, and the monster – may resemble one another in their overreaching and transgressive capacities; they differ, however, markedly in their relation to language and, too, in their relation to the novel's locus of verbal limitation, the home. Unlike Victor, both Walton and the monster crave human connection.

So, Walton, for all his desire to discover the Northwest Passage, ultimately abandons his quest for the safety of his crew. Moreover, he chooses to locate the various transgressive accounts (of foreign bodies, [non]human, as well as geographical) within his correspondence with his sister, Margaret, whose 'gentle and feminine fosterage', he writes, 'has so refined the groundwork of [his] character' (1831).[49] For Walton, the production of meaning (Western, specifically English meaning) is inextricable from human, particularly domestic, relations gendered feminine.

For the monster the equation is a bit more complex: the production of meaning is linked to the desire for a queer domestic space. The horror of the novel resides in the refusal to acknowledge and nurture as legitimate beings those who, because of their cultural or sexual production, come into existence apart from a heteronormative procreative context.[50] (This is also, arguably, Mary Shelley's horror, given the death of her mother while giving birth to her daughter and Mary's own gender-transgressive behavior, which included the mastery of several languages.[51]) With a linkage that anticipates the work of late nineteenth-century sexologists and Kafka's own literary vision in *The Metamorphosis*, the monster is, as Halberstam has noted, the product of Victor's own masturbatory and homosexual desires.[52] Stated another way, at issue is not the monster's motherless origin so much as Victor's refusal to nurture the monster because of that motherless origin. Because he is not 'of woman born',[53] but rather the product of Victor's own queer desires, the monster is abandoned, left homeless. Thus, the monster is rejected at birth by Victor, who in his linguistic authority determines not simply that the life he has made is hideous but that the technology of that production is itself neither natural nor in the service of the natural.[54] The monster yearns for a space (emotional, epistemological, and geographical) that will legitimate his queer birth and his gender otherness: within hours after coming to life the monster stretches out his hand to Victor; later he patterns his idea of family on the nurturing model followed by the motherless French family whom he encounters and from whom he learns to speak;

further on, he begs Victor to create another, female monster as a companion for him; finally, at the novel's end when Victor dies, the monster resolves to join his creator in death. Even though his pursuit of that space proves ambivalent and violent, his unrealizable desire is necessarily poignant. Much of the empathy one feels for the monster resides in this elusive yearning for a queer-inflected domesticity – elusive not because he does so much to destroy Victor's own family but because of Victor's own totalizing linguistic authority: Victor denies the monster any nourishing human connection, even at the geographical edges of European imperial interests, on basis of his scientifically engineered birth or non-normative gender.

Yet even as the monster's tragedy may be understood as the result of Victor's linguistic authority, the power of his language to define the monster's entrapment within a reality that precludes intimacy, the novel suggests the possibilities for inhabiting a queer domestic space. One such possibility is held out by the monster's encountering of the DeLacey family, themselves in flight from unjust fathers. The monster's subsequent overture to them is a reflection not only of his desire for intimacy but even more importantly of his desire to answer the linguistic tyranny that Victor exercises over his body by practicing an alternative relation between intimacy and language. In stark contrast to the parent who refuses to acknowledge him is the DeLacey family's welcome of another friendless orphan: the monster has watched the DeLaceys enact a model of family that crosses any number of conventional barriers – gender, geographic, linguistic, national, religious, and social, to name a few – in order to take into its circle the young woman Safie, whose learning of French proves the occasion for his own acquisition of the language.[55] The DeLaceys' model of family in effect counters Victor's negating own by rehabilitating cultural transgression as a dynamic ground for human intimacy rather than parental abandonment. So the kindness that the DeLaceys have shown the young woman encourages the monster to appeal to them for protection and friendship: as he explains, 'The more I saw of them, the greater became my desire to claim their protection and kindness; my heart yearned to be known and loved by these amiable creatures.'[56] Upon hearing the monster address him, the blind old man who heads the family assumes that the monster is his 'countryman', so fluent is his pitiable unsuccessful appeal: ' . . . I was educated by a French family', the monster elliptically explains, 'and understand that language only'.[57] While he has extended his knowledge by reading key European texts – Milton's *Paradise Lost*, Goethe's *The Sorrows of Young Werther*, and Plutarch's *Lives* – all in translation, as with Walton, there is no indication in the text that the monster has learned any other language. While the monster is only able to speak French and read foundational works of Western literature in translation, he nonetheless recognizes that the model of domesticity enacted by the DeLaceys, motherless and, while not corporeally, culturally, hybrid, like himself, can offer him emotional nurture, if not cultural mastery.

This reading of literature in translation, even as it marks out the limits of the monster's education and in doing so aligns him with the feminine domestic sphere,[58] offers a linguistic analogue to the model of queer domesticity set forth by the DeLacey family. Upon reading *Werther*, for example, the monster recognizes that '[t]he gentle and domestic manners it described, combined with lofty sentiments and feelings, which had for their object something out of self, accorded well with my experience among my protectors, and with the wants which were for ever alive in my own bosom'.[59] This moment is key not simply because, as with his much more critically discussed reading of *Paradise Lost*, the monster can read himself into the text or, again, read his life as an enactment of the text.[60] Translated literature also offers identification on the level of textual production: translation is the technology of reading that, enabling access to the unspeakable and unknowable foreign, renders it recognizable and familiar. In this, I am reminded of Shelley's contemporary Keats, whose sonnet 'On First Looking into Chapman's Homer', written in celebration of the power of translation, appeared in December 1816, little more than a year before *Frankenstein's* publication. In Keats's case, Chapman's translation grants the poet access to the classical literature that his spotty and class-marked education, itself figured in the mistaken reference to Cortez in the closing lines, has denied him. So, too, in Mary Shelley's novel, translation, rather than linguistic mastery and cultural fluency, proves a source of empowerment. Judith Halberstam has written that 'Gothic fiction produces monstrosity as a technology of sexuality, identity and narrative' and that this 'technology of monstrosity' is in turn 'written upon the body'.[61] In the case of *Frankenstein's* monster, I would argue that Mary Shelley encodes that technology within the figure of translation. In the novel, translation facilitates the monster's self-understanding. He can read himself, as well as the DeLacey family, in terms of Goethe's text rather than Victor's journal. Though grotesque in size and appearance, he can identify with 'the gentle and domestic' rather than the 'odious and loathsome'. Translation, then, functions as a figure of agency, answering the abjectifying power of Victor's polyglot authority.[62] In this sense, Shelley invites one to recognize the monster as himself a personification of translation: an embodied otherness that is at once approachable and readable as human.

Shelley's alignment of translation with the monster culminates in a revelatory yet little discussed moment near the end of the novel. In the final pages, Walton encounters the monster that scientist Victor Frankenstein has created. Frankenstein has just died aboard Walton's ship, and Walton finds the monster hovering over Victor's body. Walton describes the scene:

> Over [Victor] hung a form *which I cannot find words to describe*; gigantic in stature, yet uncouth and distorted in its proportions. As he hung over the coffin, his face was concealed by long locks of ragged hair; but one vast hand was extended, in colour and apparent texture like that of a mummy. When he heard the sound of my approach, he ceased to utter exclamations of grief and horror, and sprung towards the window. Never did I behold a vision so horrible as his face, of such loathsome, yet appalling hideousness. I shut my eyes involuntarily, and endeavoured to recollect what were my duties with regard to this destroyer. I called on him to stay.[63]

This scene recalls and reconfigures the monster's 'birth', in which Victor, awaking from a troubled sleep that anticipates Gregor Samsa's, beholds the monster that he created standing before him with 'one hand ... stretched out'.[64] In a metaphoric sense, the monster has arrived nowhere with his creator: at the novel's end (as well as the end of Victor's and presumably the near end of the monster's story), the monster is back where he started. Yet, there is a difference. In contrast to Victor who, once he sees his creation, runs away terrified, Walton chooses to stay and, in turn, calls on the monster to stay. Walton may initially ' ... not find words to describe' the monster; that is, he may initially represent the monster as unspeakable. Crucially, though, Walton does not pretend to exercise ultimate interpretive authority over the monster.

This moment is key to understanding the importance of translation. Walton asks the monster to stay. The monster does so, but only for a short while: within little more than three pages, the monster has left, and the novel is finished. Nonetheless, this moment indicates a fissure in the text, an opening up of narrative possibility in the very moment that the novel is closing down. That is, the moment gestures toward that alternative, albeit repressed, narrative movement for which translation itself serves as a *leitfigur*: a reordering of relations among sexual production, bodily otherness, and language so that the monster might be fully recognized as human. The moment invites a series of questions, such as those that feminist and queer critics, like Gilbert and Gubar in the mid seventies and Susan Stryker most recently, have asked. What would have happened if *Victor* had stayed? How would he, and beyond him the larger community, have received the monster's 'being'? How monstrous would the monster have been? Would his monstrosity have continued to lodge in Victor's memory of his horror of the sexual technology with which he produced him? Would the monster's physical difference, his anomalous body, have proven the essential (fundamental) barrier to his being welcomed into society? Would monstrosity have shifted and become aligned with the refusal to acknowledge and integrate the monster's corporeal exception into the community? These kinds of questions speak to the poignant concern that the monster himself voices, early in his own account: 'I was ... endowed with a figure hideously deformed and loathsome ... Was I then a monster, a blot upon the earth, from which all men fled, and whom all men disowned?'[65]

Walton's calling out to the monster is fascinating not only because of the potential alternative life story that it engenders but because Walton, or perhaps Mary Shelley herself, has left ambiguous how it is that he and the monster even communicate. In the last pages of the novel Walton returns to the frame narrative and records his encounter with the monster. All of these texts Walton apparently transmits to Margaret in English, even though Victor and the monster's native language is French, which is also, presumably, the only language that the monster knows. So we arrive at the question, how is it that Walton is able to communicate with the monster? Does Walton call out to him in simple English or broken French, or is tone enough to convey meaning? Or do he and the monster communicate 'somehow': is, in effect, Mary Shelley offering readers a translation, in which what is important is not knowledge of the original language that the two characters are speaking but rather the awareness itself of the connection that they are making? That is, is the moment indicative of a point that Mary Shelley herself is foregrounding, indicating that there is no essential, insuperable barrier between Walton and the monster; they are more alike than not? 'All understanding, and the demonstrative statement of understanding which is translation', writes George Steiner, 'starts with an act of trust'.[66] If the contrast between multilingual Victor's patriarchal rejection of the monster, on the one hand, and the French-speaking DeLaceys' queer embrace of Safie, on the other hand, is any indication, then it would seem that in Mary Shelley's novel the making of community and more particularly of intimacy depends not on a knowledge of language (or languages) and the affirmation of gender norms or a gender hierarchy but rather on what I will call a trust in translation: a recognition of a shared humanity; a commitment to good will and a desire to communicate that cuts across barriers of language, geography, gender, and sex. Discussing the potential for social change embedded within the act of translation, Emily Apter writes,

> Translation failure demarcates the limits of intersubjective communication even as it highlights that 'eureka' spot where consciousness crosses over to a rough zone of equivalency or crystallizes around an idea that belongs to no one language or nation in particular. Translation is thus a unique medium of subject re-formation and political change.[67]

The gap, or perhaps 'gradient',[68] that, within Shelley's text, discloses this trust in translation may be apparent to readers; it is not, however, recognized by either the monster or Walton. So, quite understandably, the monster proves surprised by Walton's call to stay. As the latter notes, 'He paused, looking on me with wonder'.[69]

For all his surprise, then, the monster cannot pursue the possibility for human connection that Walton's call potentially engenders. In a final, compelling soliloquy, in which he condemns himself and eulogizes Victor, he remains isolated and pitiable, begging the dead Frankenstein for forgiveness. In contrast to Susan Stryker, who, in a powerful comparison between her own experiences as a transsexual and the 'birth' of the monster, argues that, while he has made the monster's body, Frankenstein has not determined his subjectivity,[70] ultimately, neither the monster nor Walton nor Mary Shelley herself can recognize a space within community for the monster: he remains an outcast 'lost in darkness and distance'.[71] Within the classist, sexist, and queer-phobic terms of the novel's imagined reality, the monster proves an unliveable translation.

4. Dressed in translation: Pedro Almodóvar's *All About My Mother*

This is not the case for the various social monsters of Pedro Almodóvar's 1999 film *All About My Mother*,[72] whose opening shot sequence quotes the creation scene of *Frankenstein*'s monster: the credits roll, and the camera pans a hospital operating room, filled with various 'life-giving/sustaining' apparati, such as i.v. drips and medical machinery.

Here Almodóvar is making a point about the complex set of relations among gender, sexuality, space, language, and power. While, in the case of Victor Frankenstein, the laboratory is the site of Victor's phallogo-centric creation of the monster, Almodóvar immediately problematizes the authority of this space in the next sequence, inverting the various relations found in Shelley's novel. With the camera moving into the domestic space of the film's protagonist, Manuela, a transplant coor-dinator, who works in settings such as the laboratory/operating room initially seen, the domestic sphere proves a locus for claiming one's sub-jectivity. Cast in the opening scene as a performative space, linked to stage and film, the domestic functions as a site of motherhood and, more abstractly, as a site of individual engagement with literary texts and, accordingly, a proliferation of interpretations.

Seated on her living room couch, Manuela, with her son, Esteban, is watching the film *All About Eve*, Hollywood's 1950 classic exploration of female professional ambition, gender performance, and seductive (Eve-like) sexuality. Their remarks regarding the film's title inaugurate Almodóvar's exploration of translation as the critical figure for the indi-vidual claim for gender and sexual subjectivity. So, Esteban remarks on the difference between *All about Eve*'s Spanish title, *Eve Unveiled*, and the title's literal translation: 'They always change the title! *All About Eve* should be *Todo sobre Eva*.' 'But that sounds odd', Manuela responds. The camera then offers a close-up shot of Esteban writing in his notebook '*Todo*' or '*All*', followed by a shot of mother and son, with the film title superimposed. This sequence suggests that Esteban is writing the title – the literal translation – of the Hollywood film or, perhaps, the title of the screenplay of Almodóvar's film itself.

Esteban's choice of 'All About ...' is critical. As Michael Sofair notes that while 'an unveiling suggests the stripping away of superficial layers to reveal some essential core, ... "All About ..." suggests a process of elaboration which is implicitly open-ended. About such a character, story after story can be told.'[73] And indeed, the film tells story after story about 'all about'. As Almodóvar explained in a 1999 interview, the scene encodes Esteban's understanding of the link between storytelling and women. An aspiring writer, Esteban understands the importance of *All About Eve*'s dressing room scene, which he and his mother are watching: 'the story of a bunch of women talking' is the 'origin' of the film's story.[74] Thus, Esteban is making a claim not only for an understanding of gender identity as performative but also for the viability of the literal translation – no matter how foreign or unnatural it seems; how unaccommodating to prescribed expectations or social conventions it is.

This moment, particularly when sutured to the initial shot sequence, in effect offers the prism through which Almodóvar asks viewers to regard various performances of translation – surgical, theatrical, cinematic, gendered, and sexual. Translation is a figure that, as Emily Apter writes, is '[c]ast both as an act of love and as an act of disruption' and, accordingly, 'becomes a means of repositioning the subject in the world and in history'.[75] Exploring the cultural meanings – the intertexuality – of a range of bodies, corporeal as well as literary, Almodóvar's melodrama expands the conventional genre of 'woman's film'. According to Florence Jacobowitz and Lori Spring, the 'problematic' of melodrama, 'includes the expression of women's resistance to their confined and subordinated positions in a male-dominated world'.[76] Almodóvar's film, as its dedication underscores, recognizes the humanity of ' . . . all women who act, . . . men who act and become women . . . all people who want to be mothers'. *All About My Mother* is dressed in translation. As such, it claims the power – affective as well as aesthetic – of the gendered and sexual monsters that are its principal characters.

This emphasis on translation as a figure for performative identity depends upon a critical diminishment of the authority of the phallogo-centric realm of the medical laboratory. Calling to mind Susan Stryker's point that the 'consciousness shaped by the transsexual body is no more the creation of the science that refigures its flesh than the monster's mind is the creation of Frankenstein',[77] *All About My Mother*'s storyline early on underscores the limits of science's authority. So, when Manuela's son dies in an automobile accident, his death inaugurates a sequence of calls – the transplant narrative that Manuela has herself both enacted in her work and enacted in a video scenario on the process.[78] If this blurring between medical reality and video simulation proves a painful irony, it is Manuela's following of her son's heart after it's been transplanted into a middle-aged man in Coruña that brings home her loss. Hers is a melancholic reaction.[79] It is not her son's heart, after all; the doctors have kept the heart beating, and it now beats inside the older man. Her son, though, is dead.

If Esteban still lives, he does so in the memory of his mother. Yet, one might ask, is she still a mother if she is now without her child? Certainly she resembles the literal translation whose proper-ness she and Esteban debated at the outset of the film, but is she still a mother? As if spurred on by that question, Manuela begins a journey retracing her life as a mother. She leaves Madrid and travels to Barcelona, the city she had left some seventeen years before when she was pregnant. Her encounters there with people from her past, including her friend Agrado and her former husband, Esteban/Lola, and with new people, such as the actress Huma and the pregnant nun Rosa, allow her to reaffirm her role as mother and grant her a queer authority lodged not in biological fact but rather in a performativity of nation and gender – a performativity that director Almodóvar links to the realms of art and imagination, to theatre and dreams, to illusion and smoke, and, significantly, to post-Franco Spain and the modern family.

So, for example, Manuela's motherhood is powerfully intertwined with an expansive and transnational understanding of Spain. As Ernesto Acevedo-Muñoz points out,

> The significance of Manuela's travels cannot be underestimated. . . . By placing Esteban Jr's heart in Coruña, and Esteban Sr in Barcelona, Almodóvar not only displaces Madrid . . . as a synecdoche of all things Spanish, but also acknowledges a sense of inclusion of 'other things Spanish' by reconciling this bicoastal dyad. Galicia and Cataluña are steps in Manuela's healing process, in her search for and effort to 'reorganise' the body of Spain.[80]

Manuela travels first to find her son's heart and then to reaffirm her identity as mother. In the process she implicitly offers an ideological re-suturing of Spain, a vision of 'nation', once fragmented, made whole.

Importantly, her vision of nation also entails a crossing of political and geographical boundaries. As Martin D'Lugo observes,

> A new linkage through dialogue alludes to geographical sites out-side of Spain: Paris and Argentina. Years earlier, Manuela and her husband Estéban, later transformed into Lola, emigrated to Paris from their native Argentina. The unspoken assumption is that, like may Argentines of the late 1970s, they fled their homeland in the wake of the 'Proceso' (or 'Dirty War'), the series of murders, tortures, and 'disappearances' of individuals, principally younger people per-ceived as dissidents. . . . These political intertexts and the new range of non-Madrid geographic references contribute to the sense of a newly emerging style and spirit in *All About My Mother*.[81]

Manuela's travels link together parts of Spain and 'New Spain' marked by a history of political violence and cultural division, as well as by geo-graphical isolation.[82] Thus, her journeys effect a queering of nation, a re-gendering of *patria*, facilitated above all through her self-understanding as mother.

Regarding motherhood, Michael Sofair remarks, 'Characters in *All About My Mother* are at their most authentic when acting as mothers.'[83] In Barcelona Manuela enacts a queer motherhood whose key features – indiscriminate care and nurture and random comedy – counter the gender and sexual violence that permeates the lives and theatrical performances of those she meets. Huma and her drug-dependent and indifferent lover, Nina, for example, are starring as Blanche and Stella in a production of Tennessee Williams's *A Streetcar Named Desire*, a play 'all about' sexual violence. And it is as if this script in turn dictates the terms of Huma and Nina's relationship, for Nina continually abandons Huma in both their professional and private lives together. Yet, their doubled act also encodes another pairing of female roles: Huma ('Smoke'), whose stage name pays homage to Bette Davis, plays Margo Channing, a renowned role for the cigarette-smoking Davis, to Nina's seductive and treacherous Eve Harrington, from *All About Eve*. Manuela, in turn, regards *Streetcar* as a work that has marked her life,[84] and the same may be said of *All About Eve*, which frames her story within Almodóvar's film. Given their centrality for Huma as well, the two works may be read as metatexts of womanhood in general, with Manuela and Huma's continual engagement with them exposing the porous borders between art and reality. Yet, in a series of events that recall both play and film, Manuela counters the roles of treachery and betrayal that the works encode. Manuela looks after Huma and Nina before their stage appearances, and we hear that she nurses Nina during her off-stage drug episodes.

The relationship in which Manuela's queer motherhood is most apparent is that with the pregnant nun Rosa, for it is a relationship that translates Catholicism's founding story of motherhood into a context of non-normative genders and sexualities. A parodic version of the Virgin Mary, Rosa is pregnant but, technically, not by a man, since the father of her child is the transsexual Lola, formerly Esteban. The frequency and compression of coincidences, such as the sudden proliferation of Estebans and Lola's name's playful echo of the title of the Kinks' hit song, renders the crossings of lives comic, but the comedy serves to make the ethical point that people are all related, foreignness and differences notwithstanding.[85] There is a 'we', a realm of community and with it of communal responsibility, which Manuela understands. In her role as a queer mother, Manuela manifests her humanity. She takes care of Rosa during her pregnancy because the HIV positive Rosa's own mother will not, and even though Lola born Esteban also fathered her own son, Esteban (see Figure 5.1). What anger Manuela feels is fleeting, and it is reserved for Lola. Later, after having promised the dying Rosa to take

Figure 5.1:   Manuela as queer mother of Rosa. © El Deseo/Teresa Isasi.

care of the baby, also named Esteban, Manuela herself assumes the role
of Madonna, her second son the fruit not only of Rosa's virgin birth but
also of Manuela's disembodied one.

Such queering of culturally Catholic figures extends to Lola. For
Almodóvar, 'more than anything', *All About My Mother* 'talks about what
it means to bring a new life into the world, about a motherhood which
becomes a fatherhood and vice versa'. Lola is the film's 'evil' character, a Bergmanesque embodiment of death.[86] So Manuela says to her,
when she appears at Rosa's funeral, 'You're not a human being . . . you're
an epidemic.' Lola is an 'epidemic' because she has proven thoughtless
both in their marriage and in her relationship with Rosa, which culminates in Rosa's contraction of HIV and consequent death.[87] Importantly,
Lola's gender transgression is not the occasion for or sign of her evil: as
the close-up of her face directly after Manuela's pronouncement underscores, Lola has the beauty of 'someone who is sick but still desirable,
to men as well as women'.[88] Nor does her transsexuality erase her pater-
nal drive. Her identity as a transsexual exists alongside of and not in
conflict with her understanding of herself as a father. Accordingly, she
exposes not only the constructed nature of authentic genders but also
the 'natural' drive to construct authentic families. Almodóvar explains:
'there exists an animal instinct in you inciting you to procreate and to

defend your progeny, and to exercise your rights over that being. It's what Lola represents, and is perhaps what is most scandalous about the film, although I show it as natural. Lola changes her whole way of being, her entire body, yet something inside her remains intact.'[89] Or again, as he pithily remarks, 'it's possible to be self-centered, not to think about anyone else, and – with or without breasts – to want to be a father'.[90]

For Almodóvar, Manuela and Lola, along with their second son Esteban, represent the modern family:

> I wanted the audience – even if it may seem a touch forced – to see this trio as natural. Not for the audience to tolerate it but to see it as something natural. Lola, Manuela, and the second Esteban make up a new family, one that attaches importance only to essentials, one for whom external circumstances are of no importance. That's why Lola, dressed as a woman, can say to the child: 'I'm sorry to leave you such an awful inheritance' and ask Manuela if she can kiss Esteban. 'Of course you can, girl', replies Manuela, talking to Lola in the feminine with absolute naturalness. For me this very atypical family evokes the whole range of families that are possible at the end of the twentieth century. If anything is a feature of our end of century, it is precisely the break-up of the traditional family. It's now possible to create a family with different members, based on different types of biological, or other, relationships. A family should be respected whatever its make-up. What matters is that the members of the family love one another.[91]

So, this, the final scene in which Lola appears, figures Almodóvar's queer translation of the iconic 'sacred family' into modern secular terms, with neither Lola's transsexuality nor her paternity in question (see Figures 5.2 and 5.3) ... At least not in Spanish. In a chapter concerned with gender, sexuality, and translation, and, with them, the imputation of monstrosity, it is well worth noting that the subtitles accompanying the English-language version of the film translate Manuela's above response as 'of course'. Lost in translation is *'mujer'* (or 'girl'), the particular assurance of Manuela's acceptance of Lola's trans identity.

This lapse in translation not withstanding, the overall message of this scene and the film as a whole remains clear. *All About My Mother*'s multiple splicings of shots and reverse shots, which, by including cliché and comic 'birth canal'/ train-in-tunnel shot sequences, rupture real time in order to expose the fiction of reel time, continually draw attention to the cinematic production of meaning or, again, Almodóvar's translation of

Figure 5.2: Almodóvar filming in front of *La Sagrada Familia* Church in Barcelona. © El Deseo/Teresa Isasi.

reality into film, which produces comedy but also the 'truths' that art can convey. Foremost of these is that Lola, Manuela, and the baby Esteban are a family, a postmodern Spanish family. Much as Lola's embrace of her baby son choreographs the authenticity of her paternity, Manuela's series of performances as mother – with her first son Esteban, with Huma and Nina, with Rosa, and, finally, with her second son Esteban – creates her authenticity as a mother.

This connection between performance and authenticity is further underscored by Agrado, a friend whom Manuela reencounters upon her return to Barcelona, and who, like Lola, is one of the two transsexual characters (explicitly in Lola's case; implicitly in Agrado's case) with whom the film engages the question of gender and sexual monstrosity.[92] Like Manuela, Agrado, whose masculine gendered name means 'agreeable', is well aware of the gender and sexual violence that surrounds her. When she first espies Manuela after the seventeen-year absence Agrado is being beaten up by a sex client; Manuela intervenes and 'rescues'

Figure 5.3: La sagrada familia moderna – Manuela with Lola and Esteban III. © El Deseo/Teresa Isasi.

her friend. Violence is an everyday presence in Agrado's life. At one point, when the two are walking down the street, she casually refers to 'beatings [she's] taken over the last forty years' (see Figure 5.4). Later, she mentions that, had she known that her nose would be broken as many times as it has, she would never have had it 'fixed' (to create a more feminine appearance). Paradoxically, both because and irrespective of such violence, Agrado adheres to the belief that 'you are more authentic the more you resemble what you dreamed you are' (see Figure 5.5). In her case, authenticity turns on an embodied and mimed performance of womanhood.[93] That is, Agrado, a woman born a man and a woman with a penis, ruptures the narrative of 'natural' and ostensibly seamless relations among sex, gender, and sexuality. Her dream of authenticity, which she shares with a centuries-old body of comic and romantic literature,[94] offers a model for social cohesion, whereby a rigid [patriarchal] order based on gender and sexual violence gives way to an expansive [queer] order of gender and sexual variability. Much as Esteban's heart is at the core of Manuela's journey into queer motherhood, Agrado's dream is at the center of *All About My Mother*'s vision of humanity.

Let me offer one final comment about the film in particular and my chapter's argument in general: Obviously, there are limits to the reach of

Figure 5.4: Agrado and Manuela. © El Deseo/Teresa Isasi.

Figure 5.5: Agrado, l'autentica, with Pedro Almodóvar. © El Deseo/Teresa Isasi.

literature, particularly when those limits are determined by systems of distribution and production whose very aims run counter to the lessons literature has to teach us. This chapter considers the capacity or power of translation as a metaphor to answer the reduction – figurative but also social and political – of human beings to monsters. In offering my literary analysis, I have focused on the sets of relations established within the text, as well as on the relation between reader and text. Yet, it is critical to underscore that the message of any literary text, no matter the degree to which that message is acclaimed, is shaped significantly – not entirely, but nonetheless crucially – by the text's distribution and circulation. *All About My Mother* has received more awards than any other film, Spanish or otherwise.[95] The film, like Almodóvar's work as a whole, reflects the post-Franco democratization of Spain: in this sense, it is a film 'all about' democracy.[96] Yet, even though it foregrounds the figurative power of translation vis-à-vis transgressive genders, sexes, and sexualities, *All About My Mother*'s success within a US context may be understood, as Almodóvar suggests, as anomalous. While it won the Oscar for Best Foreign Film, the film, Almodóvar observes, 'remains a rarity, an oddity in American eyes'.[97] In its independent production and ethical vision, it remains foreign to the Hollywood-dominated film market. Moreover, for an American audience viewing it with English subtitles, the film's celebration of 'so-called freaks'[98] inevitably invites recognition of the anxious policing of the bounds of human community that takes place along linguistic and cultural borders within the US. The interplay between Spanish audio track and English subtitles exposes what Gayatri Spivak has called 'the general violence of culturing as incessant and shuttling translation',[99] and, in a slightly different context, singer Marianne Faithfull has named the brutal tyranny of 'broken English'.[100] In this case, the violence not only manifests itself as a discounting of the film's Spanish and a deadness to the 'ethical semiosis' of which Emily Apter has written; it also exacts cultural and geographic dislocations and compressions, whereby, for example, 'Spanish' is replaced by 'Mexican' or 'Central American' or, perhaps, 'not English'; 'not American'. In so doing the violence of translation further encodes an English-speaking American audience's anxiety *vis-à-vis* Spanish, the primary language of those other cultural monsters, those tens of thousands of illegal aliens, undocumented workers from Mexico and Central and South America, who dare to cross borders, perhaps not gender and sexual borders but certainly economic, social, and political ones, in the name of dignity and respect or again, in Agrado's terms, in the hope of realizing a dream: a life that is 'all about' authenticity.

All About My Mother captures translation's figurative empowerment of transgressive genders, sexes, and sexualities. In terms of its success within a US context, however, the film exposes the erasure and demonization of non-English-speakers and non-citizens. Even so, the message of the film still stands; indeed, it gains a painful urgency that deepens and complicates the celebratory mood, when the film's status as a work-in-translation within the American film market is recognized. *All About My Mother*, then, answers Shelley's and Kafka's earlier texts. It counters the imputation of monstrosity with an embrace of the 'deserts of the heart'; it offers an expanded definition of human community to include various members, no matter how foreign, how alien *either* their bodies *or* their languages might seem.

Notes

Introduction

1 Shane Phelan, '(Be)Coming Out: Lesbian Identity and Politics', *Signs* 18.4 (Summer 1993): 765–90.
2 Ken Plummer, *Telling Sexual Stories: Power, Change, and Social Worlds* (London and New York: Routledge, 1995).

1. Writing Sexuality: Lesbian Novels and the Progress Narrative

1. For Bunyan's influence on later writers, see, for example, Richard L. Greaves, 'Bunyan Through the Centuries: Some Reflections', *English Studies*, 64 (1983): 113–21; N. H. Keeble, ' "Of Him Thousands Daily Sing and Talk": Bunyan and His Reputation', in *Conventicle and Parnassus, Tercentenary Essays*, edited by N. H. Keeble (Oxford: Clarendon Press, 1988), 241–63; and Barry V. Qualls, *The Secular Pilgrims of Victorian Fiction* (Cambridge, UK: Cambridge University Press, 1982).
2. See my article 'The Sexed Pilgrim's Progress', *SEL* 32.3 (1992): 443–60.
3. Charlotte Brontë, *Jane Eyre* (New York: Norton, 1971), 363.
4. Ibid., 398.
5. It is Christian in Part 1 of *The Pilgrim's Progress* who battles Apollyon. In her ending to *Jane Eyre*, Charlotte Brontë imagines St John as a kind of Great-heart, the guide of Christiana, Mercy, and other pilgrims in Part 2. Brontë's splicing together of the two parts of *The Pilgrim's Progress* indicates how she uses Bunyan's text in order to underscore the particular gender difficulties that a heroine, interested in making and telling her own story, on the one hand, and negotiating larger social expectations of her submission to men, on the other hand, necessarily faces.
6. John Bunyan, *The Pilgrim's Progress* (Harmondsworth: Penguin, 1984), 172.
7. Ibid., 127.
8. It is worth noting here that while it is fairly easy to imagine Christian and Christiana as 'characters' (and so recognize how Bunyan's work came to prove so important to the development of the British novel), it is impossible to read the Flatterer as such. He seems an 'empty' or 'flat' allegory or, as I have argued in the main text, an allegory of the person without personhood. My thanks to Kirsty Milne of Oxford University, who has pushed me to think about this figure.
9. Isabel Hofmeyr, *The Portable Bunyan: A Transnational History of* The Pilgrim's Progress, (Johannesburg: Wits University Press; and Princeton, NJ: Princeton University Press, 2004), 92.
10. Ibid., 222.

11. Siobhan Somerville, 'Scientific Racism and the Invention of the Homosexual Body', *Journal of the History of Sexuality* 5.2 (1994): 243–66, 244.
12. See Nancy Leys Stepan and Sander L. Gilman, 'Appropriating the Idioms of Science: The Rejection of Scientific Racism', in *The Bounds of Race: Perspectives on Hegemony and Resistance*, edited by Dominick LaCapra (Ithaca, NY: Cornell University Press, 1991), 72–103, 73. As Stepan and Gilman point out, 'from 1870 to 1920, science became both more specialized and authoritative as a cultural resource and language of interpretation' (80). Thus scientists' claims of racial inferiority, 'pressed most insistently by the mainstream scientific community' at this time (72), were also much more difficult to refute.
13. Gertrude Stein, *Fernhurst, Q.E.D., and Other Early Writings* (New York, London: Liveright, 1996), 59 (emphasis added), 93. Q.E.D. also invests 'queer' with connotations of same-sex desire (see 77). This particular function of 'queer' is already at work in Eliza Lynn Linton's 1880 novel, *The Rebel of the Family*.
14. Edward Prime-Stevenson, *Imre* (Peterborough, ONT: Broadview, 2003), 64. Prime-Stevenson wrote under the penname Xavier Mayne.
15. See, for example, Monique Wittig, *The Straight Mind and Other Essays* (Boston: Beacon Press, 1992) and Judith Butler, *Gender Trouble: Feminism and the Subversion of Identity* (New York: Routledge, 1990).
16. For more on 'invert''s crossing with contemporary terms for sexual and gender identity, see Judith Halberstam, *Female Masculinity* (Durham and London: Duke University Press, 1998), especially Chapter 3; see also Jay Prosser, ' "Some Primitive Thing Conceived in a Turbulent Age of Transition": The Transsexual Emerging from *The Well*', in *Palatable Poison: Critical Perspectives on* The Well of Loneliness, edited by Laura Doan and Jay Prosser (New York: Columbia University Press, 2001), 129–44.
17. See, for example, James Fenton, 'Let Her Dangers Be Never So Great', *The Times Literary Supplement*, 13 April 2007. Fenton discusses Elizabeth Bishop's use of an image from *The Pilgrim's Progress* in her poem 'The Unbeliever' and makes a passing reference to Marianne Moore's knowledge of Bunyan. See also the collection by Aliki Barnstone, Michael Tomasek Manson, and Carol J. Singley, eds, *The Calvinist Roots of the Modern Era* (Hanover, NH and London, UK: University Press of New England, 1997).
18. Hofmeyr, 217.
19. The novel was available in mid July: see Diana Souhami, *The Trials of Radclyffe Hall* (London: Weidenfeld & Nicolson, 1998), 172. On 23 August 1928, *The Times* carried a letter to the editor written on behalf of Jonathan Cape, Hall's publisher, announcing the discontinued publication of the novel.
20. For the Bunyan speech, see 23 November 1928, *The Times*, 18. For the Council speech, see Souhami, 191; 15 October 1928, *The Times*.
21. Referenced in Hofmeyr, 220.
22. See, for example, Jean Walton, ' "I Want to Cross Over into Camp Ground": Race and Inversion in *The Well of Loneliness*', in Doan and Prosser, 2001, 277–99 and Sarah E. Chinn, ' "Something Primitive and Age-Old as Nature Herself": Lesbian Sexuality and the Permission of the Exotic', in Doan and Prosser, 2001, 300–15. See also Patricia E. Chu, *Race, Nationalism, and*

the State in British and American Modernism (Cambridge, UK: Cambridge University Press, 2006). See also Deborah E. McDowell, ' "It's Not Safe, Not Safe at All": Sexuality in Nella Larson's *Passing*', *Lesbian and Gay Studies Reader*, edited by Henry Abelove, Michèle Aina Barale, and David M. Halperin (New York and London: Routledge, 1993), 616–25.

23. Quoted in Hofmeyr, 226–7.
24. Radclyffe Hall, *The Well of Loneliness* (New York: Doubleday & Co., 1981), 437.
25. Bunyan, 41.
26. Walton, 298.
27. See, for example, the following moments in Hall: 'She would think with a kind of despair: "What am I in God's name – some kind of abomination? ... Why am I as I am – and what am I?" ' (152) and 'I don't know what I am ...' (201).
28. Ibid., 79.
29. Ibid., 13.
30. Ibid., 61.
31. Ibid., 11.
32. Ibid., 15.
33. Ibid., 200.
34. Ibid., 83.
35. Ibid., 79.
36. Ibid., 177.
37. Ibid., 152.
38. Bunyan, 39.
39. Dayton Haskin, 'The Burden of Interpretation in *The Pilgrim's Progress*', *Studies in Philology* 79.3 (Summer 1982): 256–78.
40. Hall, 204.
41. Ibid.
42. Ibid., 204–5.
43. Ibid, 205.
44. Ibid.
45. Ibid., 246.
46. – So much so that when she falls in love with Mary, a woman deeply devoted to her, Stephen determines that she must give her up: Mary needs to be with someone who unquestionably fits into a man's social progress narrative; someone, too, who, through marriage, can reinforce or reaffirm Mary's own location with a narrative for female progress in which her sexuality is both spiritually and socially sanctioned.
47. Hall, 52.
48. See Quentin Bailey, 'Heroes and Homosexuals: Education and Empire in E. M. Forster', *Twentieth-Century Literature* 48.3 (Fall 2002): 324–47. Quentin Bailey makes a similar argument regarding the importance of work for Maurice in the novel bearing his name: 'Is it purely coincidental that homosexuality was held to be the consequence of tardiness, rudeness, (foreign) nationalism, and effeminacy? And that these qualities were often ascribed to nonwhite or lower-class members of the British Empire (that is, those designated as inferior by the master code)? By focusing on hard work, a privileged mode of existence in the imperial

realm, Maurice hopes to overcome his surprisingly "native" predilections' (337).

49. See Chu, 145, 147; Deborah McDowell, 619; and G. F. Mitrano, *Gertrude Stein: Woman without Qualities* (Aldershot, UK: Ashgate, 2005), 122. See also Marianna Torgovnick, *Gone Primitive: Savage Intellect, Modern Lives* (Chicago: University of Chicago Press, 1991), 8. Torgovnick sees primitivism as 'fundamental to the Western sense of self and the Other'. Also see Simon Gikandi 'Africa and the Epiphany of Modernism', in *Geomodernisms: Race, Modernism, Modernity*, edited by Laura Doyle and Laura Winkiel (Bloomington and Indianapolis: Indiana University Press, 2005), 31–50; and Laura Winkiel, 'Caberet Modernism: Vorticism and Racial Spectacle', in Doyle and Winkiel, 2005, 206–24.

50. James F. Knapp, 'Primitivism and Empire: John Synge and Paul Gauguin', *Comparative Literature* 41.1 (Winter 1989): 53–68, 67.

51. Mary Gluck, 'Interpreting Primitivism, Mass Culture and Modernism: The Making of Wilhelm Worringer's Abstraction and Empathy', *New German Critique: An Interdisciplinary Journal of German Studies* 80 (Spring–Summer 2000): 149–69, 150.

52. Ibid., 152.

53. Chinn, 300.

54. Gikandi, 33. He argues that within modernism the role of the African American 'as an American ... is endowed with the value of a primitivism that is more consumable [than the role of the African] because of its Western familiarity' (33–4). Gertrude Stein's 'Melanctha' (1909), which reworks the constellation of characters in *Q.E.D.* (1903), offers an early example of a Modernist refiguration of same-sex desire in terms of race.

55. Walton, 288.

56. Hall, 362.

57. Walton, 286.

58. Ibid., 289. For a broader discussion of this dynamic of appropriation, see Patricia E. Chu, particularly the following: 'modernist primitivists construct "natives"/ nationalists as enviable for their "fortunate" *political* position: able to see and thus actively fight subjection by the state.... The primitivism I describe involves envy of an imagined ability to rebel projected onto a racial other. Primitivists were not necessarily anti-imperialists. To understand primitivism as grounded in imperial governance rather than psycho-sexual repression is to recognize one of the ways in which modernists engaged with state formations as they constructed their definitions of modernity and of themselves as "revolutionary" subjects of modernity' (147).

59. Hofmeyr, 226–7.

60. Havelock Ellis, introductory commentary, Hall.

61. See Stepan and Gilman: 'Only the trained scientist, it was claimed, was able to speak coherently and legitimately about scientific matters' (80).

62. See Somerville, 1994, 246: In her discussion of the general preface to volume one of Ellis's *Studies in the Psychology of Sex*, Somerville observes that for Ellis, 'a discourse of race – however elusively – somehow hovered around or within the study of sexuality'.

63. Margot Gayle Backus, 'Sexual Orientation in the (Post) Imperial Nation: Celticism and Inversion Theory in Radclyffe Hall's *The Well of Loneliness*', *Tulsa Studies in Women's Literature* 15.2 (Autumn, 1996): 253–66, 256.
64. Ibid.
65. Ibid., 255.
66. Ibid., 257.
67. Hall, 314.
68. Backus, 257.
69. Hall, 437.
70. Backus, 259.
71. Ibid.
72. Ibid.
73. Some of the novels that come to mind are Rita Mae Brown's *Ruby Fruit Jungle*, Leslie Feinberg's *Stone Butch Blues*, Sarah Waters' *Tipping the Velvet*, Dorothy Allison's *Bastard Out of Carolina*, and Ann-Marie MacDonald's *The Way the Crow Flies*.
74. See Chu, 111, for an explication of this distinction. See also Azar Nafisi, *Reading Lolita in Tehran* (New York: Random House, 2003), 307. Within the earlier understanding of marriage as contract, Nafisi's observations of nineteenth-century novels, Jane Austen's especially, disclose the ways in which heroines, while still adhering to the marriage plot, could claim an agency unavailable to the modernist invert Stephen: 'They put at the center of our attention … not the importance of marriage but the importance of heart and understanding in marriage; not the primacy of conventions but the breaking of conventions.'
75. Chu, 111.
76. Hall, 436.
77. Backus, 262.
78. Walton, 296.
79. Ibid., 296–7.
80. For annunciatory readings see Ed Madden, '*The Well of Loneliness* or the Gospel According to Radclyffe Hall', *Journal of Homosexuality* 33.3–4 (1997):163–86; and my own article 'Narrative Inversion: The Biblical Heritage of *The Well of Loneliness* and *Desert of the Heart*', *Journal of Homosexuality* 33.3–4 (1997): 187–206.
81. Walton, 297.
82. Hall, 437.
83. Ibid.
84. Hall, 437.
85. Backus, 261.
86. See Walton, 298.
87. While Thomas A. Luxon has made the point that the metaphor of 'the well' conveys a sense of hope not present in 'slough', it is worth noting that Beresford Eagon lampooned the novel in his 1928 cartoon titled 'The Sink of Solitude', a title, of course, that itself suggests that Hall's contemporary readers received the title negatively. (Luxon made this point after I had presented an abbreviated version of this chapter section at The Fifth Triennial International John Bunyan Society Conference, 15–19 August 2007, Dartmouth College, Hanover, New Hampshire, USA.)

88. Jane Rule, 'Radclyffe Hall', *Lesbian Images* (New York: Doubleday, 1975), 52–64, 52, 62, 64.

89. See Jane Rule, *Desert of the Heart* (London: Pandora, 1986), 52.

90. Catharine Stimpson, 'Zero Degree Deviancy: The Lesbian Novels in English', *Critical Inquiry* 8.2 (Winter, 1981): 363–79, 364.

91. Patricia Highsmith's *The Price of Salt* is another and certainly the most well known. Importantly, 1970, that is, the beginnings of the Women's Movement and the gay liberation movement inaugurated by the Stonewall Riots, and, more broadly, the intersection of those struggles with other social justice movements, such as the Civil Rights and Peace Movements, mark a shift in lesbian fiction: positive, affirming stories begin to appear regularly. Perhaps the best example is Rita Mae Brown's *Ruby Fruit Jungle*. For further discussion of lesbian pulp fiction with positive endings, see Katherine V. Forrest, 'Introduction', in *Lesbian Pulp Fiction: The Sexually Intrepid World of Lesbian Paperback Novels 1950–1965*, edited by Katherine V. Forrest (San Francisco: Cleis Press, 2005), ix–xix.

92. See Marilyn R. Schuster, *Passionate Communities: Reading Lesbian Resistance in Jane Rule's Fiction* (New York and London: New York University Press, 1999), 141.

93. For a discussion of lesbian plots, see, in addition to Schuster, Bonnie Zimmerman, *The Safe Sea of Women: Lesbian Fiction 1969–1989* (Boston: Beacon Press, 1990).

94. Jane Rule, 'On a Moral Education', in *A Hot-Eyed Moderate* by Jane Rule (Tallahassee, Fl: The Naiad Press, 1985), 136–42, 137.

95. Quoted in Schuster, 145.

96. Volker Bischoff discusses Auden's explorations of the tension between the aesthetic and social value of poetry, particularly with regard to the elegy to Yeats. Bischoff concludes that Auden, in contrast with, say, T. S. Eliot, believes in the moral and social responsibility of the poet. That responsibility, Bischoff argues, is at the centre of 'In Memory of W. B. Yeats'. In this the poem departs from the traditional pastoral elegy, which seeks to resolve the desire for immortality with the recognition of mortality. See Volker Bischoff, 'Der Dichter in der Gesellschaft: Audens "In Memory of W. B. Yeats" und seine Yeats-Aufsätze', in *Literaratur als Kritik des Lebens: Festschrift zum 65. Geburtstag von Ludwig Borinski*, edited by Ludwig Borinski, Rudolf Haas, et al. (Heidelberg: Quelle und Meyer, 1975), 264–78.

97. Edward Mendelson, *Later Auden* (New York: Farrar, Straus, and Giroux, 1999), 13.

98. Jaye Zimet, *Strange Sisters: The Art of Lesbian Pulp, 1949–1969* (New York: Viking Studio/Penguin Studio, 1999), 18.

99. Susan Stryker, *Queer Pulp: Perverted Passions from the Golden Age of the Paperback* (San Francisco: Chronicle Books, 2001), 11.

100. Betty Friedan, *The Feminine Mystique* (New York and London: W. W. Norton & Co., 1983 (1963)), 18.

101. Jane Rule, 'Lesbian and Writer', in Rule, 1985, 42–6, 44.

102. US Senate, 'Employment of Homosexuals and Other Sex Perverts in the US Government' (1950), *We Are Everywhere: A Historical Sourcebook of Gay and Lesbian Politics*, edited by Mark Blasius and Shane Phelan (New York: Routledge, 1997), 241–51, 243.

103. Audre Lorde, *Zami: A New Spelling of My Name* (Freedom, CA: The Crossing Press, 1982), 149.
104. Suzanna Danuta Walters, 'As Her Hand Crept Slowly Up Her Thigh: Ann Bannon and the Politics of Pulp', *Social Text* 23 (Autumn–Winter, 1989): 83–101, 85.
105. Stryker, 2001, 51.
106. Ibid., 2001, 52.
107. Ibid., 2001, 51.
108. Zimet, 20.
109. Ibid.
110. Walters, 84.
111. Ann Bannon, 'Introduction: The Beebo Brinker Chronicles' (2001), in *Odd Girl Out* (1957) by Ann Bannon (San Francisco: Cleis Press, 2001), v–xviii, viii.
112. Ann Bannon, 'Introduction' (2001), in *I am a Woman* (1959) by Ann Bannon (San Francisco: Cleis Press, 2002), v–xiv, ix.
113. Ann Bannon, 'Afterword' (2002), in *Women in the Shadows* (1959) by Ann Bannon (San Francisco: Cleis Press, 2002), 197–202, 200–1. See also Christopher Nealon, *Foundlings: Lesbian and Gay Historical Emotion Before Stonewall* (Durham, NC: Duke University Press, 2001), whom Bannon is paraphrasing here.
114. For a discussion of McCarthyism, see Schuster, 52–3.
115. See Schuster, especially 58: 'Many women who loved women in the 1950s and 1960s were unaware of a burgeoning lesbian subculture; isolation – because of geography or class or circumstance – kept them from any knowledge at all about lesbian possibilities. Barbara Gittings's story illustrates that one means for women to break their isolation and understand that their feelings were neither unique nor crazy was fiction; stories provided narrative form and coherence that available social scripts denied.'
116. Zimet, 21.
117. While, as Ruth Vanita points out, this trope of lesbian likeness has a well established history, it is important to recognize that Bannon's offers an immediate precedent for Rule. See Ruth Vanita, *Sappho and the Virgin Mary: Same-Sex Love and the English Literary Imagination* (New York: Columbia University Press, 1991), 100.
118. Bannon (1957), 2001, 212.
119. Rule, 1986, 244.
120. Interestingly, Donna Deitch's lesbian film *Desert of the Heart* (1986), loosely based on Rule's novel, draws further attention to the similarities between *Odd Girl Out* and *Desert of the Heart*. The ending, in which the lovers board a train together more nearly recalls Bannon's novel.
121. Schuster, 139.
122. Rule, 1986, 1.
123. Hall, 188.
124. Adrienne Rich, 'A Valediction Forbidding Mourning', in *A Will to Change* by Adrienne Rich (New York: W. W. Norton, 1971), 50. For a discussion of this poem, see Carol Bere, 'A Reading of Adrienne Rich's "A Valediction Forbidding Mourning"', *Concerning Poetry* 11.2 (1978): 33–8. Bere writes, '... it is not with the person but with the crippling, traditional

structure of marriage that Rich does battle. Her writing reflects a growing conviction that marriage constrains the creative energies of women while also revealing a sympathetic acknowledgement that both partners are caught ...' (34).

125. Portions of the following analysis of *Desert of the Heart* appeared in my essays 'Narrative Inversion: The Biblical Heritage of *The Well of Loneliness* and *Desert of the Heart*' (see note 80), and in '*Desert of the Heart*: Jane Rule's Puritan Outing', in *The Puritan Origins of American Sex: Religion, Sexuality, and National Identity in American Literature*, edited by Tracy Fessenden, Nicholas F. Radel, and Magdalena J. Zaborowska (New York and London: Routledge, 2001), 235–52.

126. Rule, 1986, 84.

127. Ibid., 195–6.

128. Ibid., 145.

129. Ibid., 112.

130. Ibid., 145.

131. Ibid., 200–1.

132. Bunyan, 345.

133. Ibid.

134. Rule, 1986, 27.

135. Ibid.

136. Ibid.

137. Ibid., 148.

138. Geoffrey Hancock, 'An Interview with Jane Rule', *Canadian Fiction Magazine* 23 (August 1976): 57–112, 98.

139. Rule, 1986, 183.

140. Ibid., 118.

141. Ibid., 120.

142. Bunyan, 39.

143. Rule, 1986, 223–4.

144. Ibid., 244.

145. Jane Rule, 'Morality in Literature', Rule, 1985, 37–41, 41.

146. Bunyan, 41.

147. E. M. Forster, *Maurice* (New York and London: W. W. Norton & Co., 1971), 165. At the end of chapter 33, Forster's narrator describes how in their marriage Clive and Anne are 'received' by 'beautiful conventions'. Forster wrote the novel between 1913 and 1914, but it was not published until after his death.

148. Rule, 1986, 244.

149. For a fascinating discussion of the novel's widespread acclaim across very different audiences, see Hilary Hinds, '*Oranges Are Not the Only Fruit*: Reaching Audiences Other Lesbian Texts Cannot Reach', in *Immortal, Invisible: Lesbians and the Moving Image*, edited by Tamsin Wilton (London and New York: Routledge, 1995), 52–69.

150. Anita Gnagnatti, 'Discarding God's Handbook: Winterson's *Oranges Are Not the Only Fruit* and the Tension of Intertextuality', in *Biblical Religion and the Novel, 1700–2000*, edited by Mark Knight and Thomas M. Woodman (Aldershot, UK: Ashgate, 2006), 121–36, 123. See also Marisol Morales Ladrón, 'Jeanette Winterson's *Oranges Are Not the Only Fruit*: A

Lesbian *Bildungsroman*', in *(Trans)Formaciones de las sexualidades y el género*, edited by Mercedes Begoechea and Marisol Morales (Alcalá de Henares, Spain: Universidad de Alcalá, 2001),167–85, 169. She writes, 'Framed in the realm of fantasy, the distinct lesbian identity "normalises" in the text forsaking its alleged "deviation" of the norm and exemplifying one of the premises of postmodern thought: that gender, reality and fiction are artificial categories which ultimately belong to the realm of language and hence stand as constructions which need to be deconstructed and contextualised.'

151. Mark Wormald, 'Prior Knowledge: Sarah Waters and the Victorians', in *British Fiction Today*, edited by Philip Tew and Rod Mengham (London and New York: 2006), 186–97, 187.

152. In a co-authored essay, Laura Doan and Sarah Waters posit that for lesbians the 'relevance of historical fiction ... may lie most fully in its capacity for illuminating the queer identities and acts against which modern lesbian narratives have defined themselves and which they perhaps continue to occlude.' See Laura Doan and Sarah Waters, 'Making Up Lost Time: Contemporary Lesbian Writing and the Invention of History', in *Territories of Desire in Queer Culture: Refiguring Contemporary Debates*, edited by David Alderson and Linda R. Anderson (Manchester, UK and New York: Manchester University Press, 2001), 12–28, 25.

153. For a discussion of *Tipping the Velvet* as both a progress and a picaresque novel 'concerned with community and care', see Emily Jeremiah, 'The "I" inside "her": Queer Narration in Sarah Waters's *Tipping the Velvet* and Wesley Stace's "Misfortune" ', *Women: A Cultural Review*, 18.2 (2007): 131–44, 132.

2. Love in the Shadows: The Same-Sex Marriage Debate and Beyond

1. See Jay Fliegelman, *Prodigals and Pilgrims: The American Revolution against Patriarchal Authority* (Cambridge, UK and New York: Cambridge University Press, 1982), particularly Chapter 5, 'Affectionate Unions and the New Voluntarism'.

2. E. J. Graff, *What is Marriage For? The Strange Social History of Our Most Intimate Institution* (Boston: Beacon Press, 1999), 250, emphasis in original.

3. George Chauncey, *Why Marriage? The History Shaping Today's Debate Over Gay Equality* (New York: Basic Books, 2004), 71.

4. Zimet, 18.

5. Bannon (2001), in Bannon, 2001, xi–xii.

6. Such resistance is a feature not solely of lesbian pulp but more broadly of women's writing. One thinks, for example, of Charlotte Brontë's *Villette*.

7. Chauncey, 2004, 9–11.

8. Stimpson, 364, quoted in Walters, 87.

9. Walters, 87.

10. Bannon (2001), in Bannon, 2001, viii.

11. Walters, 88.

12. Diane Hamer, ' "I am a Woman": Ann Bannon and the Writing of Lesbian Identity in the 1950s', in *Lesbian and Gay Writing: An Anthology of Critical*

Essays, edited by Mark Lilly (Philadelphia: Temple University Press, 1990), 47–75, 69.

13. In Colton's novel, a sympathetic doctor explains protagonist Randy Hale's homosexuality to his wife and so enables the two to continue their marriage. Smith novel's representation of 'strange marriage' is more closely related to Bannon's: in both, the 'strange marriage' is between a lesbian and a gay man. For further reading on lesbian fiction, see Forrest, ix–xix, Stryker, 2001, and Zimet, footnote 4.
14. Bannon (1959), 2002, 16.
15. Ibid., 19.
16. Ibid., 1.
17. Ibid.
18. Ibid., 9.
19. Ibid., 27.
20. Walters, 98.
21. Bannon (1959), 2002, 114, emphasis in original.
22. Ibid., 37.
23. Ibid., 116.
24. Ibid., 119.
25. Ibid., 124.
26. Ibid., 190.
27. Ibid., 93.
28. Walters, 95.
29. For a compelling discussion of Laura's, as well as Beebo's, dysphoria, see Nealon, particularly Chapter 4, 'The Ambivalence of Lesbian Pulp Fiction', 141–75.
30. Ibid., 163.
31. Bannon (1959), 2002, 57.
32. Ibid., 54.
33. Ibid., 56.
34. Ibid., 195.
35. See, for example, Frederick S. Roden, *Same-Sex Desire in Victorian Religious Culture* (Basingstoke, UK and New York: Palgrave – now Palgrave Macmillan, 2002), 194–99. Roden offers a fascinating discussion of Whym Chow, the beloved dog of the Victorian poets and lesbian couple Katherine Bradley and Edith Cooper, who wrote under the penname Michael Field.
36. Amber L. Hollibaugh, *My Dangerous Desires: A Queer Girl Dreaming Her Way Back Home* (Durham, NC and London: Duke University Press, 2000).
37. Bannon (1959), 2002, 66.
38. Ibid., 36.
39. Ibid., 163.
40. Walters, 98.
41. Chauncey, 2004, 25.
42. Bannon (1959), 2002, 115.
43. See George Chauncey, *Gay New York: Gender, Urban Culture, and the Making of the Gay Male World, 1890–1940* (New York: Basic Books, 1994), 227–44.
44. Bannon (1959), 2002, 115.
45. Ibid., 184.
46. Ibid., 193, 194.

47. Bannon (2002), in Bannon, (1959), 2002, 200.
48. Bannon (1959), 2002, 30.
49. Ibid., 69.
50. Ibid., 174.
51. Ibid.
52. Ibid., 108.
53. Nealon, 165.
54. Bannon (1959), 2002, 46.
55. Ibid., 102–3.
56. Ibid., 103.
57. Lorde, 179.
58. Bannon (2002), in Bannon (1959), 2002, 199–200.
59. Bannon (1959), 2002, 174.
60. Siobhan Somerville, *Queering the Color Line: Race and the Invention of Homosexuality in American Culture* (Durham, NC and London: Duke University Press, 2000), 84. An important point of literary comparison here is with Nella Larson's *Passing*.
61. Ibid.
62. Bannon, 1959, 2002, 106.
63. See Mary Dearborn, *Pocohontas's Daughters: Gender and Ethnicity in American Culture* (New York: Oxford University Press, 1986), 139–40, quoted in Somerville, 2000, 84. For an extended discussion of the tragic mulatta figure, see Chapter 3 (77–110) of Somerville's book.
64. Bannon, 1959, 2002, 45.
65. Chauncey, 2004, 95.
66. Ibid., 42–3.
67. Ibid., 96.
68. Ibid., 97.
69. Evan Wolfson, *Why Marriage Matters: America, Equality, and Gay People's Right to Marry* (New York: Simon & Schuster, 2004), 7.
70. Chauncey, 2004, 108.
71. Ibid.
72. Dorothy Allison, 'Mama and Mom and Dad and Son', in *This is What Lesbian Looks Like*, edited by Kris Kleindienst (Ithaca, NY: Firebrand, 1999), 16–23, 20.
73. Ibid.
74. Ibid., 22.
75. Andrew Sullivan, *Virtually Normal: An Argument About Homosexuality* (New York: Alfred A. Knopf, 1995), 182, emphasis added.
76. Chauncey, 2004, 71.
77. Judith Stacey, *In the Name of the Family: Rethinking Family Values in the Postmodern Age* (Boston: Beacon Press, 1996), 80.
78. Mattie Richardson, 'What You See is What You Get: Building a Movement Toward Liberation in the Twenty-First Century', in Kleindienst, 210–19, 217.
79. For discussions of the policies of marriage promotion, see Legal Momentum, Marriage and Welfare (a), 'Marriage Promotion: What the Administration is Already Doing', www.legalmomentum.org/issues/wel/marriagepromotion.shtml, date accessed 20 April 2006 and Legal Momentum, Marriage and Welfare (b), 'Why NOW Legal Defense Opposes Federal Marriage Promotion

in TANF Reauthorization', www.legalmomentum.org/issues/wel/ marriage-promotion.shtml, date accessed 20 April 2006.

80. See Diana M. Zuckerman, 'The Evolution of Welfare Reform: Policy Changes and Current Knowledge', *Journal of Social Issues*, 56.4 (December 2000): 811–20, 817. Zuckerman, President and Director of the National Center for Policy Research for Women and Families, points out that the welfare reforms passed during the Clinton administration have had an adverse effect on women and children, as well as on legal immigrants. Citing the findings of the Children's Defense Fund (CDF), Zuckerman notes, 'larger families that leave welfare struggle more, because welfare benefits were more generous for families with more children; in contrast, employers do not offer larger salaries to workers with more children. Although these "larger" families average only 3.5 children, many single mothers are unable to earn salaries large enough to make up for the loss of slightly larger welfare benefits.' One can understand, then, how, beginning in the mid 1990s, welfare reformers would meet the problem facing single mothers by advocating a reconfiguration of family, whereby there would be two rather than one income earner. The Bush marriage programs are, in other words, an outgrowth of the reforms enacted during Clinton's years in office.

81. Jennifer Levin, 'Beebo Lives', *The Harvard Gay and Lesbian Review* 2.2 (Spring 1995), 1, 53–4, 54, emphasis in original.

82. Michael Warner, *The Trouble with Normal: Sex, Politics, and the Ethics of Queer Life* (New York: The Free Press, 1999), 82, emphasis in original.

83. John D'Emilio, 'Capitalism and Gay Identity', in *Powers of Desire: The Politics of Sexuality*, edited by Ann Snitow, Christine Stansell, and Sharan Thompson (New York: Monthly Review Press, 1983), 100–13.

84. Jane Rule, 'The Heterosexual Cage of Coupledom', *BC Bookworld*, Spring 2001. Reprinted in Rick Bebout, 'Lives of Our Own Invention', http://www.rbebout.com/getfree/jane.htm, date accessed 22 December 2007.

85. Wolfson, 7.

86. One needs, for example, to consider how marriage debates depend on a notion of two sexes and in turn give way to two complementary genders. Thus, people who are transgendered, transsexual, or intersexual necessarily haunt the discourse of same-sex marriage debates. See Anne Fausto-Sterling, *Sexing the Body: Gender Politics and the Construction of Sexuality* (New York: Basic Books, 2000), 107 and 112.

87. See Warner, 1999. See, too, Gayle Rubin, 'Thinking Sex: Notes for a Radical Theory of the Politics of Sexuality', in *Pleasure and Danger: Exploring Female Sexuality*, edited by Carole S. Vance (Boston: Routledge, Kegan, and Paul, 1984), 267–319.

88. Douglas Crimp, 'Melancholia and Moralism', in *Loss: The Politics of Mourning*, edited by David L. Eng and David Kazanjian (Berkeley: University of California Press), 2003, 188–202, 199.

89. Sullivan, 199.

90. Butler, *Undoing Gender* (New York and London: Routledge, 2004), 26–7.

91. United States Conference of Catholic Bishops, 'Between Man and Woman: Questions and Answers About Marriage and Same-Sex Unions', *United States Conference of Catholic Bishops*, 12 November 2003, http://www.usccb.org/laity/manandwoman.htm, date accessed 3 February 2004.

92. George Bush, 'President's State of the Union Message to Congress and the Nation', *New York Times*, 21 January 2004, sec. A, 14–15.
93. Ibid., sec. A, 15.
94. Mab Segrest, 'Hawai'ian Sovereignty/Gay Marriage: *Ka Huliau*', in Kleindienst, 231–41, 240, emphasis in original.
95. Segrest, 235.
96. Wolfson, 178. Wolfson is careful to draw distinctions between the Civil Rights struggle and the movement for gay and lesbian equality. He writes, 'Let us note, however, that the comparison to Rosa Parks is not a perfect fit. This is not just because the violence and exclusion African-Americans confronted in Montgomery, Alabama, in the 1950s were so massive. Although the lives of human rights pioneers such as Phyllis and Del have ample resonance with the example of Rosa Parks, the decisions made by Mayor Newsom and the elected officials and clerks around the country to issue marriage licenses to committed same-sex couples is not, in my view, best understood as civil disobedience, a venerable and valid form of activism. Rather, it is constitutional *obedience* – these officials are following, not flouting the law. By issuing licenses without discrimination, they are doing what the law permits and the Constitution requires. And far from refusing to obey an unjust law, they are submitting the question to the courts, who will decide, as the courts should, whether there is sufficient reason to continue the exclusion of same-sex couples or, rather, whether constitutional guarantees of equality under the law mean that marriage discrimination must end. (Wolfson, 170–1)
97. Some 20,000 same-sex marriages had been performed over the six months when they were recognized; their status remains unclear. The ACLU, Lambda Legal, and the National Center for Lesbian Rights (NCLRights) have filed a petition with the California Supreme Court to invalidate Proposition 8. According to a November 5, 2008 press release from the NCLRights, 'The petition charges that Proposition 8 is invalid because the initiative process was improperly used in an attempt to undo the constitution's core commitment to equality for everyone by eliminating a fundamental right from just one group – lesbian and gay Californians. Proposition 8 also improperly attempts to prevent the courts from exercising their essential constitutional role of protecting the equal protection rights of minorities.' See the press release NCL, 'Legal Groups File Lawsuit Challenging Proposition 8, Should It Pass', 5 November 2008, www.nclrights.org, accessed 24 November 2008.
98. Wolfson, 138, emphasis in original.
99. GLAD, 'A Brief Q&A for Couples About Marriage for Same-Sex Couples in Connecticut', 14 October 2008, www.glad.org, 5, date accessed 14 November, 2008.
100. Ibid., 4.
101. The full list of authors is as follows: Katherine Acey, Terry Boggis, Debanuj Dasgupta, Joseph N. DeFilippis, Lisa Duggan, Kenyon Farrow, Ellen Gurzinsky, Amber Hollibaugh, Loraine Hutchins, Surina Khan, Richard Kim, Kerry Lobel, Alice M. Miller, JD, Ana Oliviera, Cori Schmanke Parrish, Suzanne Pharr, Nancy Polikoff, Achebe Betty Powell, Ignacio Rivera, Kendall Thomas, Kay Whitlock, and Beth Zemsky. 'Beyond Same-Sex Marriage: A New Strategic Vision for All Our Families and Relationships', which I accessed on

26 April 2008 at beyondmarriage.org, is no longer available at that site. It is available at mrzine.monthlyreview.org/beyondmarriage080806.html. *Studies in Gender and Sexuality* 9.2 (April 2008): 158–60 includes a copy of the executive statement.

102. Ibid., 1.
103. For an extensive list, see ibid., 2.
104. Ibid., 4, emphasis added.
105. Bannon (1959), 2002, 186.

3.   Reading for Fantasy in 'Rip Van Winkle' and *The Farewell Symphony*

1. Gayle Rubin, in Hollibaugh, 146.
2. Dorothy Allison, in Dorothy Allison et al., 'On Contemporary Lesbian Literature in the United States: A Symposium with Dorothy Allison, Blanche McCrary Boyd, Nicole Breedlove, Melanie Kaye/Kantrowitz, and B. Ruby Rich', in *Queer Representations: Reading Lives, Reading Cultures*, edited by Martin Duberman (New York and London: New York University Press, 1997), 356–61, 360.
3. Butler, 2004, 27.
4. Thomas Piontek, *Queering Gay and Lesbian Studies* (Urbana and Chicago: University of Illinois Press, 2006), 82–3.
5. David Leavitt, 'Out of the Closet and Off the Shelf', *The New York Times Book Review*, 17 July 2005, 7–8, 7.
6. Ibid., 8. Borders is a chain bookstore – superstore – in the US, as well as in Australia, New Zealand, and Singapore.
7. – And my students are pro-choice. (It is interesting and significant, I think, that pro-choice is readily used in such contexts as these, and that the earlier pro-choice usage has morphed into pro-abortion.)
8. Alexandra Jacobs, 'A Feminist Classic Gets a Makeover', *The New York Times Book Review*, 17 July 2005, 27.
9. This is to name just some of the overlapping categories of people affected.
10. Dorothy Allison, 'Puritans, Perverts, and Feminists', 93–100, in *Skin: Talking About Sex, Class, and Literature* (Ithaca, NY: Firebrand, 1994), 95.
11. So-called 'lesbian' sex scenes within straight pornography are often read in terms of male desire to dominate and objectify the women he watches. Their sex or, again, sexuality gains validity and meaning through his gaze. I, in turn, would like to propose another, potentially simultaneous possibility: that the girl-on-girl sex act is a standard feature of straight pornography narratives might well speak to the reading practices of straight men. That is, much as gay men and lesbians can read themselves into straight plots, I am suggesting that straight men might very well fantasize about themselves as lesbians.
12. Betrayal is a vexed issue, particularly, I find, among feminists and lesbians. See Hollibaugh, 157. Hollibaugh contrasts gay male culture with lesbian culture (broadly defined): 'The concept of betrayal usually is based on very different kinds of ideological assumptions, and a partner being sexual with someone else is not an assumption of betrayal or lack of commitment.'

13. For engaging discussions of these issues, see Carol Queen and Lawrence Schimel, eds, *Pomosexuals: Challenging Assumptions about Gender and Sexuality* (San Francisco: Cleis Press, 1997). See especially the essay 'The Personals' by David Harrison, 129–137.
14. Mari Ruti, 'From Melancholia to Meaning: How to Live the Past in the Present', *Psychoanalytic Dialogues* 15.5 (2005): 637–60, 645.
15. Gayle Salamon, 'Melancholia, Ambivalent Presence and the Cost of Gender Commentary on Paper by Meg Jay', *Studies in Gender and Sexuality* 8.2 (Spring 2007): 149–64, 152. Salamon is herself drawing on the work of David L. Eng and David Kazanjian, 'Introduction: Mourning Remains', in *Loss: The Politics of Mourning*, edited by David L. Eng and David Kazanjian, 1–28 (Berkeley: University of California Press, 2003). Eng and Kazanjian write, 'As both a formal relation and a structure of feeling, a mechanism of disavowal and a constellation of affect, melancholia offers a capaciousness of meaning in relation to losses encompassing the individual and the collective, the spiritual and the material, the psychic and the social, the aesthetic and the political' (3).
16. It is important to note here that Irving wrote 'Rip Van Winkle' while living in England. The story itself is based on a German folktale. These conditions of composition prove crucial for readers to consider: Irving was fashioning a distinctly American tale, when his definition of Americanness relied at least in part on European social and literary contexts. For discussions of Irving's departures from his source text, see, for example, Steven Blakemore, 'Family Resemblances: The Texts and Contexts of "Rip Van Winkle"', *Early American Literature* 35 (2000), 187–212, 208, footnote 8 and Michael Warner, 'Irving's Posterity', *ELH* 67 (2000): 773–99, 787.
17. See, for example, Leslie Fiedler, *Love and Death in the American Novel* (New York: Criterion, 1960), xx–xxi: 'Ever since ["Rip Van Winkle"], the typical male protagonist of our fiction has been a man on the run, harried into the forest and out to sea, down the river or into combat – anywhere to avoid "civilization", which is to say, the confrontation of a man and woman which leads to the fall to sex, marriage, and responsibility' (quoted in Michael Warner, 2000, 785).
18. Bryce Traister, 'The Wandering Bachelor: Irving, Masculinity, and Authorship', *American Literature* 74.1 (March 2002): 111–37, 112.
19. Robert Burton, epigraph for *The Sketch Book of Geoffrey Crayon, Gent.*, in Washington Irving, *The Legend of Sleepy Hollow and Other Stories [The Sketch Book of Geoffrey Crayon, Gent.]* (New York: Penguin, 1988).
20. I say partial because Burton is wonderfully verbose.
21. Warner, 2000, 773.
22. Ibid., 785. Warner continues, 'Literary reproduction is, for Irving, the ultimate form of surrogacy: a mode of cultural reproduction in which bachelors are, at last, fully at home' (792).
23. Ruti, 644.
24. Ibid., 639. Ruti is drawing on Freud's 1917 work 'Mourning and Melancholia', *Standard Edition*, 14: 243–58 (London: Hogarth Press, 1955).
25. Andrew Burstein, *The Original Knickerbocker: The Life of Washington Irving* (New York: Basic Books, 2007), 128.
26. Washington Irving, 'Rip Van Winkle' (1819–1820), in Irving, 28–42, 30.
27. Ibid., 29.

28. Ibid., 30.
29. Ibid.
30. There is a whole history on the use/uselessness trope. One thinks of Shakespeare's sonnets and Wilde's response in the preface to *The Picture of Dorian Grey*. Basically, though, what I am saying here is that queer fantasies do not allow one readily to figure desire in terms of this trope. Further, if people's oppression turns in part on the eradication of the signs of their labor – or on the erasure of any signs of value of that labor, one might begin also to understand how the absence or redirection of the productivity trope has widespread cultural resonance.
31. Irving, 29, emphasis added. Other meanings of 'vapours' seem also to be at work here. In addition to 'mists' and 'melancholy', the OED suggests that 'vapours' may signal 'something unsubstantial or worthless', or again, 'a fancy or fantastic idea'.
32. Irving, 32.
33. Ibid., 30.
34. Butler, 2004, 28–9.
35. Ruti, 645.
36. Irving, 32, emphasis added.
37. Ruti, 645.
38. See John K. Howat, *The Hudson River and Its Painters* (New York: Viking Press, 1972), 174. Howat makes this connection between Cole's painting (alternately titled *Sunny Morning on the Hudson*) and Bryant's description of the Catskills. Because Howat's version of the Bryant passage is not quite correct, I quote directly from William Cullen Bryant, *The American Landscape, No. 1* (New York: E. Bliss, 1830), 9–10. Finally, Irving's description of the Catskills appears in the first paragraph of 'Rip Van Winkle'. See Irving, 29.
39. For a compelling discussion of Cole's landscape paintings and temporality, see Bernd Herzogenrath, 'Looking Forward/Looking Back: Thomas Cole and the Belated Construction of Nature', in *From Virgin Land to Disney World: Nature and Its Discontents in the USA of Yesterday and Today*, edited by Bernd Herzogenrath (Amsterdam: Rodopi, 2001), 83–103.
40. See Stephen Fender, 'American Landscape and the Figure of Anticipation: Paradox and Recourse', in *Views of American Landscapes*, edited by Mick Gigley and Robert Lawson-Peebles (Cambridge: Cambridge University Press, 1989), 51–63, 53–4. Fender offers a very different reading of Rip's relation to the landscape. Citing in particular 'The Author's Account of Himself', at the beginning of *The Sketch Book*, Fender argues that '... *The Sketch Book* never really escapes from under the cloud of anxiety that Americans might be radically cut off from whatever gives meaning to the ordinary events of their lives.' Consequently, for Fender, ' "Rip Van Winkle" ... is about a man who stands on the cusp precisely between "the sublime and beautiful of natural scenery", but who fails to make the association, falls into a stupor and awakes to a shoddy present-day America stripped of the icons of its inheritance.'
41. Irving, 34.
42. See Susan Sontag, 'Melancholy Objects', *On Photography* (New York: Farrar, Straus and Giroux, 1974), 49–82, 65–6, emphasis in original. Thank you to Mena Mitrano for this reference.

43. Irving, 34.
44. Butler, 2004, 29.
45. Ibid.
46. Judith Butler, *The Psychic Life of Power* (Stanford, CA: Stanford University Press, 1997), 140.
47. Ibid., 142. Psychologist Meg Jay summarizes criticisms levelled against Butler's work on melancholy gender. That work is seen as 'a product of the humanities', operating at a remove from 'lived experience', the importance of her work for gender studies remains undeniable, precisely because it invites consideration of the lived experiences of LGBTQ people. For Jay herself, the 'link that Butler makes between the loss of same-sex desire and a resulting gender identification is a stunning insight ... At the same time, the clinical application of the theory is somewhat limited by the language of melancholy gender and, I argue, by the vague use of the word foreclosure.' See Meg Jay, 'Melancholy Femininity and Obsessive-Compulsive Masculinity: Sex Differences in Melancholy Gender', *Studies in Gender and Sexuality* 8.2 (Spring 2007): 115–35, 117, 130. See also the earlier critique in Toril Moi, *What is a Woman?* (New York: Oxford University Press, 1999). For a compelling response to such criticisms, see Salamon.
48. Ruti, 642.
49. Traister, 120: 'Historical evidence remains insufficient to argue that Irving was himself homosexual. At the same time, his bachelor status and, indeed, the term *bachelor* itself, may well have functioned as suggestive cultural code, if not specifically for the antebellum inchoate gay male subject, then for an essential sexual vagueness whose very ambiguity reflected the "namelessness" of same-sex genital desires. At the very least, it is productive to read the bachelor as sexually ambiguous.'
50. Lauren Berlant, 'America, post-Utopia: Body, Landscape, and National Fantasy in Hawthorne's *Native Land*', *Arizona Quarterly* 44.4 (Winter 1989): 14–54, 26.
51. Ibid.
52. Compare this formulation as well to Ernest Renan's point: 'Forgetting ... is a crucial factor in the creation of a nation'. Ernest Renan, 'What is a Nation?' in *Nation and Narration*, edited by Homi K. Bhabha (London: Routledge, 1990), 8–22, 11, (quoted in Herzogenrath, 88).
53. Butler, 1997, 147.
54. Irving, 37.
55. Ibid., 40.
56. Ibid., 41.
57. Ibid.
58. For a different and fascinating approach to the relation between national and domestic politics in 'Rip Van Winkle', see Fliegelman, Chapter 5. Fliegelman notes that in revolutionary America, '[w]hether separation was a justifiable response to ... domestic tyranny was a question with great political ramifications' (123). As editor of *The Pennsylvania Magazine*, Thomas Paine regularly offered essays on marriage, politics, and linkages between the two. Fliegelman continues, 'The journal's featured contributor, "The Old Bachelor", believed all reasonable men would agree with him when he declared, "I had rather be a solitary bachelor than a miserable married

man"' (124). For Fliegelman, Rip van Winkle 'is a direct descendant of the plaintive persona of Tom Paine' (293, footnote 5).

59. Irving., 40.
60. Ibid.
61. Ibid.
62. Ibid., 41.
63. See Edmund White, 'The Personal is Political: Queer Fiction and Criticism', in *Queer Ideas: The David R. Kessler Lectures in Lesbian and Gay Studies*, edited by Martin Duberman (New York: The Feminist Press, 2003), 41–50, 48. White uses the phrase to characterize Jean Genet's novels.
64. Prime-Stevenson, 34, emphasis added.
65. Ann Pellegrini and Janet R. Jakobsen, 'Melancholy Hope and Other Psychic Remainders: Afterthoughts on *Love the Sin*', *Studies in Gender and Sexuality* 6.4 (Fall 2005): 423–44, 439.
66. Edmund White, *The Farewell Symphony* (New York: Vintage Books, 1997), 19.
67. Ruti, 660.
68. Eng and Kazanjian, 5.
69. Ibid., 649.
70. White, 1997, 4.
71. This is a common feature of lesbian and gay fiction. See especially Carolyn Allen, *Following Djuna: Women Lovers and the Erotics of Loss* (Bloomington and Indianapolis: Indiana University Press, 1996) and Terry Castle, *The Apparitional Lesbian: Female Homosexuality and Modern Culture* (New York: Columbia University Press, 1993).
72. Butler, 2004, 17–19.
73. In the final movement of the 'Farewell' Symphony, one by one the musicians stop playing, snuffing out the candles on their music stands. With this feature of Haydn's work acting as an objective correlative for decades of homophobic intolerance within the US, White's novel may be said to operate contrapuntally, illuminating each queer life overlooked, vilified, or prematurely extinguished.

    It is worth recalling here that White's title sustains the musical motif found in many works of gay literature, including E. M. Forster's *Maurice* and Edward Prime-Stevenson's *Imre*.
74. White, 1997, 365.
75. Larry Kramer, 'Sex and Sensibility', *The Advocate* 773 (27 May 1997): 59–70. Kramer rhetorically asks the following of White, with regard to his then forthcoming novel: 'Is it not incumbent, particularly in the time of a plague that has been spread by our own callous indifference to ending it, that those of us who are read and listened to perceive of ourselves as fuller human beings and capable of writing about far more than just what sex we had night after night for thirty years? It is impossible for me to believe that this book [*The Farewell Symphony*] represents to Edmund or that this is the kind of tribute he wishes to leave to all his dead friends and lovers or, indeed, that this is all that becoming our most esteemed and respected writer has meant to him. I found this book an irresponsible piece of work indeed.' See Douglas Crimp's response in Douglas Crimp, 'Melancholia and Moralism', in Eng and Kazanjian, 188–202.

76. David L. Eng and Shinhee Han, 'A Dialogue on Racial Melancholia', *Psychoanalytic Dialogues*, 10.4 (2000): 667–700, 695. See also David L. Eng, 'Melancholia in the Late Twentieth Century', *Signs: Journal of Women in Culture and Society* 25.4 (2000): 1275–81. Eng asks, 'Why is it that women, homosexuals, people of color, and postcolonials seem to be at greatest risk for melancholia and depression in contemporary society? How do we account for the fact that it is these minoritarian groups and not normative heterosexual male subjects who bear the greatest burden of unresolved grief?' (1278). He answers, 'As a psychic paradigm in which the lost object holds pride of place, melancholia's tenacious attachment to objects of loss convinces us, finally, of something we might otherwise doubt: our enduring attachment to (disparaged) others' (1280).

77. White, 1997, 340.

78. Ibid., 364.

79. Ibid., 92.

80. Butler, 2004, 29.

81. White, 1997, 116.

82. Pat Califia, 'Feminism and Sadomasochism' (1980), in *Public Sex: The Culture of Radical Sex* (San Francisco: Cleis Press, 1994), 165–74, 168, emphasis in original.

83. Gayle Rubin, 'Misguided, Dangerous and Wrong: An Analysis of Anti-Pornography Politics', in *Gender, Race and Class in Media*, edited by Gail Dines and Jean M. Humez (Thousand Oaks, London, and New Delhi: Sage, 1995), 244–53, 246. See also Califia, 170: 'S/M eroticism focuses on forbidden feelings or actions and searches for a way to obtain pleasure from them.'

84. Laura Kipnis, 'Fantasy in America: *The United States v. Daniel Thomas DePew*', in *Bound and Gagged: Pornography and the Politics of Fantasy in America* by Laura Kipnis (Durham, NC: Duke University Press, 1999), 3–63, 7.

85. See Hollibaugh, 139–40. As Jewelle Gomez observes, this is a feminist issue: '... gay men exist in their sexuality in the privilege of having sex free of politics – in a way ... they're not suffering under a recognizable form of sexism throughout their growing up, through their adolescence and into adulthood, so that their practice of sex is privileged in a way that women have had to work through to get to in our practice of sex'.

86. Rubin, 1995, 246.

87. White, 1997, 327.

88. Gayle Rubin, with Judith Butler, 'Sexual Traffic', *differences: A Journal of Feminist Cultural Studies* 6.2–3 (1994): 62–99, 96.

89. Leopold von Sacher-Masoch's 1870 novella *Venus in Furs* might offer an interesting point of comparison for this moment in White's novel. In Sacher-Masoch's work, the erotic fantasy of domination reveals more than the interplay between national and individual identities. Within the context of the late nineteenth-century Hapsburg Empire, the fantasy also offered coherence to those identities, necessarily complex given their multi-lingual and multi-ethnic features that, in turn, often delineated different social and class positions. Fantasy offered a space for engaging and resisting (and so potentially destabilizing) the hegemonic forces of empire. In addition to the novella itself, see Larry Wolff, 'Introduction', in *Venus in Furs* by Leopold von Sacher-Masoch (Harmondsworth and New York: Penguin, 2000), vii–xxviii.

90. I am thinking here of the important work of Dorothy Allison on fantasy, in particular in her novel *Bastard Out of Carolina* (New York: Penguin, 1993), which I discuss in Chapter 4. See also Hollibaugh.

91. Relevant here is the discussion of SM in Carole S. Vance, 'Negotiating Sex and Gender in the Attorney General's Commission on Pornography', in *The Gender and Sexuality Reader*, edited by Roger N. Lancaster and Micaela di Leonardo (New York and London: Routledge, 1997), 440–52.

92. See Pellegrini and Jakobsen, 433. They write, ' "Making love" too quickly closes the book on what sex can mean or do, whereas "making sex" makes room for the recognition, both elated and pained, that what we make of sex and how sex makes and remakes "us" are not set in advance'.

93. Crimp, 191.

94. Butler, 2004, 29.

95. I am taking this heading, not from John Donne's but rather from Adrienne Rich's 'A Valediction: Forbidding Mourning'. Rich's poem is a leave-taking from marriage. With this reference I am suggesting how reading for fantasy allows one to take leave of stable identity categories. Please see a related discussion in *Desert of the Heart* section of Chapter 1.

96. Blanche McCrary Boyd, quoted in Duberman, 1997, 356.

97. Adrienne Rich, 'A Valediction Forbidding Mourning'.

98. Edmund White, in Duberman, 2003, 50. See also Adrienne Rich, 'When We Dead Re-Awaken: Writing as Re-vision', in *Arts of the Possible* by Adrienne Rich (New York and London: W. W. Norton, 2001), 10–29.

4. Remaking Gendered Systems of Story

1. bell hooks, 'talking back', in *Talking Back: Thinking Feminist, Thinking Black* (Boston: South End Press, 1989), 5–9, 8.

2. All page references are to the following editions: Allison, 1993 and Ann-Marie MacDonald, *The Way the Crow Flies* (New York: HarperCollins, 2003).

3. See Estelle B. Freedman, *No Turning Back: The History of Feminism and the Future of Women*, (New York: Ballantine Books, 2002), 284. As Freedman observes, 'Rape continues to target women who deviate from heterosexual norms'. Her chapter 'Gender and Violence' (276–302) is particularly useful. For discussions of harassment and violence against lesbians and gay men, see the following. G. M. Herek, 'The Psychology of Sexual Prejudice', *Current Directions in Psychological Science* 9 (2000): 19–22. Herek writes that up to 92% of gay men and lesbians have experienced verbal harassment that is linked to their sexual orientation. See also G. M. Herek, 'Hate Crimes against Lesbians and Gay Men: Issues for Research and Policy', *American Psychologist* 44.6 (1989): 948–55. In this article he notes that 'as many as 24% [of lesbians and gay men] report physical attacks because of their sexual orientation'. See also Keren Lehavot and Alan J. Lambert, 'Toward a Greater Understanding of Antigay Prejudice: On the Role of Sexual Orientation and Gender Role Violation', *Basic and Applied Social Psychology* 29.3 (2007): 279–92; Valerie Jenness, 'Social Movement Growth, Domain Expansion, and Framing Processes: The Gay/Lesbian Movement and Violence Against Gays

and Lesbians as a Social Problem', *Social Problems* 42.1 (February 1995): 145–70; and Gary David Comstock, *Violence Against Lesbians and Gay Men* (New York: Columbia University Press, 1991).

Unsurprisingly, violence is a standard feature of much LGBT fiction. Leslie Feinberg's *Stone Butch Blues* provides a particularly haunting example. For essays that incorporate memories of violence into understandings of lesbianism broadly defined, see Leslie Feinberg, 'We Are All Works in Progress', in Kleindienst, 80–9 and Deke Law, 'Evolution', in Kleindienst, 136–45. See also Hollibaugh.

4. See Plummer, 1995, 87. Writing of the importance of storytelling within gay and lesbian contexts, sociologist Ken Plummer explains, 'My argument is simple. I will suggest – just as I have for rape stories – that for narratives to flourish there must be a community to hear; that for communities to hear, there must be stories which weave together their history, their identity, their politics.' For a literary discussion of the importance of storytelling within queer contexts also see my essay ' "Falling into a Place": Reading for Renewal as Queer Pedagogy'. *Journal of Gay, Lesbian, and Bisexual Identity* 3.3 (July 1998): 233–44. See also Leigh Gilmore, 'Limit-Cases: Trauma, Self-Representation, and the Jurisdictions of Inability', *Biography* 24.1 (Winter 2001): 128–39. Gilmore writes, 'I am interested in the coincidence of trauma and self-representation and what it reveals about the cultural and psychic work of autobiography, its internally fractured histories, and especially, its limits' (129).

5. Allison, 'Femme', Allison, 1994, 151–64, 157.

6. Ibid., 153.

7. Allison, 'Puritans, Perverts, and Feminists', in Allison, 1994, 93–100, 94.

8. Ibid., 97.

9. Ibid., 98.

10. Ibid., 100.

11. According to studies by Rusell (1983), Finkelhor (1978), and DeFrancis (1969), one in four girls will be sexually abused by the age of eighteen. See Rape and Sexual Assault Center, http://www.rasac.or/education/statistics.html, date accessed 28 January 2006. Department of Justice statistics are that one in six women in the US has been raped. See, too, Freedman, 285 and 298. She cites the Center for Disease Control and Prevention findings that 'one in five women had experienced a rape or attempted rape at some point in her life'. She cites comparably high statistics for sexual abuse of children: According to a 1995 UN report, between one-fourth and one-third of the women in Barbados, Canada, the Netherlands, New Zealand, Norway, and the United States reported sexual abuse as children or adolescents. Other US studies place the figure somewhere between 12 and 20 percent.'

12. For a discussion of the 'narrative of determinism', see Walters, 89ff. See as well Linda Garnets, Gregory M. Herek, and Barrie Levy, 'Violence and Victimization of Lesbians and Gay Men: Mental Health Consequences', *Journal of Interpersonal Violence* 5.3 (September 1990): 366–83, 379. The authors conclude, 'The trauma associated with anti-gay victimization may become linked to survivors' homosexuality. Although this often results in intensification of psychosocial problems associated with being gay or lesbian, it also

may lead to further consolidation of the survivor's gay or lesbian identity and involvement in her or his community.' While trauma can beget trauma, those who have experienced violence can draw strength from their understanding of themselves as members of a larger LGBT community. Queerness, in other words, becomes the sign of mental health, with queer identification the healthy response to the disease of homophobia.

13. Allison, 'Believing in Literature', in Allison, 1994, 165–81, 166.
14. For the passage in question, see Virginia Woolf, *To the Lighthouse* (San Diego, New York, and London: Harcourt, 1989), 100.
15. Allison, 1993, 46.
16. Ibid., 246.
17. Dorothy Allison, quoted in Duberman, 1997, 358. Allison is in effect writing for a startling number of girls. In 1995, AMA President Lonnie Bristow said, 'Sexual assault ... represent[s] the most rapidly growing crime in America, claiming a victim every four seconds. Over 61% of female victims are under the age of eighteen ...', (See Rape and Sexual Assault Center, http://www.rasac.org/education/statistics.html, date accessed 28 January 2006.
18. Allison, 1993, 2.
19. Ibid., 2–3.
20. Ibid., 3.
21. Dorothy Allison, quoted in Duberman, 1997, 357.
22. Allison, 1993, 30.
23. Ibid., 54.
24. Ibid., 121.
25. Ibid., 111.
26. Glen's investment in those norms is also apparent in the kinds of houses he chooses to rent for his family: 'tract houses with white slatted walls and tin-roofed carports'; houses that 'always looked naked and abandoned' (Allison, 1993, 79). These houses stand in sharp contrast to the Boatwrights' with their wide porches, the locus for family connection, storytelling, and safety. For a discussion of the importance of porches in Southern culture and, specifically, within the novel, see Jocelyn Hazelwood Donlon, ' "Born on the Wrong Side of the Porch": Violating Traditions in *Bastard out of Carolina*', *Southern Folklore* 55.2 (1998): 133–44.
27. Allison, 1993, 98.
28. Ibid., 102.
29. Ibid., 110.
30. Ibid., 100.
31. Ibid., 3.
32. Ibid., 44.
33. Ibid., 46–7.
34. Ibid., 246–7.
35. Ibid., 283; 284, emphasis in original.
36. It is vital to see how Allison's strategy to link incest here with the drive toward heteronormativity rather than with lesbianism.
37. Allison, 1993, 262.
38. Ibid., 111.
39. Ibid., 53.

40. Ibid., 118–19.
41. Ibid., 63.
42. Ibid., 112–13.
43. For specific discussions of sexual trauma, see J. Brooks Bouson, ' "You Nothing But Trash": White Trash Shame in Dorothy Allison's *Bastard Out of Carolina*', *Southern Literary Journal* 34.1 (Fall 2001): 101–23, particularly 111–12; see as well Ann Cvetkovich, 'Sexual Trauma/Queer Memory: Incest, Lesbianism, and Therapeutic Culture', in *Incest and the Literary Imagination*, edited by Elizabeth Barnes (Gainesville: University of Florida Press, 2002), 329–57. For more general discussions of sexual shame see Hollibaugh and Warner, 1999.
44. The conference, held on 24 April 1982, was titled 'The Scholar and the Feminist IX – Toward a Politics of Sexuality'.
45. Dorothy Allison, 'Public Silence, Private Terror', in Allison, 1994, 101–19, 102.
46. Blanche McCrary Boyd, 'Dorothy Allison, Crossover Blues', *The Nation*, 5 July 1993: 20, 22.
47. For a discussion of the sex wars, see Lisa Duggan and Nan D. Hunter, *Sex Wars; Sexual Dissent and Political Culture* (New York and London: Routledge, 1995).
48. For a discussion of the mid 1980s alliance between political conservatives and feminists on the issue of pornography, see Vance.
49. Boyd, 20, 22.
50. Ibid.
51. For a discussion of the demonization of pro-sex lesbians within feminist and lesbian contexts during the late 1970s and early 1980s, see Gayle Rubin, 'The Leather Menace: Comments on Politics and S/M', *The Body Politic*, April 1982: 33–5. See also Rubin, 1984, as well as Rubin with Butler, 1994. For a discussion of late 1980s and early 1990s tensions between the 'responsible' and the 'dangerous' homosexual, see Anna Marie Smith, 'Resisting the Erasure of Lesbian Sexuality: A Challenge for Queer Activism', in *Modern Homosexualities: Fragments of Lesbian and Gay Experience*, edited by Ken Plummer (New York and London: Routledge, 1992), 200–13, 205. Smith writes, 'These demonizations are organized around an extremely mysogynist, anti-"left", anti-working class, and pro-American nationalism agenda.'
52. See Alice Walker, 'In Search of Our Mothers' Gardens', in *In Search of Our Mothers' Gardens* by Alice Walker (New York: Harcourt, Brace, Jovanovich, 1983), 231–43.
53. I'm using 'witness' here as a spiritually charged term that recalls Bone's connection to gospel music. I am also thinking of the complicated ways in which Anney understands Bone's pain.
54. Vincent King, 'Hopeful Grief: The Prospect of a Postmodernist Feminism in Allison's *Bastard Out of Carolina*', *The Southern Literary Journal* 33.1 (2000): 122–40, 136.
55. Allison, 1993, 262.
56. Ibid., 300.
57. Ibid., 309.
58. Ibid.

59. See King, 136. As King has argued, *Bastard* 'unlike the other stories that Bone creates, is a tale that does not "glare" at anyone'.
60. Allison, in Allison, 1994, 157–8.
61. MacDonald, 3.
62. Juliet Waters, 'Killing with Sunshine: Anne-Marie MacDonald Finds a Different Way to Spook in *The Way the Crow Flies*', *Montreal Mirror*, 23–9 October 2003 (19.19).
63. So, for example, in *A Room of One's Own*, Virginia Woolf describes the creative thought as a 'little fish', and in his afterword to *Maurice* E. M. Forster recalls the 'touch on the backside' that generated the novel. See Virginia Woolf, *A Room of One's Own* (San Diego, New York, and London: Harcourt, 1989) and Forster, 249.
64. Crows have excellent memory. See For the Love of Crows, http://zeebyrd.com/corvi29/, date accessed 13 February 2006 and BBC News, 'Crows Prove They Are No Birdbrains', 8 August 2002, http://news.bbc.co.uk/1/hi/sci/tech/2178920.stm, date accessed 12 February 2006.
65. MacDonald, 41.
66. Ibid.
67. I am of course thinking of McCarthyism here.
68. MacDonald, 170, 218
69. Ibid., 193.
70. Ibid., 234–5.
71. Ibid., 250.
72. Ibid., 122.
73. Ibid., 253–4.
74. Ibid., 300–1.
75. Ibid., 703–4.
76. Ibid., 619, 623, for example.
77. Ibid., 749.
78. Ibid., 700.
79. Ibid.
80. Ibid., 701, 744.
81. Ibid., 701.
82. Ibid.
83. Ibid., 704.
84. Ibid., 748.
85. Ibid.
86. Ibid.
87. Ibid., 749.
88. Ibid.
89. Ibid., 750, 763.
90. Ibid., 793.
91. Ibid., 590.
92. Allison, 1994, 113.
93. See bell hooks, ' "whose pussy is this?": a feminist comment', in hooks, 1989, 134–41, especially 138–9. hooks discusses the representation of rape in Spike Lee's film *She's Gotta Have It*.
94. Allison, 1994, 177.

5. Trussed/Trust/Dressed in Translation

1. Butler, 2004, 228. Butler is speaking of the work of Gloria Anzaldúa.
2. Judith Halberstam, *Skin Shows: Gothic Horror and the Technology of Monsters* (Durham, NC and London: Duke University Press, 1995), 37.
3. The Kinks, 'Lola', 1970.
4. Edward J. Ingebretsen, *At Stake: Monsters and the Rhetoric of Fear in Public Culture* (Chicago: University of Chicago, 2001), 4.
5. Ibid., 3.
6. See Shane Weller, 'In Other Words: On the Ethics of Translation', *Angelaki* 10.3 (December 2005): 171–86. Specifically, see Weller's conclusion: 'Literal translation, as Benjamin conceives it, involves both the *threat* of meaning's disappearance and the *promise* of a language that does not lack meaning but is beyond meaning: in other words, Scripture' (182). See Walter Benjamin, 'The Task of the Translator' (1923), translated by Harry Zohn. *Illuminations: Essays and Reflections*, edited by Hannah Arendt (New York: Schocken, 1968), 69–82. The essay is quoted in Weller, 176. See also Stephen Yao, 'The *Unheimlich* Manuever; or the Gap, the Gradient, and the Spaces of Comparison', *Comparative Literature* 57.3 (Summer 2004): 246–55. Yao writes, '... Nor does it rely on the assertion, à la Walter Benjamin, of a dubious, metaphysical unity underlying all languages' (252, footnote 10). Both Weller and Yao discuss Benjamin.
7. See note 6.
8. Halberstam, 1995, 45.
9. Franz Kafka, *The Metamorphosis* (1915), edited and translated by Stanley Corngold (New York: Bantam, 1972), 3.
10. Ibid.
11. Ibid., 51. (In the German it is clear from the beginning of the novella that Gregor is an 'es' or 'it'.)
12. Ibid., 35.
13. See Sander Gilman, *Freud, Race, and Gender* (Princeton, NJ: Princeton University Press, 1993), especially 39–40, 60–1, for a discussion of masturbation.
14. See my discussion in *Butler Matters*: Margaret Sönser Breen, *'Gender Trouble* in the Literature Classroom: Unintelligible Genders in *The Metamorphosis* and *The Well of Loneliness'*, in *Butler Matters: Judith Butler's Impact on Feminist and Queer Studies*, edited by Margaret Sönser Breen and Warren J. Blumenfeld (Aldershot, UK: Ashgate, 2005), 147–60.
15. Ibid, particularly 153 and note 9 for my discussion of transfiguration.
16. Gayatri Spivak, 'Translation as Culture', *parallax* 6.1 (2000): 13–24, particularly 14.
17. This phrase obviously pays homage to Judith Butler's work.
18. This is David Rousset's term. See David Rousset, *L'univers concentrationnaire* (Paris: Éditions du Pavois, 1946) (*The Other Kingdom*, translated by Ramon Guthrie (New York: Reynal and Hitchcock, 1947)).
19. Rousset, *Other Kingdom*, cit. Lynn M. Gunzberg, 'Down among the Dead Men: Levi and Dante in Hell', *Modern Language Studies* 16.1 (Winter, 1986): 10–28, 10.

20. Janet R. Jakobsen, 'Queers Are Like Jews, Aren't They? Analogy and Alliance Politics', in *Queer Theory and the Jewish Question*, edited by Daniel Boyarin, Daniel Itzkovitz, and Ann Pelligrini, (New York: Columbia University Press, 2003), 64–89, 80.

21. The 'Canto' was not included in the first edition of the memoir, published in 1947; Levi added it to the 1958 Einaudi edition.

22. Specifically, as Valerio Ferme argues, translating Ulysses' words 'on what it means to be human', in Dante's text allows Levi to resist a Nazi definition of Jews as non-human. It also allows him to affirm his masculinity on three fronts: as a partisan (citizen-soldier in the tradition of the great soldier of classical literature), as a reader of literature (specifically the 'masterpiece' of one of the 'fathers' of Italian culture), and as a man drawn by affection and protectiveness toward another man (who 'did not neglect his human relationships with less privileged comrades'). See Valerio Ferme, 'Translating the Babel of Horror: Primo Levi's Catharsis through Language in the Holocaust Memoir *Se questo è un uomo*', *Italica* 78.1 (Spring, 2001): 53–73, 62. Quotations from the English-language version of *Se questo è un uomo* (1958) are from Primo Levi, *Survival in Auschwitz* (New York: Simon & Schuster, 1996), 110.

23. Levi, 114.

24. Butler, 2004, 29, emphasis added.

25. Emily Apter, 'Afterlife of a Discipline', *Comparative Literature* 57.3 (Summer 2005): 201–6, 205.

26. See, for example, Halberstam, 1995, 36. See, also, Sandra M. Gilbert and Susan Gubar, *The Madwoman in the Attic: The Woman Writer and the Nineteenth-Century Literary Imagination* (New Haven and London: Yale University Press, 1979), Chapter 7, 'Horror's Twin: Mary Shelley's Monstrous Eve', for their discussion of 'bibliogenesis'.

27. Gayatri Spivak, 'Three Women's Texts and a Critique of Imperialism', *Critical Inquiry* 12.1 (Autumn 1985): 243–61, 259.

28. Judith Butler, *Bodies That Matter: On the Discursive Limits of Sex* (New York and London: Routledge, 1993), 16.

29. Halberstam, 1995, 35.

30. Unless otherwise noted, all *Frankenstein* quotations are based on the 1818 text used in Mary Shelley, *Frankenstein*, edited by J. Paul Hunter (New York and London: W. W. Norton & Co., 1996). See Shelley, 1996, 32.

31. See, for example, Gilbert and Gubar, 237.

32. See Gilbert and Gubar, 672, note 21. They are quoting Marc A. Rubenstein, ' "My Accursed Origin": The Search for the Mother in *Frankenstein*', *Studies in Romanticism* 15.2 (Spring 1976): 165–94, 173.

33. Rubenstein, 153.

34. Halberstam, 1995, 31.

35. Ibid., 33.

36. The 1831 text is used in the following edition: Mary Shelley, *Frankenstein*, edited by Johanna M. Smith (Boston and New York: Bedford/St. Martin's, 2000), 38.

37. Ibid., 70.

38. Shelley, 1996, 13.

39. Ibid., 10.

40. Shelley, 2000, 38.
41. Ibid., 39.
42. Shelley, 1996, 10
43. Ibid., 23.
44. Ibid., 43.
45. Butler, 2004, 228, emphasis in original.
46. Shelley, 1996, 87–8.
47. Susan Stryker, 'My Words to Frankenstein above the Village of Chamounix: Performing Transgender Rage', in *The Transgender Studies Reader*, edited by Susan Stryker and Stephen Whittle (New York and London: Routledge, 2006), 244–56, 253.
48. The monster's gender is not clear. Born an 'it', he then becomes a 'he'. See Stryker. See also Fausto-Sterling, 67. She discusses psychologist John Money's position regarding intersexuals and gender. Regarding his (in)famous John/Joan case, Money wrote, 'To use the Pygmalion allegory, one may begin with the same clay and fashion a god or a goddess.' In allocating gender assignment to the doctor, Money recalls Victor Frankenstein. The realms of gothic horror novel and modern-day science are not so far apart after all.
49. Shelley, 2000, 31.
50. I propose this, rather than arguing, as Anne K. Mellor does, that '[o]ne of the deepest horrors of this novel is Frankenstein's implicit goal of creating a society for men only'. See Anne K. Mellor, 'Possessing Nature: The Female in *Frankenstein*', in *Romanticism and Feminism*, edited by Ann K. Mellor (Bloomington: Indiana University Press, 1988), 220–32, 230.
51. See Ellen Moers, 'Female Gothic: The Monster's Mother', *New York Review of Books* 21.4 (21 March 1974). (This essay is reprinted in Shelley, 1996, 214–24).
52. See Halberstam, 1995, 42. She writes, 'His creation of a being "like myself" hints at both masturbatory and homosexual desires which the scientist attempts to sanctify with the reproduction of another being. The suggestion that a homosexual bond in fact animates the plot adds an element of sexual perversity to the monster's already hybrid form.'
53. With this phrase I am obviously playing off of both Adrienne Rich and *MacBeth*. Arguably, Mary Shelley was herself not 'of woman born', since her mother, Mary Wollestonecraft Godwin, died in childbirth.
54. Contrast this sense with Stryker, 2006. Stryker regards the surgeon's intervention as facilitating the transsexual's embodiment of 'natural' sex.
55. See Joseph W. Lew, 'The Deceptive Other: Mary Shelley's Critique of Orientalism in *Frankenstein*', *Studies in Romanticism* 30.2 (Spring 1991): 255–83, 30. Regarding the gender barriers, it is important here that the DeLacey family is motherless. I read the DeLacy family as queer in part because of their incorporation of Safie. For a contrasting argument see Lew's article, in which, according to Halberstam, 'this family represents itself as the safe haven of the Oriental woman from the barbarity of the East'.
56. Shelley, 1996, 89.
57. Ibid., 90.
58. See, for example, Barbara Johnson, 'My Monster/My Self', *Diacritics* 12.2 (Summer 1982): 2–10, 9–10. Limited education was not Mary Shelley's

actual experience, but it was certainly the specter held out to her and the lived reality of countless nineteenth-century women.

59. Shelley, 1996, 86.
60. See Gilbert and Gubar, 224: 'It is a female fantasy of sex and reading, then, a gothic psychodrama reflecting Mary Shelley's own sense of what we might call bibliogenesis, that *Frankenstein* is a version of the misogynistic story implicit in *Paradise Lost*.'
61. Halberstam, 1995, 106.
62. I am reminded here of how horror, powerlessness, and evil can find roots in the lack of translation. Kafka's text provides one example of this possibility. One might also think of Primo Levi's *Survival in Auschwitz*: Levi likens the Carbide Tower in the middle of the Buna work camp in Auschwitz to the Tower of Babel. 'Its bricks were called *Ziegel, briques, tegula, cegli, kamenny, mattoni, téglak*, and they were cemented by hate; hate and discord, like the Tower of Babel, and it is this that we call it: – *Babelturm, Bobelturm* and and in it we hate the insane dream of grandeur of our masters, their contempt for God and men, for us men' See Levi, 73.
63. Shelley, 1996, 152, emphasis added.
64. Ibid., 35.
65. Shelley, 1996, 80–1.
66. George Steiner, *After Babel: Aspects of Language and Translation* (Oxford: Oxford University Press, 1975), 296.
67. Apter, 205.
68. See Yao, 249, 250. Yao proposes the term gradient as a counter to the problematic understanding of linguistic knowledge, as if there were 'only two possible states . . . : mastery or ignorance'. Yao offers the gradient 'as a way to conceptualise the category of difference, both for marking distinctions in levels or degrees of multilingualism . . . By "gradient", I mean to designate a conception of difference that operates not through absolute, fixed distinctions, but rather by means of relative, phased dimensions.'
69. Shelley, 1996, 153.
70. Stryker, 2006, 248.
71. Shelley, 1996, 156.
72. Pedro Almodóvar, dir, *All About My Mother* (*Todo sobre mi Madre*), Madrid: El Deseo S. A., 1999, distributed in the US by Sony Pictures Classics.
73. Michael Sofair, Review of *All About My Mother*, *Film Quarterly* 55.2 (Winter 2001–2002): 40–7, 42.
74. See Guillermo Altares, 'An Act of Love toward Oneself', 1999 interview, translated by Paula Willoquet-Maricondi, in *Pedro Almodóvar: Interviews*, edited by Paula Willoquet-Maricondi (Jackson: University Press of Mississippi, 2004), 139–53, 146–7.
75. Apter, 205.
76. Florence Jacobowitz and Lori Spring, 'Unspoken and Unsolved: Tell Me a Riddle', in *Issues in Feminist Film Criticism*, edited by Patricia Erens (Bloomington and Indianapolis: Indiana University Press, 1991), 353–64, 356.
77. Stryker, 2006, 248.
78. The scene also recalls one from Almodóvar's 1996 film *Flower of My Secret*. See Frédéric Strauss, ed., *Almodóvar on Almodóvar, Revised Edition*, translation

of additional material by Richard Same, 2006 (New York and London: Faber and Faber, Ltd, 2006), 189. Almodóvar explains, 'As it happens, the character Manuela was there already in *The Flower of My Secret* and even had the same name. She was the nurse who did a simulation with the doctors, one of those role-plays to teach doctors how best to break the news of decease. In *All About My Mother* I wanted, almost for moral reasons, to show why such doctors do simulations. It's because they have only a few hours to get a donor organ from A to B, knowing that a transplant patient can sometimes live very far.'

79. In an unpublished paper, Lourdes Estrada López argues that in relation to her son's death, and particularly in her ability to recount that death, Manuela moves from melancholia to mourning. See Lourdes Estrada López, 'Re-membering the Body, the Family, and the Nation in Almodóvar's *All About My Mother*', unpublished paper, University of Connecticut, Spring 2008.

80. Ernesto Acedvedo- Muñoz, *Pedro Almodóvar* (London, UK and Berkeley, CA: BFI, 2007), 223. My thanks to J. D. Gutierrez-Albilla of the University of Newcastle for making me aware of Acevedo-Muñoz's book.

81. Martin D'Lugo, *Pedro Almodóvar* (Urbana and Chicago: University of Illinois Press, 2006), 100.

82. Within this context, the importance of Argentina is underscored by the actress who plays Manuela. Cecilia Roth, who has appeared in several Almodóvar films, is herself Argentinian.

83. Sofair, 46.

84. Altares, 145. Almodóvar observes, particularly with regard to Tennessee Williams's play *A Streetcar Named Desire*, the following: '... they are tools for the film. Which is to say that Williams's masterpiece, *A Streetcar Named Desire*, is no more a tribute to Williams, who appeals to me tremendously, than Marisa's interpretation of the role is a tribute to Blanche – and she is truly great and right for the part. What matters is that when Cecilia was young she was in the play, and she has already rehearsed the lines she will be repeating, in real life, while pregnant. In this case, however, since in the play she is holding the child in her arms, she is going to turn toward her house and say: "I will never come back to this house, never again," thus abandoning a mate who is her husband, whom she will eventually abandon in the same way. It's as if, all of a sudden, she had rehearsed in this play something that will happen to her in real life. But, on top of that, *A Streetcar Named Desire* becomes a streetcar that runs into the flow of her life, destroying it each time it appears since, after that, she is going to go see it with her son on the same night he dies. Since she says it so spontaneously, it's a play, a situation that has marked her life. It's as if the streetcar had run into her several times, every time it and crossed her life.'

85. See, for example, Strauss, 183. In his interviews, Almodóvar explains that both the Lola and Agrado characters were drawn from real life.

86. This is Almodóvar's point in his interview with Strauss, 185–6.

87. Manuela's calling Lola an 'epidemic' stands in sharp contrast to the reaction of Rosa's mother. After Rosa's death, her mother sees Lola kissing baby Esteban, and asks Manuela who the woman is. When Manuela tells her that

she is the boy's father, Rosa's mother cries out, 'That monster is the one who killed my daughter?' Manuela responds, 'Don't think about that ...'.

88. Montano, 135.
89. Strauss, 185.
90. Alicia G. Montano (1999), 'Almost All About Almodóvar', translated from Spanish by Linda M. Willem, in *Pedro Almodóvar: Interviews*, edited by Paula Willoquet-Maricondi (Jackson: University Press of Mississippi, 2004), 130–8, 131.
91. Strauss, 186.
92. I am using the term 'transsexual' even as 'transgender' would also work.
93. Sofair, 45. Sofair continues that it is Agrado's dream that makes her womanhood authentic.
94. One thinks here, for example, of Shakespeare's comedies.
95. D'Lugo, 105: *All About My Mother*'s awards 'include an Oscar for the Best Foreign Language Film, Best Director, and Ecumenical Award at Cannes; the French César for Best Foreign Film; a Golden Globe for Best Foreign Film; a British Academy Award; a British Independent Film Award for Best Foreign Film, and a Twelfth Annual European Film Award'.
96. For discussions of the film's relation to Spain, see the following: D'Lugo and Allinson. See also Ernesto R. Acevedo-Muñoz, 'The Body and Spain: Pedro Almodóvar's *All About My Mother*', *Quarterly Review of Film and Video*, 21 (2004): 25–38, especially 27: 'In *All About My Mother* the role of transgender and transitory bodies of fathers, mothers, and children becomes a sign of Almodóvar's effort to resolve some issues of national identity seen in his previous films. My analysis of the story ... and the extended body/nation metaphor ... suggests a move toward an understanding of identity as something ambiguous (sexually, culturally) and problematic, yet ultimately functional.' See also Ernesto R. Acevedo-Muñoz, *Pedro Almodóvar* (London, UK and Berkeley, CA: BFI, 2007).
97. Strauss, 210.
98. Ibid.
99. Spivak, 2000, 15. Spivak underscores the danger here of translation wiping out the 'original'. See, too, note 62, in which I mention Primo Levi's point about Buna work camp within Auschwitz as a site of Babel or again the camp's destruction of culture through the fragmentation of languages. It seems to me that language or the cohesion that the subject gains through locating him-/herself within language can be eroded, destroyed even, through both of these processes.
100. Marianne Faithful, 'Broken English', 1979.

Bibliography

Acevedo-Muñoz, Ernesto R. 'The Body and Spain: Pedro Almodóvar's *All About My Mother*'. *Quarterly Review of Film and Video* 21 (2004): 25–38.

——. *Pedro Almodóvar*. London, UK and Berkeley, CA: BFI, 2007.

Acey, Katherine, Terry Boggis, et al. 'Beyond Same-Sex Marriage: A New Strategic Vision for All Our Families and Relationships'. mrzine.monthlyreview.org/beyondmarriage080806.html.

——. *Pedro Almodóvar*. London, UK and Berkeley, CA: BFI, 2007.

——. 'Beyond Same-Sex Marriage: A New Strategic Vision for All Our Families and Relationships'. Executive Statement. *Studies in Gender and Sexuality* 9.2 (April 2008): 158–60.

Allen, Carolyn. *Following Djuna: Women Lovers and the Erotics of Loss*. Bloomington and Indianapolis: Indiana University Press, 1996.

Allison, Dorothy. *Bastard Out of Carolina*. New York: Penguin, 1993.

——. *Skin: Talking About Sex, Class, and Literature*. Ithaca, NY: Firebrand, 1994.

——. 'Mama and Mom and Dad and Son'. In *This is What Lesbian Looks Like*, edited by Kris Kleindienst, 16–23. Ithaca, NY: Firebrand, 1999.

Allison, Dorothy et al. 'On Contemporary Lesbian Literature in the United States: A Symposium with Dorothy Allison, Blanche McCrary Boyd, Nicole Breedlove, Melanie Kaye/Kantrowitz, and B. Ruby Rich'. In *Queer Representations: Reading Lives, Reading Cultures*, edited by Martin Duberman, 356–61. New York and London: New York University Press, 1997.

Almodóvar, Pedro, dir. *All About My Mother* (*Todo sobre mi Madre*). Madrid: El Deseo S. A., 1999. Distributed in the US by Sony Pictures Classics.

Altares, Guillermo. 'An Act of Love toward Oneself'. 1999 interview, translated by Paula Willoquet-Maricondi. In *Pedro Almodóvar: Interviews*, edited by Paula Willoquet-Maricondi, 139–53. Jackson: University Press of Mississippi, 2004.

Apter, Emily. 'Afterlife of a Discipline'. *Comparative Literature* 57.3 (Summer 2005): 201–6.

Backus, Margot Gayle. 'Sexual Orientation in the (Post) Imperial Nation: Celticism and Inversion Theory in Radclyffe Hall's *The Well of Loneliness*'. *Tulsa Studies in Women's Literature* 15.2 (Autumn, 1996): 253–66.

Bailey, Quentin. 'Heroes and Homosexuals: Education and Empire in E. M. Forster'. *Twentieth-Century Literature* 48.3 (Fall 2002): 324–47.

Bannon, Ann. *Odd Girl Out* (1957). San Francisco: Cleis Press, 2001.

——. *I am a Woman* (1959). San Francisco: Cleis Press, 2002.

——. *Women in the Shadows* (1959). San Francisco: Cleis Press, 2002.

Barnstone, Aliki, Michael Tomasek Manson, and Carol J. Singley, eds. *The Calvinist Roots of the Modern Era*. Hanover, NH and London, UK: University Press of New England, 1997.

BBC News. 'Crows Prove They Are No Birdbrains'. 8 August 2002. http://news.bbc.co.uk/1/hi/sci/tech/2178920.stm.

Bebout, Rick. 'Lives of Our Own Invention'. http://www.rbebout.com/getfree/jane.htm.

Benjamin, Walter. 'The Task of the Translator' (1923), translated by Harry Zohn. *Illuminations: Essays and Reflections*, edited by Hannah Arendt, 69–82. New York: Schocken, 1968.

Bere, Carol. 'A Reading of Adrienne Rich's "A Valediction Forbidding Mourning"'. *Concerning Poetry* 11.2 (1978): 33–8.

Berlant, Lauren. 'America, post-Utopia: Body, Landscape, and National Fantasy in Hawthorne's *Native Land*'. *Arizona Quarterly* 44.4 (Winter 1989): 14–54.

Bischoff, Volker. 'Der Dichter in der Gesellschaft: Audens "In Memory of W. B. Yeats" und seine Yeats-Aufsätze'. In *Literaratur als Kritik des Lebens: Festschrift zum 65. Geburtstag von Ludwig Borinski*, edited by Ludwig Borinski, Rudolf Haas, et al., 264–78. Heidelberg: Quelle und Meyer, 1975.

Blakemore, Steven. 'Family Resemblances: The Texts and Contexts of "Rip Van Winkle,"' *Early American Literature* 35 (2000), 187–212.

Bouson, J. Brooks. ' "You Nothing But Trash": White Trash Shame in Dorothy Allison's *Bastard Out of Carolina*'. *Southern Literary Journal* 34.1 (Fall 2001): 101–23.

Boyd, Blanche McCrary. 'Dorothy Allison, Crossover Blues'. *The Nation*, 5 July 1993: 20, 22.

Breen, Margaret Sönser. 'The Sexed Pilgrim's Progress'. *SEL* 32.3 (1992): 443–60.

——. 'Narrative Inversion: The Biblical Heritage of *The Well of Loneliness* and *Desert of the Heart*'. *Journal of Homosexuality* 33.3–4 (1997): 187–206.

——. ' "Falling into a Place": Reading for Renewal as Queer Pedagogy'. *Journal of Gay, Lesbian, and Bisexual Identity* 3.3 (July 1998): 233–44.

——. '*Desert of the Heart*: Jane Rule's Puritan Outing'. In *The Puritan Origins of American Sex: Religion, Sexuality, and National Identity in American Literature*, edited by Tracy Fessenden, Nicholas F. Radel, and Magdalena J. Zaborowska. New York and London: Routledge, 2001.

——. '*Gender Trouble* in the Literature Classroom: Unintelligible Genders in *The Metamorphosis* and *The Well of Loneliness*'. In *Butler Matters: Judith Butler's Impact on Feminist and Queer Studies*, edited by Margaret Sönser Breen and Warren J. Blumenfeld, 147–60. Aldershot, UK: Ashgate, 2005.

Brontë, Charlotte. *Jane Eyre*. New York: Norton, 1971.

Bryant, William Cullen. *Picturesque America; Or, the Land We Live In*. New York: D. Appleton and Co., 1872–1874.

Bunyan, John. *The Pilgrim's Progress*. Harmondsworth: Penguin, 1984.

Burstein, Andrew. *The Original Knickerbocker: The Life of Washington Irving*. New York: Basic Books, 2007.

Butler, Judith. *Gender Trouble: Feminism and the Subversion of Identity*. New York: Routledge, 1990.

——. *Bodies That Matter: On the Discursive Limits of Sex*. New York and London: Routledge, 1993.

——. *The Psychic Life of Power*. Stanford, CA: Stanford University Press, 1997.

——. *Undoing Gender*. New York and London: Routledge, 2004.

Califia, Pat. 'Feminism and Sadomasochism' (1980). In *Public Sex: The Culture of Radical Sex*, 165–74. San Francisco: Cleis Press, 1994.

Castle, Terry. *The Apparitional Lesbian: Female Homosexuality and Modern Culture*. New York: Columbia University Press, 1993.

Chauncey, George. *Gay New York: Gender, Urban Culture, and the Making of the Gay Male World, 1890–1940*. New York: Basic Books, 1994.

——. *Why Marriage? The History Shaping Today's Debate Over Gay Equality*. New York: Basic Books, 2004.

Chinn, Sarah E. ' "Something Primitive and Age-Old as Nature Herself": Lesbian Sexuality and the Permission of the Exotic'. In *Palatable Poison: Critical Perspectives on* The Well of Loneliness, edited by Laura Doan and Jay Prosser, 300–15. New York: Columbia University Press, 2001.

Chu, Patricia E. *Race, Nationalism, and the State in British and American Modernism*. Cambridge, UK: Cambridge University Press, 2006.

Comstock, Gary David. *Violence Against Lesbians and Gay Men*. New York: Columbia University Press, 1991.

Crimp, Douglas. 'Melancholia and Moralism'. In *Loss: The Politics of Mourning*, edited by David L. Eng and David Kazanjian, 188–202. Berkeley: University of California Press, 2003.

Cvetkovich, Ann. 'Sexual Trauma/Queer Memory: Incest, Lesbianism, and Therapeutic Culture'. In *Incest and the Literary Imagination*, edited by Elizabeth Barnes, 329–357. Gainesville: University of Florida Press, 2002.

Dearborn, Mary. *Pocohontas's Daughters: Gender and Ethnicity in American Culture*. New York: Oxford University Press, 1986.

D'Emilio, John. 'Capitalism and Gay Identity'. In *Powers of Desire: The Politics of Sexuality*, edited by Ann Snitow, Christine Stansell, and Sharan Thompson, 100–13. New York: Monthly Review Press, 1983.

D'Lugo, Martin. *Pedro Almodóvar*. Urbana and Chicago: University of Illinois Press, 2006.

Doan, Laura and Sarah Waters, 'Making Up Lost Time: Contemporary Lesbian Writing and the Invention of History'. In *Territories of Desire in Queer Culture: Refiguring Contemporary Debates*, edited by David Alderson and Linda R. Anderson, 12–28. Manchester, UK and New York: Manchester University Press, 2001.

Donlon, Jocelyn Hazelwood. ' "Born on the Wrong Side of the Porch": Violating Traditions in *Bastard out of Carolina*'. *Southern Folklore* 55.2 (1998): 133–44.

Duggan, Lisa and Nan D. Hunter. *Sex Wars; Sexual Dissent and Political Culture*. New York and London: Routledge, 1995.

Eng, David L. 'Melancholia in the Late Twentieth Century'. *Signs: Journal of Women in Culture and Society* 25.4 (2000): 1275–81.

—— and Shinhee Han. 'A Dialogue on Racial Melancholia'. *Psychoanalytic Dialogues* 10.4 (2000): 667–700.

——. and David Kazanjian. 'Introduction: Mourning Remains'. In *Loss: The Politics of Mourning*, edited by David L. Eng and David Kazanjian, 1–28. Berkeley: University of California Press, 2003.

Estrada López, Lourdes. 'Re-membering the Body, the Family, and the Nation in Almodóvar's *All About My Mother*'. Unpublished paper. University of Connecticut, Spring 2008.

Fausto-Sterling, Anne. *Sexing the Body: Gender Politics and the Construction of Sexuality*. New York: Basic Books, 2000.

Feinberg, Leslie. 'We Are All Works in Progress'. In *This is What Lesbian Looks Like*, edited by Kris Kleindienst, 80–9. Ithaca, NY: Firebrand, 1999.

Fender, Stephen. 'American Landscape and the Figure of Anticipation: Paradox and Recourse'. In *Views of American Landscapes*, edited by Mick Gigley and Robert Lawson-Peebles, 51–63. Cambridge: Cambridge University Press, 1989.

Fenton, James. 'Let Her Dangers Be Never So Great'. *The Times Literary Supplement*, 13 April 2007.

Ferme, Valerio. 'Translating the Babel of Horror: Primo Levi's Catharsis through Language in the Holocaust Memoir *Se questo è un uomo*'. *Italica* 78.1 (Spring, 2001): 53–73.

Fiedler, Leslie. *Love and Death in the American Novel*. New York: Criterion, 1960.

For the Love of Crows. http://zeebyrd.com/corvi29/.

Forrest, Katherine V., ed. *Lesbian Pulp Fiction: The Sexually Intrepid World of Lesbian Paperback Novels 1950–1965*. San Francisco: Cleis Press, 2005.

Friedan, Betty. *The Feminine Mystique* (1963). New York and London: W. W. Norton & Co., 1983 (1963).

Freud, Sigmund. 'Mourning and Melancholia' (1917). *Standard Edition*, 14: 243–58. London: Hogarth Press, 1955.

Fliegelman, Jay. *Prodigals and Pilgrims: The American Revolution against Patriarchal Authority*. Cambridge, UK and New York: Cambridge University Press, 1982.

Forster, E. M. *Maurice*. New York and London: W. W. Norton & Co., 1971.

Freedman, Estelle B. *No Turning Back: The History of Feminism and the Future of Women*. New York: Ballantine Books, 2002.

Garnets, Linda, Gregory M. Herek, and Barrie Levy. 'Violence and Victimization of Lesbians and Gay Men: Mental Health Consequences'. *Journal of Interpersonal Violence* 5.3 (September 1990): 366–83.

Gikandi, Simon. 'Africa and the Epiphany of Modernism'. In *Geomodernisms: Race, Modernism, Modernity*, edited by Laura Doyle and Laura Winkiel, 31–50. Bloomington and Indianapolis: Indiana University Press, 2005.

Gilbert, Sandra M. and Susan Gubar. *The Madwoman in the Attic: The Woman Writer and the Nineteenth-Century Literary Imagination*. New Haven and London: Yale University Press, 1979.

Gilman, Sander. *Freud, Race, and Gender*. Princeton, NJ: Princeton University Press, 1993.

Gilmore, Leigh. 'Limit-Cases: Trauma, Self-Representation, and the Jurisdictions of Inability'. *Biography* 24.1 (Winter 2001): 128–39.

GLAD. 'A Brief Q&A for Couples About Marriage for Same-Sex Couples in Connecticut'. 14 October 2008. www.glad.org.

Gluck, Mary. 'Interpreting Primitivism, Mass Culture and Modernism: The Making of Wilhelm Worringer's Abstraction and Empathy'. *New German Critique: An Interdisciplinary Journal of German Studies* 80 (Spring–Summer 2000): 149–69.

Gnagnatti, Anita. 'Discarding God's Handbook: Winterson's *Oranges Are Not the Only Fruit* and the Tension of Intertextuality'. In *Biblical Religion and the Novel, 1700–2000*, edited by Mark Knight and Thomas M. Woodman, 121–36. Aldershot, UK: Ashgate, 2006.

Graff, E. J. *What is Marriage For? The Strange Social History of Our Most Intimate Institution*. Boston: Beacon Press, 1999.

Greaves, Richard L. 'Bunyan Through the Centuries: Some Reflections'. *English Studies*, 64 (1983): 113–21.

Gunzberg, Lynn M. 'Down among the Dead Men: Levi and Dante in Hell'. *Modern Language Studies* 16.1 (Winter, 1986): 10–28.

Halberstam, Judith. *Skin Shows: Gothic Horror and the Technology of Monsters*. Durham, NC and London: Duke University Press, 1995.

——. *Female Masculinity*. Durham and London: Duke University Press, 1998.

Hall, Radclyffe. *The Well of Loneliness*. New York: Doubleday & Co., 1981.

Hamer, Diane. ' "I am a Woman": Ann Bannon and the Writing of Lesbian Identity in the 1950s'. In *Lesbian and Gay Writing: An Anthology of Critical Essays*, edited by Mark Lilly, 47–75. Philadelphia: Temple University Press, 1990.

Hancock, Geoffrey. 'An Interview with Jane Rule'. *Canadian Fiction Magazine* 23 (August 1976): 57–112.

Harrison, David. 'The Personals.' In *Pomosexuals: Challenging Assumptions about Gender and Sexuality*, edited by Carol Queen and Lawrence Schimel, 129–37. San Francisco: Cleis Press, 1997.

Haskin, Dayton. 'The Burden of Interpretation in *The Pilgrim's Progress*'. *Studies in Philology* 79.3 (Summer 1982): 256–78.

Herek, G. M. 'Hate Crimes against Lesbians and Gay Men: Issues for Research and Policy'. *American Psychologist* 44.6 (1989): 948–55.

——. 'The Psychology of Sexual Prejudice'. *Current Directions in Psychological Science* 9 (2000): 19–22.

Herzogenrath, Bernd. 'Looking Forward/Looking Back: Thomas Cole and the Belated Construction of Nature', in *From Virgin Land to Disney World: Nature and Its Discontents in the USA of Yesterday and Today*, edited by Bernd Herzogenrath, 83–103. Amsterdam: Rodopi, 2001.

Hinds, Hilary. '*Oranges Are Not the Only Fruit*: Reaching Audiences Other Lesbian Texts Cannot Reach'. In *Immortal, Invisible: Lesbians and the Moving Image*, edited by Tamsin Wilton, 52–69. London and New York: Routledge, 1995.

Hofmeyr, Isabel. *The Portable Bunyan: A Transnational History of* The Pilgrim's Progress. Johannesburg: Wits University Press; and Princeton, NJ: Princeton University Press, 2004.

Hollibaugh, Amber L. *My Dangerous Desires: A Queer Girl Dreaming Her Way Home*. Durham, NC and London: Duke University Press, 2000.

hooks, bell. *Talking Back: Thinking Feminist, Thinking Black*. Boston: South End Press, 1989.

Howat, John K. *The Hudson River and Its Painters*. New York: American Legacy Press, 1972.

Ingebretsen, Edward J. *At Stake: Monsters and the Rhetoric of Fear in Public Culture*. Chicago: University of Chicago, 2001.

Irving, Washington. *The Legend of Sleepy Hollow and Other Stories [The Sketch Book of Geoffrey Crayon, Gent.]* New York: Penguin, 1988, 28–42.

Jacobowitz, Florence and Lori Spring. 'Unspoken and Unsolved: Tell Me a Riddle'. In *Issues in Feminist Film Criticism*, edited by Patricia Erens, 353–64. Bloomington and Indianapolis: Indiana University Press, 1991.

Jacobs, Alexandra. 'A Feminist Classic Gets a Makeover'. *The New York Times Book Review*. 17 July 2005, 27.

Jakobsen, Janet R. 'Queers Are Like Jews, Aren't They? Analogy and Alliance Politics', in *Queer Theory and the Jewish Question*, edited by Daniel Boyarin, Daniel Itzkovitz, and Ann Pelligrini, 64–89. New York: Columbia University Press, 2003.

Jay, Meg. 'Melancholy Femininity and Obsessive-Compulsive Masculinity: Sex Differences in Melancholy Gender'. *Studies in Gender and Sexuality* 8:2 (2007): 115–35.

Jenness, Valerie. 'Social Movement Growth, Domain Expansion, and Framing Processes: The Gay/Lesbian Movement and Violence Against Gays and Lesbians as a Social Problem'. *Social Problems* 42.1 (February 1995): 145–70.

Jeremiah, Emily. 'The "I" inside "her": Queer Narration in Sarah Waters's *Tipping the Velvet* and Wesley Stace's "Misfortune"'. *Women: A Cultural Review*, 18.2 (2007): 131–44.

Johnson, Barbara. 'My Monster/My Self'. *Diacritics* 12.2 (Summer 1982): 2–10.

Kafka, Franz. *The Metamorphosis* (1915), edited and translated by Stanley Corngold. New York: Bantam, 1972.

Keeble, N. H. ' "Of Him Thousands Daily Sing and Talk": Bunyan and His Reputation'. In *Conventicle and Parnassus, Tercentenary Essays*, edited by N. H. Keeble, 241–63. Oxford: Clarendon Press, 1988.

King, Vincent. 'Hopeful Grief: The Prospect of a Postmodernist Feminism in Allison's *Bastard Out of Carolina*'. *The Southern Literary Journal* 33.1 (2000): 122–40.

Kipnis, Laura. *Bound and Gagged: Pornography and the Politics of Fantasy in America*. Durham, NC: Duke University Press, 1999.

Knapp, James F. 'Primitivism and Empire: John Synge and Paul Gauguin'. *Comparative Literature* 41.1 (Winter 1989): 53–68.

Kramer, Larry. 'Sex and Sensibility'. *The Advocate* 773 (27 May 1997): 59–70.

Law, Deke. 'Evolution'. In *This is What Lesbian Looks Like*, edited by Kris Kleindienst, 136–45. Ithaca, NY: Firebrand, 1999.

Leavitt, David. 'Out of the Closet and Off the Shelf'. *The New York Times Book Review*. 17 July 2005, 7–8.

Legal Momentum. Marriage and Welfare (a). 'Marriage Promotion: What the Administration is Already Doing'. www.legalmomentum.org/issues/wel/marriagepromotion.shtml.

———. Marriage and Welfare (b). 'Why NOW Legal Defense Opposes Federal Marriage Promotion in TANF Reauthorization'. www.legalmomentum.org/issues/wel/marriagepromotion.shtml.

Lehavot, Keren and Alan J. Lambert. 'Toward a Greater Understanding of Antigay Prejudice: On the Role of Sexual Orientation and Gender Role Violation', *Basic and Applied Social Psychology* 29.3 (2007): 279–92.

Levi, Primo. *Survival in Auschwitz*. New York: Simon & Schuster, 1996.

Levin, Jennifer. 'Beebo Lives'. *The Harvard Gay and Lesbian Review* 2.2 (Spring 1995), 1, 53–4.

Lew, Joseph W. 'The Deceptive Other: Mary Shelley's Critique of Orientalism in *Frankenstein*'. *Studies in Romanticism* 30.2 (Spring 1991): 255–83.

Lorde, Audre. *Zami: A New Spelling of My Name*. Freedom, CA: The Crossing Press, 1982.

MacDonald, Anne-Marie. *The Way the Crow Flies*. New York: HarperCollins, 2003.

Madden, Ed. '*The Well of Loneliness* or the Gospel According to Radclyffe Hall'. *Journal of Homosexuality* 33.3–4 (1997):163–86.

McDowell, Deborah E. ' "It's Not Safe, Not Safe at All": Sexuality in Nella Larson's *Passing*', *Lesbian and Gay Studies Reader*, edited by Henry Abelove, Michèle Aina Barale, and David M. Halperin, 616–25. New York and London: Routledge, 1993.

Mellor, Anne K. 'Possessing Nature: The Female in *Frankenstein*', in *Romanticism and Feminism*, edited by Ann K. Mellor, 220–32. Bloomington: Indiana University Press, 1988.

Mendelson, Edward. *Later Auden*. New York: Farrar, Straus, and Giroux, 1999.

Mitrano, G. F. *Gertrude Stein: Woman without Qualities*. Aldershot, UK: Ashgate, 2005.

Moers, Ellen. 'Female Gothic: The Monster's Mother'. *New York Review of Books* 21.4 (21 March 1974).

Moi, Toril. *What is a Woman?* New York: Oxford University Press, 1999.

Montano, Alicia G. (1999). 'Almost All About Almodóvar'. Translated from Spanish by Linda M. Willem. In *Pedro Almodóvar: Interviews*, edited by Paula Willoquet-Maricondi, 130–8. Jackson: University Press of Mississippi, 2004.

Morales Ladrón, Marisol. 'Jeanette Winterson's *Oranges Are Not the Only Fruit*: A Lesbian *Bildungsroman*'. In *(Trans)Formaciones de las sexualidades y el género*, edited by Mercedes Begoechea and Marisol Morales, 167–85. Alcalá de Henares, Spain: Universidad de Alcalá, 2001.

Nafisi, Azar. *Reading Lolita in Tehran*. New York: Random House, 2003.

Nealon, Christopher. *Foundlings: Lesbian and Gay Historical Emotion Before Stonewall*. Durham, NC: Duke University Press, 2001.

NCL. 'Legal Groups File Lawsuit Challenging Proposition 8, Should It Pass'. 5 November 2008. www.nclrights.org.

Pellegrini, Ann and Janet R. Jakobsen. 'Melancholy Hope and Other Psychic Remainders: Afterthoughts on *Love the Sin*'. *Studies in Gender and Sexuality* 6:4 (Fall 2005): 423–44.

Phelan, Shane. '(Be)Coming Out: Lesbian Identity and Politics'. *Signs* 18.4 (Summer 1993): 765–90.

Piontek, Thomas. *Queering Gay and Lesbian Studies*. Urbana and Chicago: University of Illinois Press, 2006.

Plummer, Ken. *Telling Sexual Stories: Power, Change, and Social Worlds*. London and New York: Routledge, 1995.

Prime-Stevenson, Edward. *Imre*. Peterborough, ONT: Broadview, 2003.

Prosser, Jay. ' "Some Primitive Thing Conceived in a Turbulent Age of Transition": The Transsexual Emerging from *The Well*'. In *Palatable Poison: Critical Perspectives on* The Well of Loneliness, edited by Laura Doan and Jay Prosser, 129–44. New York: Columbia University Press, 2001.

Qualls, Barry V. *The Secular Pilgrims of Victorian Fiction*. Cambridge, UK: Cambridge University Press, 1982.

Queen, Carol and Lawrence Schimel, eds. *Pomosexuals: Challenging Assumptions about Gender and Sexuality*. San Francisco: Cleis Press, 1997.

Rape and Sexual Assault Center. http://www.rasac.org/education/statistics.html.

Renan, Ernest. 'What is a Nation?' In *Nation and Narration*, edited by Homi K. Bhabha, 8–22. London: Routledge, 1990.

Rich, Adrienne. *A Will to Change*. New York: W. W. Norton, 1971.

———. 'When We Dead Re-Awaken: Writing as Re-vision'. In *Arts of the Possible* by Adrienne Rich, 10–29. New York and London: W. W. Norton, 2001.

Richardson, Mattie. 'What You See is What You Get: Building a Movement Toward Liberation in the Twenty-First Century'. In *This is What Lesbian Looks Like*, edited by Kris Kleindienst, 210–19. Ithaca, NY: Firebrand, 1999.

Roden, Frederick S. *Same-Sex Desire in Victorian Religious Culture*. Basingstoke, UK and New York: Palgrave – now Palgrave Macmillan, 2002.

Rousset, David. *L'univers concentrationnaire*. Paris: Éditions du Pavois, 1946.

Rousset, David. *The Other Kingdom*, translated by Ramon Guthrie. New York: Reynal and Hitchcock, 1947.

Rubenstein, Marc A. '"My Accursed Origin": The Search for the Mother in *Frankenstein*'. *Studies in Romanticism* 15.2 (Spring 1976): 165–94.

Rubin, Gayle. 'The Leather Menace: Comments on Politics and S/M'. *The Body Politic*, April 1982: 33–5.

——. 'Thinking Sex: Notes for a Radical Theory of the Politics of Sexuality'. In *Pleasure and Danger: Exploring Female Sexuality*, edited by Carole S. Vance, 267–319. Boston: Routledge & Kegan, Paul, 1984.

—— with Judith Butler. 'Sexual Traffic'. *differences: A Journal of Feminist Cultural Studies* 6.2–3 (1994): 62–99.

——. 'Misguided, Dangerous and Wrong: An Analysis of Anti-Pornography Politics'. In *Gender, Race and Class in Media*, edited by Gail Dines and Jean M. Humez, 244–53. Thousand Oaks, London, and New Delhi: Sage, 1995.

Rule, Jane.*Lesbian Images*. New York: Doubleday, 1975.

——. *A Hot-Eyed Moderate*. Tallahassee, Fl: The Naiad Press, 1985.

——. *Desert of the Heart*. London: Pandora, 1986.

——. 'The Heterosexual Cage of Coupledom'. *BC Bookworld* Spring 2001.

Ruti, Mari. 'From Melancholia to Meaning: How to Live the Past in the Present'. *Psychoanalytic Dialogues* 15.5 (2005): 637–60.

Salamon, Gayle. 'Melancholia, Ambivalent Presence and the Cost of Gender Commentary on Paper by Meg Jay'. *Studies in Gender and Sexuality* 8.2 (2007): 149–64.

Schuster, Marilyn R. *Passionate Communities: Reading Lesbian Resistance in Jane Rule's Fiction*. New York and London: New York University Press, 1999.

Segrest, Mab. 'Hawai'ian Sovereignty/Gay Marriage: *Ka Huliau*'. In *This is What Lesbian Looks Like*, edited by Kris Kleindienst, 231–41. Ithaca, NY: Firebrand, 1999.

Shelley, Mary. *Frankenstein* (1818), edited by J. Paul Hunter. New York and London: W. W. Norton & Co., 1996.

——. *Frankenstein* (1831), edited by Johanna M. Smith. Boston and New York: Bedford/St. Martin's, 2000.

Smith, Anna Marie. 'Resisting the Erasure of Lesbian Sexuality: A Challenge for Queer Activism'. In *Modern Homosexualities: Fragments of Lesbian and Gay Experience*, edited by Ken Plummer, 200–13. New York and London: Routledge, 1992

Sofair, Michael. Review of *All About My Mother*. *Film Quarterly* 55.2 (Winter 2001–2002): 40–7.

——. 'Scientific Racism and the Invention of the Homosexual Body'. *Journal of the History of Sexuality* 5.2 (1994): 243–66.

Somerville, Siobhan. *Queering the Color Line: Race and the Invention of Homosexuality in American Culture*. Durham, NC and London: Duke University Press, 2000.

Sontag, Susan. 'Melancholy Objects'. In *On Photography* by Susan Sontag, 49–82. New York: Farrar, Straus and Giroux, 1974.

Souhami, Diana. *The Trials of Radclyffe Hall*. London: Weidenfeld & Nicolson, 1998.

Spivak, Gayatri. 'Three Women's Texts and a Critique of Imperialism'. *Critical Inquiry* 12.1 (Autumn 1985): 243–61.

——. 'Translation as Culture'. *parallax* 6.1 (2000): 13–24.

Stacey, Judith. *In the Name of the Family: Rethinking Family Values in the Postmodern Age*. Boston: Beacon Press, 1996.

Stein, Gertrude. Fernhurst, Q.E.D., *and Other Early Writings.* New York, London: Liveright, 1996.

Steiner, George. *After Babel: Aspects of Language and Translation.* Oxford: Oxford University Press, 1975.

Stepan, Nancy Leys and Sander L. Gilman. 'Appropriating the Idioms of Science: The Rejection of Scientific Racism'. In *The Bounds of Race: Perspectives on Hegemony and Resistance,* edited by Dominick LaCapra, 72–103. Ithaca, NY: Cornell University Press, 1991.

Stimpson, Catharine. 'Zero Degree Deviancy: The Lesbian Novels in English'. *Critical Inquiry* 8.2 (Winter, 1981): 363–79.

Strauss, Frédéric, ed., *Almodóvar on Almodóvar, Revised Edition.* Translation of additional material by Richard Same, 2006. New York and London: Faber and Faber, Ltd, 2006.

Stryker, Susan. *Queer Pulp: Perverted Passions from the Golden Age of the Paperback.* San Francisco: Chronicle Books, 2001.

——. 'My Words to Frankenstein above the Village of Chamounix: Performing Transgender Rage'. In *The Transgender Studies Reader,* edited by Susan Stryker and Stephen Whittle, 244–56. New York and London: Routledge, 2006.

Sullivan, Andrew. *Virtually Normal: An Argument About Homosexuality.* New York: Alfred A. Knopf, 1995.

Torgovnick, Marianna. *Gone Primitive: Savage Intellect, Modern Lives.* Chicago: University of Chicago Press, 1991.

Traister, Bryce. 'The Wandering Bachelor: Irving, Masculinity, and Authorship'. *American Literature* 74.1 (March 2002): 111–37.

United States Conference of Catholic Bishops. 'Between Man and Woman: Questions and Answers About Marriage and Same-Sex Unions'. *United States Conference of Catholic Bishops.* 12 November 2003. http://www.usccb.org/laity/manand woman.htm.

US Senate. 'Employment of Homosexuals and Other Sex Perverts in the US Government' (1950). Reprinted in *We Are Everywhere: A Historical Sourcebook of Gay and Lesbian Politics,* edited by Mark Blasius and Shane Phelan, 241–51. New York: Routledge, 1997.

Vance, Carole S. 'Negotiating Sex and Gender in the Attorney General's Commission on Pornography'. In *The Gender and Sexuality Reader,* edited by Roger N. Lancaster and Micaela di Leonardo, 440–52. New York and London: Routledge, 1997.

Vanita, Ruth. *Sappho and the Virgin Mary: Same-Sex Love and the English Literary Imagination.* New York: Columbia University Press, 1991.

Walker, Alice. 'In Search of Our Mothers' Gardens'. In *In Search of Our Mothers' Gardens* by Alice Walker, 231–43. New York: Harcourt, Brace, Jovanovich, 1983.

Walters, Suzanna Danuta. 'As Her Hand Crept Slowly Up Her Thigh: Ann Bannon and the Politics of Pulp'. *Social Text* 23 (Autumn–Winter, 1989): 83–101.

Walton, Jean. ' "I Want to Cross Over into Camp Ground': Race and Inversion in *The Well of Loneliness'.* In *Palatable Poison: Critical Perspectives on* The Well of Loneliness, edited by Laura Doan and Jay Prosser, 277–99. New York: Columbia University Press, 2001.

Warner, Michael. *The Trouble with Normal: Sex, Politics, and the Ethics of Queer Life.* New York: The Free Press, 1999.

——. 'Irving's Posterity.' *ELH* 67 (2000): 773–99.

Waters, Juliet. 'Killing with Sunshine: Anne-Marie MacDonald Finds a Different Way to Spook in *The Way the Crow Flies*'. *Montreal Mirror*, 23–9 October 2003 (19.19).

Weller, Shane. 'In Other Words: On the Ethics of Translation'. *Angelaki* 10.3 (December 2005): 171–86.

White, Edmund. *The Farewell Symphony*. New York: Vintage Books, 1997.

——. 'The Personal is Political: Queer Fiction and Criticism', in *Queer Ideas: The David R. Kessler Lectures in Lesbian and Gay Studies*, edited by Martin Duberman, 41–50. New York: The Feminist Press, 2003.

Winkiel, Laura. 'Caberet Modernism: Vorticism and Racial Spectacle'. In *Geomodernisms: Race, Modernism, Modernity*, edited by Laura Doyle and Laura Winkiel, 206–24. Bloomington and Indianapolis: Indiana University Press, 2005.

Wittig, Monique. *The Straight Mind and Other Essays*. Boston: Beacon Press, 1992.

Wolff, Larry. 'Introduction.' In *Venus in Furs* by Leopold von Sacher Masoch, vii–xxviii. Harmondsworth and New York: Penguin, 2000.

Wolfson, Evan. *Why Marriage Matters: America, Equality, and Gay People's Right to Marry*. New York: Simon & Schuster, 2004.

Woolf, Virginia. *A Room of One's Own*. San Diego, New York, and London: Harcourt, 1989.

——. *To the Lighthouse*. San Diego, New York, and London: Harcourt, 1989.

Wormald, Mark. 'Prior Knowledge: Sarah Waters and the Victorians'. In *British Fiction Today*, edited by Philip Tew and Rod Mengham, 186–97. London and New York: Continuum, 2006.

Yao, Steven. 'The *Unheimlich* Manuever; or the Gap, the Gradient, and the Spaces of Comparison', *Comparative Literature* 57.3 (Summer 2004): 246–55.

Zimet, Jaye. *Strange Sisters: The Art of Lesbian Pulp, 1949–1969*. New York: Viking Studio/Penguin Studio, 1999.

Zimmerman, Bonnie. *The Safe Sea of Women: Lesbian Fiction 1969–1989*. Boston: Beacon Press, 1990.

Zuckerman, Diana M. 'The Evolution of Welfare Reform: Policy Changes and Current Knowledge'. *Journal of Social Issues*, 56.4 (December 2000): 811–20.

Index

Jakobsen, Janet R.   84, 90, 122, 162
James, Henry   82
Jane Eyre (Brontë)   9–11, 12
Jews   120, 122–3, 170
Johnson, J. Rosamond   20
Journey to a Woman (Bannon)   31, 45
Joynson-Hicks, Sir William   14–15, 146

Kafka, Franz   7, 118–19, 119–24, 128, 144, 169, 172
Kazanjian, David   85, 156, 159, 162
Keats, John   130
King, Vincent   103, 167, 168
Kinsey, Alfred   27
Kipnis, Laura   89, 163
Knapp, James F.   19, 148
knowledge, sexual   40
Krafft-Ebing, Richard von   17–18, 21
Kramer, Larry   86

Lambda Legal Defense   59
Lambda Lesbian Fiction Award   102
landscape   79–82, **80, 81**; and melancholy   80–2
language   117; of abjection   90; access to   124; development of 12–13, 85–6; grammatical structure 22–3; lack of   82–4, 92, 110; learning   126–7; limitation of 120, 122; possession of   126–30
Leavitt, David   73, 158
legitimate acts   74
lesbian baby boom   56, 58–9, 70
lesbian desire   6
lesbian fiction: and the progress novel 3–4, 8–41, 105–6; pulp   28–30, 42, 46; relevance of *Pilgrim's Progress* 8–12
Lesbian Images (Rule)   25, 149
lesbianism, definitions of   102
Levi, Primo   122–3, 156, 169, 170, 172, 174
Levin, Jennifer   63, 156
life-writing   6
linguistic power   127–30
literature   94–5, 118; role in interdisciplinary studies   1–2; translated   129–31

Lorde, Audre   28, 54, 150, 155
loss   75, 82–4, 86
love, loss of   82–4

MacDonald, Anne-Marie   6, 92, 94, 95, 105, 106, 108, 113, 114, 115, 149, 164, 168. *see also The Way the Crow Flies*
'Mama and Mom and Dad and Son' (Allison)   59–60
marginalization   7, 23
marriage   3. *see also* same-sex marriage; and the church   66–7; as cultural ideal   61–2; Defense of Marriage Act (DOMA) (USA)   69; defining   66–7; and *Desert of the Heart*   33, 42; and discrimination 55; equality movement   5; exclusionary power   63–4; and identity   73–4; inter-racial   43, 52–5; and lesbian progress novels 42–3; and melancholy   76; and separation   58–9; status of   63–4; and United States of America 43–4; the wedding vow   68; and *The Well of Loneliness*   23–4, 33, 42; in *Women in the Shadows*   47, 48, 50–2, 52–5, 69
masculinity   21, 76, 77–9, **79**, 82, 83, 98–9, 120, 123
masturbation   85, 101, 120, 128
Meaker, Marijane   29
meaning, production of   128–9
melancholia   5, 75, 77, 79–2, 84–6, 90, 135, 156, 159, 162, 163, 173
melancholy gender   75–84, 86, 161
'Melancholy Objects' (Sontag)   81–2, 160
melodrama   135
memory   106, 110–13, 115
Mendelson, Edward   27, 150
Metamorphosis, The (Die Verwandlung) (Kafka)   7, 118–19, 119–24, 128
middle-class gender norms   95–100, 102, 104
Milton, John   129, 130
mirrors, symbolism   35
Modernist primitivism   15, 19, 20, 21, 49, 150